PRAISE FOR O

This is indeed a story wo.. .....
churches welcomes this wonderfully expressed record.

Canon Aled Edwards OBE,
CEO Cytûn: Churches Together in Wales

What a moving story... This book is the appropriate history of a movement.

The unique complementary qualities of the writer John Morgans and the photographer Peter Noble allow us to re-visit with them the living heritage of our Christian Welsh communities. This publication is not just a history book among many others but a re-telling of the story in a way our ancestors would have done from generation to generation. This story has the ability to open the heart of our nation.

We are invited (challenged, in a way) to listen carefully and to be questioned radically as the story uncovers the common ground ('this ground you are standing on is Holy ground...') of our Welsh Christian experience.

It is when the churches act together that they become inheritors of the whole history of the People of God. If the churches search together into their common story and celebrate that story together, it could lead to a reinvigorated and united Christian life.

This book is about our common story that was born of Love, called to growth in Love, and to be blessed and transformed anew by Love. This story has to be told because it is worth telling as it sheds light and meaning on our holy Land...

Daniel, Abbot of Caldey
The Rt. Rev. Dom Daniel OCSO

'Gwyn ei byd y genedl y mae'r Arglwydd yn Dduw iddi' meddai'r Salmydd ac fe ddengys cyfrol Dr John Morgans gymaint yw dylanwad Cristionogaeth ar fywyd y genedl ac mae'n gofnod gwerthfawr o'r dystiolaeth i'r Efengyl ar hyd y canrifoedd. Meddai Gwenallt,

> Duw a'th wnaeth yn forwyn iddo,
> Galwodd di yn dyst,
> Ac argraffodd Ei gyfamod
> Ar dy byrth a'th byst.

Mae'r awdur a'r gyfrol yn haeddu pob gwerthfawrogiad.

('Blessed is the nation whose God is the Lord' said the Psalmist and Dr John Morgans' volume shows how much Christianity influences the life of the nation and it's a valuable record of the testimony of the Gospel over the centuries. The poet D. Gwenallt Jones said,

> God made you his maiden,
> He called you a witness,
> And impressed His covenant
> On your gates and posts.

The author and book merit all of our appreciation.)

The Rev. Gareth Morgan Jones,
President Free Church Council for Wales

I wonder whether I have been invited to comment on *Our Holy Ground* because I like to consider myself to be amongst those 'in 21st-century Wales who are determined not to allow ourselves to be incessantly divided between people of the north and the south and the forgotten middle'.

For some years, I have been working within a group that has been trying to do something tangible about this dividedness in Wales, and in this book the Revs John Morgans and Peter Noble have supplied one of the dimensions that had been missing from our work.

Having questioned many residents of Wales over many years in order to try and discover what enables them to identify with Wales, I had reached the clear conclusion that what could enable the widest range of residents of Wales to identify with the country was its landscape.

And so this group of 'unifiers' proceeded to devise a railway route with some arteries that would link together as many regions of Wales as possible so as to enable travellers to get a 'sense' of the country – north, south and mid Wales.

Such a scheme produces a map, but a map, like an icon in an Orthodox Church, is deliberately two dimensional. For map and icon alike, depth is missing, and in the case of the icon, depth is considered to be absent in order to be replaced by the Eternal dimension.

Our Holy Ground has added to our attempt at a geographically widely-encompassing map precisely that which two dimensional depictions are able to invite in – the Eternal dimension. The book invites us to take a look at the inspiring dimension of Divine, saving history within this land, and it does so with the wisdom, discernment and sensitivity to the work of the Spirit that one can expect from these two greatly loved servants of the Lord who have served God and the people of Wales so faithfully and pioneeringly.

They hope that the book 'will help us rediscover out roots and prepare us to face God's future humbly and confidently'. No-one could be better placed than John Morgans and Peter

Noble to lead us on this remarkable geographical, historical and spiritual pilgrimage or to give us a book that I believe has the potential to achieve their stated aim. This is a story that can both inspire us and teach us – a story certainly worth telling. It is a book well worth reading. May our hearts be open to the wisdom and openness of the authors and their love of the Kingdom of God and its historical and cultural manifestations in this land. This is a dimension truly worthy of our embrace.

Tad Deiniol, Blaenau Ffestiniog
The Very Rev. Archimandrite Father Deiniol of Manod

OUR HOLY GROUND

The Welsh Christian Experience

To Hilda,

Thank you for your
company this evening,
alpha, Builth
16.V.17

John I. Morgans.
Peter C Noble

OUR HOLY GROUND

The Welsh Christian Experience

JOHN I. MORGANS, WRITER

PETER C. NOBLE, PHOTOGRAPHER

First impression: 2016

© Copyright John I. Morgans /
Peter C. Noble and Y Lolfa Cyf., 2016

Cover photographs of Our Lady of Penrhys
and the Guardian of the Valleys: Peter C. Noble
Cover design: Y Lolfa

Every attempt was made to ascertain and contact
the source of all the photographs in this book

ISBN: 978 1 78461 280 1

Published and printed in Wales
on paper from well-maintained forests by
Y Lolfa Cyf., Talybont, Ceredigion SY24 5HE
website www.ylolfa.com
e-mail ylolfa@ylolfa.com
tel 01970 832 304
fax 832 782

CONTENTS

PREFACE

ANCIENT STONES SPEAK. Living stones speak even more eloquently. Two images haunted us. Two contexts haunted us. There was both simplicity and mystery. The writer and the photographer were intrigued, beguiled, awed. What were these images telling us? They spoke with power and compassion to their neighbours and neighbourhoods. Were they also speaking to today's Wales? Both reached out from the past. One was speaking from a mysterious, Christian medieval Wales dismantled by a king; the other from an industrial Wales which was on the cusp of being ruthlessly destroyed.

This Lady of Medieval pilgrimage had 'answered the prayers of the labourers, who in hosts are ever at Penrhys'.[1] Was she continuing to embrace the people of this mid-twentieth century housing estate which had won architectural prizes but failed its residents? What was the Mother of Jesus trying to say? Was the Lady of the Magnificat continuing to disturb the status quo? Was she keeping her promise to bring down the powerful from their thrones and lift up the lowly? Is she filling the hungry with good things and sending the rich away empty? Will she call us to remember the mercy of the God of Israel and Ishmael, the Father of her Son?

Who is this hero embracing the community of Six Bells? I will hold you in the palm of my hand. I will love you to the end of time. Who is this courageous suffering miner? Is he Ivor and Daniel and James? Is he cutterman and collier haulier and repairer? Is he the Welsh miner? Is he the miner? Is he the workman? Is he everyman? Or 'Perhaps a woman hanging out the wash... a silence, before sirens cried... before she finished hanging out her sheets.'[2] He is everywoman. She is everyman. The Guardian is the Nameless One with many names calling out to remember me, remember us.

On our journeys through Wales, we searched for historic places significant in the story of the Welsh Christian experience. We found many places which touched us deeply. Even more significant is that in many places there are people living, with enthusiasm, the old story day by day. They are the bearers of treasures for the people of Wales. We were inspired by the places and even more inspired by the people. They helped us see long history from fresh angles.

At Tŷ Mawr Wybrnant, the birthplace of William Morgan, Gerwyn Edwards, 'Will Tŷ Mawr,' proudly showed two William Morgan Bibles, one bought recently from the library of Coleg Harlech, and also quietly pointed out that he was one of a group responsible for the re-opening for worship (after a closure of ten years) the church of Saint Tudclud, Penmachno, a treasury of ancient stones and contemporary mission.

At the Cathedral of Our Lady of Sorrows, Wrexham, we respected the quiet and unassuming reverence of those who knelt before the relics of Saint Richard Gwyn, born in Llanidloes and martyred in Wrexham in 1584.

Sion Tomos greeted us at Trawsfynydd. He is the local enthusiastic guide and caretaker of Llys Ednowain, the new heritage centre and hostel in the centre of the village. There we explored the exhibitions on Hedd Wyn and John Roberts. Hedd Wyn – Ellis Humphrey Evans – a shepherd from Trawsfynydd who was killed at Pilkem Ridge in July 1917, only a month after sailing to France. Posthumously, he won the chair at the Birkenhead National Eisteddfod for his poem 'Yr Arwr' (The Hero). The chair was draped in black. John Roberts, born at Rhiw Goch, Trawsfynydd, a convert to Catholicism, was executed at Newgate on 10 December 1610. He was canonised on 25 October 1970.

Pennant Melangell is a special place. The twelfth-century shrine of Melangell is one of the 'holiest places' in Wales. What a sense of peace, especially when one receives the healing oil and the Eucharist from the resident priest.

Hans Schmeinck, a 90-year-old member of the chapel took

us around Jerusalem, Yr Efail, Berriew, the home chapel of the Calvinistic Methodist, Thomas Jones, the first missionary to Khasia Hills in India in 1841. Hans was a German prisoner-of-war who married a local Welsh girl and settled in Montgomeryshire.

Epynt is a sacred mountain. Cilmeri is the memorial to the death in 1282 of Llywelyn ap Gruffydd, the last native prince of Wales. 'Ys terfyn byd? Is it the end of the world?' was the despairing elegiac cry of Bleddyn Fardd. Nearly 700 years later, in 1940, at the other end of Epynt, Babell Calvinistic Methodist Chapel was closed, the land confiscated and the people evicted when the government demanded the land for military training. Iorwerth Peate records an 82-year-old lady of Hirllwyn farm, saying to him, 'It is the end of the world here.' Epynt is also the birthplace of John Penri of Cefn Brith, hanged for his faith in London in 1593. He is 'the morning star of Protestant Nonconformity in Wales'.[3]

It is a joy to partake of Holy Communion with a living congregation at Maesyronnen in Radnorshire, the oldest and best preserved Nonconformist chapel in Wales. Probably a converted Elizabethan barn, the church has worshipped there since 1697, but the cause dates back to much earlier.

The enthusiasm and hospitality of the Williams family of Pantycelyn is gracious and overwhelming. They invite you into their home which is a national treasure. The family includes Cecil, Aled, and three-year-old Hefin, the sixth, seventh and eighth generations of William Williams, 'y pêr ganiedydd, the sweet singer of Wales'.[4]

'Is it nothing to you, all you who pass by?' Rawlins White, a Welsh Protestant martyr was executed in Cardiff on 30 March 1555. He is remembered and forgotten in a premier Cardiff departmental store.

It was a privilege to converse with John Williams of Cefn Brith, the birthplace of John Penri, the Puritan martyr. John Williams wisely commented: 'They executed John Penri in 1593 – it was too late! The Bible had been translated in 1588.'

These are just ten of our hundreds of experiences of the living history which is Wales today. The ancient stones became living stones. *Our Holy Ground* is for all who live in Wales and all who are interested in the distinctive story of the different nations on these islands. We trust it will help us rediscover our roots and prepare us to face God's future humbly and confidently.

This pilgrimage of creativity has been taking place in two dimensions. John has read and re-read the eminent Welsh scholars of the last half-century and has written and re-written the story over the past 15 years. Peter, accompanied at times by John as an eager passenger, has been on a physical journey with his camera, crossing and re-crossing our land. We have both found ourselves discerning the action of God. While it would seem that John was making journeys into the past and Peter was on pilgrimage through present-day Wales, in fact we both found ourselves exploring past and present and preparing ourselves for the future.

We are both from mining valleys: John from Tylorstown and Peter from Brynmawr. We were both nurtured in the Congregational Way and are ministers ordained in the Reformed tradition. We both began our ministries in Powys and between us we have served in Wales for 80 years. We have both found ourselves served by the community of Penrhys. Above all, we rejoice in our commitment to the one, holy, catholic and apostolic church. We offer our exploration and our discoveries to the wider community, and trust our readers and viewers find their own encouragement to discover many bright fields.

What we have written and photographed present glimpses of a history which belongs to all of us who care about Wales. We are grateful to the great line of historians who have stimulated and challenged us. Our intention is to seek to share a broad sweep of the story. John has found his journeys into the past, humbling, exciting and joyous. Peter has found his journeys across Wales an equally humbling, exciting and joyous pilgrimage. We have been stimulated by what we have learned from each other and how the conversation between text and image has stimulated our sense of inhabiting God's story. We wish to share our adventure.

In our exploration we have discerned the finger of God guiding the people of Wales throughout their history. We align ourselves with all, in twenty-first-century Wales, who are determined not to allow ourselves to be incessantly divided between people of the north and the south and the forgotten middle. Neither will we in the church allow ourselves to live continually in our historic denominational straitjackets. We look forward to the day when the people of Wales will discover and celebrate the wholeness of their Christian story. We are grateful that we see Jesus in the midst of human life. *Our Holy Ground* is an attempt to recognise how God is always with his people. That surely will give us confidence to be discerning and courageous as we seek to be faithful in God's today and tomorrow.

And so we set out on our journey. The photographer and the writer were sent to hear the message of the Lady and the nameless one. Would we find anything? Would there be anything at the end of the quest? Would it all end in a vanity of vanities? Or would the ancient stones speak. Would living stones speak even more eloquently? Yes they did – both stones and living stones. Were we surprised? Overwhelmed? Grateful? Yes!

The gift of God came literally on our final journey together. It had taken several years to get there. Many times we had travelled the length and breadth of Wales. It had involved thousands of miles to get there. And what did God reveal to us at the end of the journey? Come with us and be prepared to be surprised by joy.

John I. Morgans, Newchapel, Llanidloes
Peter C. Noble, Llanbradach
Dydd Gŵyl Dewi 2016

15

1

ORIGINS OF A PEOPLE

WHEN E.G. BOWEN, Gregynog professor of geography and anthropology at Aberystwyth, died in 1983, his obituarist in *The Times* wrote, Bowen 'was quintessentially Welsh. Short and dark, dressed in bible black from shoes to hat, he was as distinctive as he was distinguished.'[1]

What is it to be 'quintessentially Welsh'? Welsh people are not caricatures of characters in Dylan Thomas' *Under Milk Wood*. Who are the people of Wales? What is this land called Wales? Gwyn Alf Williams' wonderfully polemical and incisive history of Wales is entitled *When was Wales?*[2] The title raises a series of puzzles. When did a Wales recognizable today come into existence? Can Wales be geographically defined as the mountainous land west of the boundary of Offa's Dyke (Clawdd Offa), built by a Mercian king in the eighth century? To what extent has the Dyke shaped our view of the extent and identity of Wales? Is Wales, and are the Welsh shaped by the strength and sound of the sea, modelled by their proximity to sea-routes, and have its peoples always been influenced by an oceanic consciousness? Are the people of Wales the direct descendants of pre-historic peoples, creators of Megalithic and Neolithic marvels? To what extent have these indigenous peoples been changed by the engrafting of Celtic incomers during the millennium before the Christian era? Re-shaped by the arrival of would-be conquering Romans and Normans? Changed radically by the flood of immigrants from other parts of the British Isles, Italy and Spain during the industrial revolution? Influenced by economic migrants from the

Caribbean and southern Asia, and English recreational arrivals in the post second world war period? And in this twenty-first century, receiving new peoples from the old nations of Eastern Europe and refugees from the catastrophic warfare and economic inequalities which are destroying much of our contemporary world? Despite the long and chequered story of many communities living in this land, it has been argued that the distinctiveness of the Welsh was shaped in the period when their ancient language and culture were decisively formed during the era historians once called the 'Dark Ages', that era between the retreat of militaristic Romans and the arrival of equally militaristic Normans? When did Wales begin to emerge as Wales? When did the Welsh begin to see themselves as Welsh?

The people of Wales first knew themselves as Britons, Brythoniaid, deriving from the Brittonic Prytani (people of Britain). They also saw themselves as Cymry (Cymry first appears in Welsh poetry in the seventh century), a word which means fellow countrymen. It was not until the twelfth century that the incoming Normans used the derogatory term 'Wales and the Welsh', meaning foreign land and foreigners. What was it that gave the people of this land a sense of belonging? An argument is made that this distinctiveness emerged during the centuries which immediately follow the retreat of Rome and the advance of the Anglo-Saxons.

> The years 400–600 are wholly central to the history of Wales and Britain. That was the era when Britain came to be divided into a Brythonic west, a Teutonic east and a Gaelic north, and when the nations of the Welsh, the English and the Scots crystallized. It was the era which saw the establishment of the dynasties of the main kingdoms of Wales and the transformation of Brittonic into a language which can be recognized as Welsh. It was also the age when Christianity so pervaded Wales that most of its parishes came to bear the names of the glorious army of the saints.[3]

The Land and Peoples of Early Wales

Although the land of Wales with its people of a distinctive language, religion and culture emerged during the post Roman period, the previous millennia had left their mark on the landscape of Wales and the inscape of the Welsh. Inhabitants and visitors embarking upon a historical and geographical magical mystery tour through Wales should begin with the Palaeolithic limestone caves of Pontnewydd in the Elwy valley, Denbighshire, where Ice Age hunters were present 225,000 years ago. The journey continues to the extreme south, to Paviland cave in Gower where the remains of the 'Red Lady', a young man from 24,000 years BCE, were discovered. Travel eastwards and towards our own days and find the footprints of a family walking towards the sea at Uskmouth about 9,000 years ago. Excitement will mount as the enquirer moves from the Palaeolithic to the Neolithic age and discovers some of Wales' most startling gifts. Chambered tombs dating from 4500 to 3500 BCE are the oldest surviving standing structures in Europe. It is an awesome experience to walk into the heart of Bryn Celli Ddu in Anglesey, or to survey from Pentre Ifan in Pembrokeshire, the vast panorama of the Welsh coast and the seas stretching westwards to Ireland, or to stumble upon hidden Tinkinswood and St Lythan's in the Vale of Glamorgan. And then to acknowledge in wonder that these are but four of 150 such tombs which survive in this small country.

The Early Bronze Age presents the construction of cairns, barrows, stone and timber circles and, above all, standing stones and stone circles. The Iron Age, beginning about 700 BCE, saw the creation of more than 600 defensive hill-forts, among which are the elaborate forts of Llanymynech, Breiddin and Ffridd Maldwyn along the eastern borders and the awesome Tre'r Ceiri perched above Trefor on Llŷn. This period witnessed the arrival of the Celtic peoples who merged with the indigenous Britons. The traditional theory was that they arrived and conquered soon after 700 BCE, but 'The general trend nowadays is to view the arrival of Celtic-speaking peoples and their rich and diverse material culture as a gradual process which occurred over thousands of years. This culture, in turn, was assimilated, adapted and developed by native societies over a long period of time.'[4] The Celts bequeathed the gift of their languages, two branches of which survived as Brittonic (P Celtic) whose descendants are Welsh, Breton, Cornish and Cumbrian, and Goedelic (Q Celtic) from which emerged Irish and Scottish Gaelic and the language of Manx.

Into this land of the Brythoniaid/Celtic people marched the Romans under Aulus Plautius. From the year 43 CE the tribes living in Wales were confronted by Roman legions. After facing generations of resistance, the armies of Rome conquered the Deceangli of the north coast, the highland Ordovices, the Silures of the south-east and the Demetae of the south-west. Victory was accomplished by the combination of military successes and building permanent fortresses and marching camps connected by brilliantly engineered roads. The two major Roman fortresses at Chester (Deva) and Caerleon (Isca) were linked with auxiliary fortresses at Caernarfon (Segontium) and Carmarthen (Moridunum Dematarum). Alongside the military subjugation came civilian administration centred on Caerwent (Venta Silorum) and Carmarthen, which claims to be the oldest town in Wales. These towns were the exception within Welsh Roman life. During the 350 years of Roman occupation, it was only the south-east corner of Wales which was 'Romanized'. The native heartland continued much as it had been before the arrival of the Roman invaders. However, part of the inheritance passed on by the Romans after they left in 383 was a religion which had begun as a cult within Judaism but had become recognised as the official religion of the Empire by Emperor Constantine in 312. Christianity had arrived in Wales.

The Forming of Wales

What is meant by the Dark Ages? The period after the retreat of Rome was termed 'dark' by many historians because of the comparative lack of documentary evidence. On the contrary, the centuries separating the Romans and the Normans provided the space for Wales to emerge into the light. Between 383, when Macsen Wledig (Magnus Maximus) ordered the removal of the Roman legions and 1066, when William I seized the English throne, came the 'heroic age'. Wales emerged as a territorial, cultural entity created by a range of factors.

The post-Roman period saw the transformation of tribal groups into the more stable kingdoms of Gwynedd, Powys, Dyfed and Glywysyng (the forerunner of Morgannwg). Under the leadership of kings, princes and heroes like Cunedda, Rhodri Fawr, Hywel Dda and Gruffydd ap Llewelyn, they resisted the incursions of the Anglo-Saxons from the east and the Vikings from the north and west. Independence was maintained for many centuries, until the double blow of the death of Llywelyn ap Gruffydd, the last native prince of Wales at Cilmeri in 1282, and the imposition of the Acts of Union (the annexation of Wales) in 1536 and 1542 by Henry VIII, a descendant of the Welsh Tudors of Anglesey.

The struggle against the pressures of the Saxons in the east, the Irish in the west, and the Vikings from the north and west saw the seeds of a nation taking root as a geographical entity. This land of mountains and forests was bounded on the east by Offa's Dyke and on the north, west and south by the seas. Protected and isolated from the east by its mountains, the Welsh turned to the seas as their highways, especially to contact other Celtic peoples of the islands of Britain and of continental Brittany.

These centuries witnessed the development of a canon of Welsh native law, traditionally codified at a great synod at Hendy-gwyn (Whitland) in the 940s. The Laws of Hywel (Cyfraith Hywel Dda) emphasized kinship, neighbourhood, trust, compensation and reconciliation. Cyfraith Hywel Dda held sway throughout most of Wales until it was finally suppressed by the Acts of Union.

The Welsh language emerged from Brittonic and matured into a culturally rich and legally acknowledged language for the majority of people who lived in Wales. The earliest body of Welsh verse, that of Taliesin and Aneirin, dates to the sixth century and there has been an unbroken thread which continues to flourish with the Welsh Renaissance of the twentieth and twenty-first centuries. Welsh, the language of the people of Wales, was never under threat until the Acts of Union outlawed Welsh from public affairs, and the Education Acts of the late nineteenth century focused on learning through the medium of the English language.

The period is also described as the age of the saints when Wales became 'Christianized'. The Cymry emerged during this period of 700 years, and critical to their sense of identity was the creation of a form of Christianity in touch with the developments of wider faith communities on the Celtic western seaboards, in continental Europe and the eastern Mediterranean, and at the same time indigenous to the land of Wales. The form of Christianity which emerged was faithful to the text of the Gospel and the context of its community and remained a critical influence on the people of Wales through nearly two millennia until its erosion during the past century.

In our story, we will look at the interweaving of these elements in the shaping of the nation of Wales.

2

THE SHAPING OF A CHRISTIAN PEOPLE, c.200–1066

The Arrival of Christianity

Jesus was a country-man. Most of his life and ministry was exercised in rural Galilee and many of his disciples were fishermen. Jerusalem, the ancient religious and political capital of Judea, witnessed his betrayal, arrest, illegal trial and execution. The immediate reaction of his followers was to retreat to their familiar life by the shores of Lake Galilee. It was the resurrection of Jesus and the empowering of his spirit which changed fearful disciples into fearless apostles. These apostles moved from their rural background to share the gospel in an urban setting. Paul, born in the 'no mean city' of Tarsus and educated 'at the feet of Gamaliel' in Jerusalem, moved from city to city, from Jerusalem to Antioch, Ephesus, Athens and Corinth, and ended his life in Rome. Christianity was the religion of the urban Roman world, moving onwards by road and sea. Rural people remained pagans.

Who were the people of Wales during the period of Roman occupation? They were indistinguishable from the other Brithonic-Celtic inhabitants of southern Britain. Before Emperor Claudius ordered the invasion of Britain in 43 CE, the British people shared the same 'British-Celtic' language and, by the year 400, most of the educated inhabitants of 'southern Britain' spoke Latin and British-Celtic. Some, particularly the inhabitants of Dyfed and Brycheiniog, added the Irish language to their accomplishments during the sixth century and can be described as trilingual. By about 700, British Latin had died out but the inhabitants of Wales continued to share a common language with the peoples of Strathclyde, the Isle of Man, Cornwall and Brittany. They knew themselves to be different from the Picts in the north, the Irish in the west and the English in the east. These were the centuries when a more distinctive people began to be recognized within the land we now know as Wales. By the ninth century the Cymry had become monolingual, using the language of Cymraeg, one of the languages emerging from British. Neither Latin nor Irish were commonly spoken, although Latin remained the language of liturgy and learning. By this time, those who lived west of the Mercian boundary of Offa's Dyke began to grasp that they were a distinctive people. It was the consequence of a combination of several factors: the shaping of a common language, the formation of more stable kingdoms, the development of a canon of Welsh native law and the flourishing of a form of Christianity shaped by native, Roman and Eastern influences.

The Formative Period

> Christianity was first introduced into this country before the Welsh, as a separate people, could properly be said to exist. It was brought by anonymous Roman traders and soldiers when Britain was still a remote province of the Empire. During the era of imperial rule it remained very much a religion of the towns and the civilian settlements, of which there were relatively few in Wales. When the Roman legions departed in the fifth century AD and left the inhabitants of Britain to fend for themselves, Christianity undoubtedly survived – in Wales as well as in the more intensively Romanized areas of south-east Britain.[1]

When and how did this new faith arrive in Wales? The heritage of British Christianity stretches back to the days of Roman occupation. Ancient legends weave stories of Joseph of Arimathea arriving in Glastonbury, and even of a missionary journey by Paul to Llantwit Major! The ninth-century *Historia*

Brittonum includes the story of the British king Lucius sending a delegation to Rome in 167 CE and, as a consequence, the Christian faith was established in Britain.

The period of Roman occupation bears witness to the two first known 'Welsh' martyrs, Julius and Aaron, in the City of the Legions (Caerleon). Gildas records that they were victims of Emperor Diocletian's persecution (303–5), but modern historians suggest they were probably martyred during earlier persecutions, under Decius (250–1) or Valerian (257–9). Bishops played a defining role in the ministry of the Early Church. Three bishops from Britain were present when the Council of Arles debated the problem of puritanical Donatism in 313. Three others were at the Council which met at Rimini to deal with the Arian heresy in 359.

What is the physical evidence for an early Christian presence in Wales? There are few Romano-Christian remains. The apse building at Caerwent may have been a church erected in about 400. Caerwent has also yielded a pewter bowl bearing a Christian monogram. Graves near the villa at Llantwit Major (Llanilltud Fawr) may be aligned in a Christian fashion. An undoubted treasure of Welsh history and culture is the survival of between 450 and 500 stone monuments. These inscribed stones, also found in Ireland and along the western coasts from Brittany to Argyll, provide the most important material evidence for life in Wales for the half-millennia after the fall of the Roman Empire.

The earliest stones which date from 400–600 CE reflect the legacy of Roman culture. This was a key period when the Welsh nation was beginning to emerge and when Christianity was deepening its roots throughout the country. Most of the inscriptions are carved in Latin although 40 stones bear the influence of both Ireland / the Atlantic seaboard and Roman / Irish styles. Their inscriptions are in Latin and Ogham (an ancient Irish form of writing). These are found particularly in the south-west and in Breconshire (Brycheiniog). Most of these are commemorations of the dead. The early medieval stones, surviving from the seventh to the ninth centuries are elaborate and free-standing, usually in the form of an incised cross, while a few have names. One, at Tywyn in Meirionethshire, dating from the eighth century includes the earliest example of written Welsh. One of the most significant is Eliseg's Pillar, erected about 854 near Llangollen. The inscription, now indecipherable, commemorates the glory of the rulers of Powys. The later monuments, dating from the ninth to the eleventh centuries are also free-standing, but these stone crosses are more elaborately carved, revealing Celtic graphic influences. Some of these include memorials to leading rulers. Particularly spectacular are the crosses at Penmon in Anglesey, Llanbadarn Fawr in Ceredigion, Nevern and Carew in Pembrokeshire and at Margam, Llanilltud Fawr and Llangyfelach in Glamorgan.

Documentary evidence of the existence of a flourishing British Christianity comes from various sources. Pelagius (c. 360–c. 420) was a Brythonic Christian whose theological views were condemned as heretical at the Council of Carthage in 418. Followers of the ideas of Pelagius were exiled by the emperor and many took refuge in Britain. There they created such a strong network of sympathizers that Garmon (Germanus) of Auxerre was sent, in 429, by the Pope to extirpate this 'heretical' movement. Another early thinker was Faustus, who was born in Britain at the beginning of the fifth century. He became abbot of Lérins, an island off the coast of Provence in 429. A third figure was Gildas (c. 495–c. 570). His *De Excidio Britanniae* (On the Destruction of Britain, c. 540) gives a vivid picture of the period between the erosion of Latin influence and the emergence of early Welsh culture. Probably born near the Clyde, Gildas became a monk at Llanilltud Fawr where, along with David and Samson, he was educated by Illtud. His use of the Bible, Virgil and the Letters of Ignatius of Antioch reflects a scholarly education. Modelled on the prophecies of Jeremiah, *De Excidio* contains a history of Britain and views of contemporary kings, judges and churchmen. Britain is a latter-day Israel, being punished by the invading pagans for its infidelity. All three, Pelagius, Faustus and Gildas, reveal the existence of a vibrant Christian life in the immediate post-Roman period.

The influence of Latin culture affected only a minority of literate people, largely confined to the south-east of Wales or in the vicinity of Roman forts and towns. This remained a period when Wales had no distinctive boundaries, its peoples were consciously tribal, and there was no common recognisable language. But all was about to change. During the centuries between the departure of the Roman conquerors and the arrival of the Norman invaders, Wales came into existence. This was partly the consequence of the life and work of the Christian movement.

The Romanized South-East: Dyfrig

If Christianity was brought into Wales by Roman merchants, soldiers, civil servants and housewives, we should not be surprised if there was some continuity of witness and practice in the ancient Romanized territories of Gwent, Erging and Glywysing in south-east Wales which survived the arrival of the new pagan barbarians from Europe. Gwent, formed around Caerwent, claimed Caradog as its first king. Erging, or Archenfield, between the Monnow and the Wye, traditionally recognized Ariconium as its centre, and was a region (which included western Herefordshire) where Welsh was spoken until the eighteenth century. Glywysing, between the Tawe and the Usk claimed the fifth-century Glywys as its first king, and Cadog, a Welsh saint as the grandson of Glywys. The uniqueness of this south-eastern corner and the border country was the cradle of Christianity in Wales, and was the starting point of a missionary movement which revitalized much of Western Europe.

Amongst the first saints of the church emerging from this Romanized background was Dubricius or Dyfrig (c.425–c.505). Possibly born at Madley, near Hereford, he is reputed to have founded monasteries at Hentland on the Wye and Moccas, also near Hereford, before he withdrew to Bardsey (Ynys Enlli) where he died and was buried. *The Life of St. Samson*, dating from 610 and written in Brittany, refers to him as papa Dyfrig.

A Bridge from Roman to Celtic: Illtud

The early saints felt compelled to communicate the faith to the vast majority of the people of Wales who had always lived outside the Romanized south-east. A key monk/missionary was Illtud (died early sixth century), a successor of Dyfrig. Like Dyfrig, Illtud is also mentioned in *The Life of St. Samson*. He was heir of the monastic tradition of Anthony of Egypt (before 310), Martin of Tours and Honoratus of Lérins. An ascetic and scholar, Illtud, 'was the renowned master of the Britons [and] learned in the teachings of the Church, in the culture of the Latins and in the traditions of his own people.'[2] His base was the community of Llanilltud Fawr, near the ancient villa of Llantwit, and not far from Dinas Powys, the seat of the kings of Glywysing where objects from Bordeaux, Athens and Alexandria were in use. Llanilltud was the Christian axis of the Celtic-speaking peoples. Llanilltud has often been described as the University of the Atlantic (or the missionary-seminary of the Atlantic) of the Celtic period. Dyfrig and Illtud were two of the earliest leaders of the Celtic tradition who successfully fused a native emphasis with the intellectual traditions of the wider European church. Samson, a student at Llanilltud, left for Dol about 520 to become the father of Breton monasticism. Dyfrig, Gildas and Samson are all linked with Caldey Island (Ynys Bŷr), the one place in Wales where there has been a continuing monastic tradition, even until this third Christian millennium (with interruptions caused by Vikings and the Reformation!). Two of Samson's fellow students at Llanilltud Fawr were Paul Aurelian of Llandovery, a leading figure in the Cornish church and Gildas, the author of *De Excidio Britanniae*.

27

A Celtic Tradition Emerges: Dewi

The mood changed after 500. The Roman world had collapsed. Paganism was on the march, destroying an ancient civilization. Now the emphasis was holding on to the faith. How was the faith, handed down by the saints, to be preserved and passed on? The strategy now was for survival and a return to the basics of faith and ethics. The vogue was a new puritanism, and ascetics searched out desolate retreats. By 550, perhaps also as a result of plagues, ascetic monasticism had become the Christian norm. This age of saints witnessed a Christian spirit which helped shape the life of the people of Wales. The most famous of all Welsh saints, the patron saint of Wales, is Dewi (David, 530–589). Sixty churches are dedicated to his name between Pembroke and Hereford. Fact and legend are interwoven in the *Life of St David*, written by Rhygyfarch of Llanbadarn in 1090, in the work of Gerallt Gymro (Giraldus Cambrensis, c.1146–1223) and in *The Book of the Anchorite* (1346) of Llanddewibrefi. Tradition suggests that Dewi was the son of Non and Sant, king of Ceredigion. Dewi belonged to the ascetic branch of the monastic tradition. He presided at the synod at Llanddewibrefi where he combatted Pelagianism. There he is said to have raised a hill so that the crowd could hear him more clearly. Dewi's asceticism was reflected in his hard work, vegetarianism and temperance. Many present-day Christians who applaud the primacy of Dewi would hesitate at his ethical stance, but there are many in the green lobby, eager to live in tune with nature and to preserve our environment who would find much to commend in this old-fashioned puritan. It is to the Llanddewi hermit that we owe the famous final words of Dewi: 'Lords, brothers and sisters, be joyful and keep your faith and your belief, and do the little things that you have heard and seen from me.'

The Nature of Early Christian Communities

Christianity inherited a world view in which the material and the spiritual were intertwined. The human drama was depicted as a combat between the absolutes of good and evil. Spiritual forces were embattled in an eternal struggle for the possession of the human soul. Life was poor, nasty, brutish and short. Famine, plague and war were constant realities. The final scenes in the Christian drama were death, judgment, heaven and hell, and those exercising the powers of blessing and cursing possessed the ultimate weapons. This was the context in which the church embarked on its nurture and mission.

Llan

The 'llan' was at the heart of the life of early Christianity in Wales. Llan was originally a word meaning an enclosure of any kind, as, for example, 'y gwinllan' (vineyard) or 'y berllan' (orchard), but llan came to be applied to an enclosed burial ground and therefore to the church built within it. Llan is common in place-names in Wales. Of the 1,132 names of Welsh parishes listed in the tithe schedules of the 1830s and 1840s (stretching row after row in the National Library of Wales in Aberystwyth), 40 per cent begin with llan. 'Clues to an early medieval date for church sites include defended enclosures in close association with circular or curvilinear churchyards, churches, housing, early Christian monuments, and early dedications.'[3]

The cultural geography of Wales is impossible to understand without reference to the hundreds of llannau found throughout the country. Llan holds together the sense of a community and a place. It was both a community founded and shaped by the Gospel as embodied in a Welsh saint and is also identified with a place, located in the secular world of space and time. Llanwynno in north Glamorgan is typical of hundreds of llannau. Founded by Gwynno, its church is built near an ancient holy well, it possesses an incised ring-cross, retains an atmosphere of sacredness and remains a place of worship and pilgrimage. It is the inheritance of sixth-century Gwynno for the post-industrial Rhondda, Clydach and Cynon valleys and post-Victorian Christianity.

The physical shape of the llan was concentric. The whole area was deemed to be a sacred place (noddfa or nawdd). Within the noddfa was the cemetery (mynwent), and at the centre was the llan itself, the residence of the saint and a place of worship. The llan met the needs of the community. These holy places, often at 'the world's end, some at the sea jaws, or over a dark lake, in a desert or a city'[4] offered protection against the power of cursing. They provided sanctuary in an age when the power of the curse and the invocation of evil spirits held sway in people's everyday lives. Here was a safe place, revered because it offered protection. Many Christian sanctuaries were built on the site of a pre-Christian holy place where there had been stone circles, as at Yspyty Cynfyn in Ceredigion. This emphasis on the holy place, the security of the womb, the place where the divine presence is experienced has validity in all cultures, not least in our own. The llan was also the place where the liturgy was celebrated. No-one had to travel far to avail themselves of the sacramental life.

Clas

Although the majority of llannau were small and served by an ascetic hermit-monk, they were linked into a federation of daughter churches, members of a saint-cult dependent on a central clas-church. Large houses such as Llanilltud and Bangor-is-y-coed (where Bede suggests there were 2,000 monks) were normally located on good lands, around the sea coasts, along the valleys and near usable tracks. Only a few, like Llangurig in northern Powys, were found in the remote high uplands. The clas was the critical source of inspiration, fellowship and training. Although the clas was organized in accordance with Roman law, it also anticipated what developed into Irish canon law. The clas served as a bridge between ancient classicism and the emerging world of the Celtic-British peoples of the Atlantic coasts. These centres of learning taught the faith and trained the missionary saints for their life-work of sharing the Gospel.

The clas was a major church, usually headed by an abbot and consisting of a community living in individual cells. Probably some of these Christian communities had survived from the days of Romanitas. Others came into existence during the fifth century but the most rapid advance was between 550 and 650. At least 36 clasau (including Glasbury and Glascwm, both in Radnorshire) have been recognised throughout Wales, from Penmon in Anglesey to Caerwent in Gwent, and from Bangor-is-y-coed, near Wrexham, to St Davids in Pembrokeshire.

The community of the clas, led by the abbot included the *sacerdos* (presbyter) to celebrate the liturgy, the *lector* (scriba or athro) responsible for teaching and the *oeconomus* who cared for the economic life. The clas, usually associated with a major figure, would be linked with daughter houses, often sharing the same name and perhaps reflecting a similar theological, liturgical and ethical emphasis. Eminent saints included Illtud, with his clas at Llanilltud Fawr, Teilo at Llandeilo, Padarn at Llanbadarn, and Beuno at Clynnog Fawr. Llannau were linked in a connexional way with the mother house, and not necessarily in a diocesan or territorial manner. They shared relationships and specific local histories, stemming from a named saint. The diocese and the parish were shaped in the twelfth century, the gifts of a more organized Norman mentality. There then emerged a quite different way of seeing the church.

The saints dominated popular religion. Although many Welsh churches were dedicated to the Virgin Mary, Peter or Michael, as in other European countries, most were associated with national saints like Dewi, Beuno or Cadog, or to local saints like Idloes, Melangell, Gwynno and Tyfodwg. Curig's llan was at Llangurig, but he also had his 'resting place' at Eisteddfa Gurig where he meditated and prayed in solitariness. The close association between the saint and the llan was forged by

31

charters, by the saint's celebration in a hagiographical 'Life', by being commemorated in the liturgical calendar and as a place of pilgrimage. Journeys to these places were part of the international practice of pilgrimages. St David is reputed to have visited Jerusalem, where he was believed to have been created archbishop by the patriarch. Hywel Dda made a pilgrimage to Rome in 928. St Davids and Bardsey (Ynys Enlli) were famed places of pilgrimage. The saints and their followers lived in the community of the llan, but that community included those who felt a particular allegiance to the saint and even extended to those who had died. The saint was invoked on many occasions, but particularly during times of crisis. After the saint's death, his holiness continued in places with which he had been identified. Relics were treasured. As early as the sixth century, shrines were constructed to safeguard saintly remains, and many wished to be buried near the saint, such as at the notable Christian cemetery at Arfryn in Anglesey or near the bell of Cadog at Llancarfan in Glamorgan.

One thousand, one hundred wells have been located in Wales, of which 437 have been dedicated to saints. Many of these springs were sacred in pagan times and were Christianized. This may be the case at Penrhys where the ancient well (now associated with the medieval cult of the Blessed Virgin Mary) is near the only crossing-place between the two Rhondda valleys, on the saddle between the rivers Rhondda Fawr and Rhondda Fach. Control of such key places was central in the expansion of any new faith. The battle for the spring between the Christian and the pagan was often arduous, and was followed by the building of a chapel, as at the sixth-century chapels of St Seiriol in Anglesey and Ffynnon Cybi in Caernarfonshire.

Conflict between Celtic and Latin Traditions

The emergence of Wales as a land and people, with its law, leadership, culture and language seemed to crystallize at the same time as the formation of the Christian faith as a 'national' religion. As a consequence, the Christian religion was part of the essence of being Welsh. The heritage of British Christianity stretched back to the days of Roman occupation. It is possible that the church in south Wales had a consistent ecclesiastical structure from the Roman era to the arrival of the Normans. There is a possible connection between Caerwent as the capital of the Silures and Llandaff, and between Moridunum as the capital of the Demetae with St Davids. The British were Christian long before the arrival of Anglo-Saxons who were new, unwelcome and pagan arrivals. It was not surprising that the British considered themselves to be a chosen people, a latter-day Israel, an elect nation called by God to preserve and share the Gospel.

Augustine, an Italian by birth, was appointed in 596 by Pope Gregory to re-establish the church in England. Augustine landed at Ebbsfleet (Kent) in 597. Gregory's intention was to create an administrative system of bishops and provinces mirroring the towns and provinces of the empire. Augustine was given authority over British bishops who were expected to co-operate with the new archbishop and be subject to the new see of Canterbury. Not for the first, and certainly not for the last, time was the church to divide nations, communities and cultures by its insistence on only one form of church government. Bede records that two conferences between Augustine and the Welsh bishops took place in 602–3 at Aust near the mouth of the Severn, and near Bangor-is-y-coed. Both meetings broke down in mutual intransigence and alienation. Augustine claimed authority over the British bishops and, according to Bede, he did not rise to greet them when they arrived. This affront to the dignity of the church marked the beginning of a failure to cooperate between the churches in Britain and the church in England. By the 670s, the English church regarded the Britons as heretics. Their history was dismissed as irrelevant, and Christian Britain and English Britain became coterminous in the eyes of York and Canterbury.

Disagreements centred upon the tonsure of monks, the practice of baptism and the calculation of the Easter cycles. The churches of Britain and Ireland adhered to a system devised by the western church in 314, while Rome followed a novel system adopted there in 457. The disagreement over the date of Easter was settled when Christians in Celtic lands changed to the Roman system – in Ireland in 630, Northumbria at the Synod of Whitby in 664, Iona in 716 and Wales as late as 768. Celtic practices were later eliminated by the Norman invasion in the eleventh century. How different were the two forms of Christianity? Was it only a matter of dates and habits? Or was it more fundamental? Charles-Edwards suggests that the 'British Church was more dependent on Biblical scholarship than were its continental counterparts, while it was increasingly, and soon wholly, dependent on its teachers to provide clergy who were *litterati*.'[5] Probably this was the reason that British and Irish synods were composed of bishops, abbots *and* teachers. Both the episcopal and teaching orders were important in the government of the church. Pennar Davies argues:

> There was therefore a difference of theological outlook between the Christian life of Wales and the Rome-centred organization which confronted it in the person of Augustine... it differed completely from traditional episcopacy in that the episcopal and priestly functions were subordinated to the missionary and monastic activities of the 'saints' and that the pattern was not diocesan but connexional in the freest sense. And it could be added that the whole movement was politically aware and vigorous...[6]

Nurture

It is nothing short of miraculous that a tradition of learning and scholarship was maintained in Wales, despite the hammering on the eastern frontier by pagan Anglo-Saxons, and on the coasts by the savage maritime onslaughts of Scandinavian raiders. The tradition of scholarship survived by the content of learning being passed on from one generation to the next. At the heart of the teaching ministry of the clasau was the stability of the classical curriculum, the *trivium* which remained basically unchanged from the fifth to the eleventh century. Its foundation was the *rudimenta* or the egwyddorion (the abecadarium) when the novice was taught to read and write Latin, recite the Latin psalms by heart and learn 'the rudiments, the psalms, the readings of the whole year, the masses, and the divine office'.[7] Built on the foundation of the rudimenta was the stage of learning *grammar*, during which the pupil was taught central texts like Virgil's *Aeneid* and Christian Latin poets. The third stage was *rhetoric*, learning to communicate clearly and forcefully what had been received through the process of rudimenta and grammar. The study of Scripture was central to the whole shaping of education, and therefore to the nurture of the members of the monastic community. The 'saint' was prepared for the work of mission.

Learning was communicated from master to apprentice. The tradition had been passed on to Illtud by Garmon, the defender of orthodoxy against Pelagianism, and in turn Illtud, at his famous school at Llanilltud Fawr, taught Samson of Dol (*c*.485–565), Gildas (sixth century) and Maelgwyn Gwynedd (d. 547), prince of north Wales. Asser (d. 909), from St Davids diocese, was invited by Alfred the Great to improve standards of learning for his subjects. The clergy of Gwynedd maintained close contacts with scholars in Ireland and on the Continent. Sulien the Wise (*c*.1010–91) established Llanbadarn Fawr as a centre of learning, and the tradition was continued by his four sons, Rhygyfarch, Ieuan, Daniel, and Arthen, and by their sons, Sulien, Cydifor and Henry. Among the manuscripts associated with Llanbadarn is Ieuan's copy of Augustine's *De Trinitate* and Rhygyfarch's translation of the *Hebrew Psalter*, his *Lament* on the invasion of the Normans and his *Life of St David* (1094).

The programme of education remained intact at Llanbadarn Fawr in Ceredigion and at Llancarfan in Glamorgan until the eleventh century. Members of the clas at Llancarfan may have been involved in the creation of the *Liber Landavensis* (The Book of Llandaff). Llanbadarn was a prominent centre of education until the Norman invasion of Dyfed in 1093 which proved disastrous for both the traditional programme of nurture and for the families which exercised that ministry. Rhygyfarch wrote a lament for a Wales subjected to the Norman yoke:

> Nothing is of any use to me now but the power of giving: neither the law, nor learning, nor great fame, nor the deep-resounding glory of nobility, not honour formerly held, not riches, not wise teaching, not deeds nor arts, not reverence of God, not old age; none of these things retains its station, nor any power. Now the labours of earlier days are despised; the people and the priest are despised by the word, heart and work of the Normans.[8]

Mission

Mission was at the heart of the great enterprise. The whole of Wales was effectively evangelized during the two centuries following the departure of the Romans. The faith needed to be shared. The monk who carried his staff/cross changed standing-stones into crosses and Christian grave-markers. He built his llan in the centre of stone circles, turned pagan holy places into Christian holy places, helped change sinners into saints and sought to make the people of Wales a holy nation. Although many of the saints prayed and worked on the very edges of their world in the wildernesses of upland and highland Wales, the heart of the faith beat primarily in the monastic settlements at the crossroads of the Celtic world. Jesus moved from Galilee to Jerusalem, where the Cross was raised high; Paul moved along the Roman highways and seaways, creating Christian communities in city after city; the Welsh saints transformed the community and Christianized pagan rocks, wells and shrines. The British church was not seriously reversed after the withdrawal of the Romans in 367. It is a story of gradual advance. The Church was both at the centre and on the margins of the world. The links between Welsh and Irish Christianity remained strong from the fifth century until the arrival of the Normans. Patrick took the faith to the Atlantic coast of Ireland. In 563, Columba left Ireland with twelve companions for Iona.

Aidan, monk of Iona, came to England in 635 and became the first bishop and abbot of Lindisfarne. Columbanus left Ireland for Gaul in 590, also with twelve companions. The Welsh were involved in missions to Ireland, Cornwall, Brittany and Galicia in north-western Spain. The faith needed to be shared.

This was the era when seeds planted during the Roman period sent their roots deep into the soil, and strong plants emerged which would flourish for generations. Some claim that the form of Christianity shaped during the Celtic period has retained its influence down through the centuries even to the present. The saints went from area to area sharing the Gospel. They were fired by the evangel. Most were wandering monks, often associated with the Celtic areas of Ireland, western Scotland and the Isles, the Isle of Man, parts of northern England, Wales, Cornwall, and Brittany.

Strong links existed between continental Europe, the Mediterranean, and the western edge of Britain. This connection can only be understood when we grasp the importance of the seaboard. The coasts were the route-ways. The interior, locked in by forests, was off the beaten track. The land of the Angles and Saxons was even more inhospitable. St Davids was the meeting place of the sea-roads from the north and west of the islands of Britain and Ireland with the ancient lands of Christendom. Was the uniqueness of the Christian witness in Wales the consequence of the intermingling of western and eastern traditions with the Celtic context? A pattern of faith, 'catholic and orthodox', was totally contextualized by the Welsh landscape and inscape. The church grasped the opportunities of mission because its faith was formed by the combination of the text received by the fathers and mothers of the Church with a careful rooting into the here and now of the context of post-Roman Wales.

It is for this reason that a contemporary eastern monk, Deiniol of Manod, seeks inspiration from the most ancient Welsh traditions. Saint Aristobulus of Britannia, one of the 70 disciples, is regarded as the founder of the British church.

Similarly, the Cistercian community on Caldey, founded by Pyro in the sixth century, is grateful that it inherits the earliest traditions of the Church. As the Church of twenty-first-century Wales seeks a new shape of belief, ethic and ecclesiology, it could do well to look at the process by which the Church rooted itself into the life of an emerging Wales. New life will not breathe into the dead bones of today's Church by inventing a Celtic romanticism or by any single denomination claiming to be the true and sole inheritor of the Celtic Church. The Church will be renewed by putting the Church's history alongside the story of where the people of Wales believe themselves to be today. From that conversation there may emerge a way of being tomorrow's Church today.

> They not only inherited the earlier Christian tradition from Roman Britain but were also candescently inspired by the infusion into their midst of the ascetic ideals of eastern Christianity, which spread into Britain via France... there survived among them long afterwards an intense awareness of what they believed to be their association with Romanitas; their Christian superiority over the pagan and barbarian milieu of the Anglo-Saxons... [These saints] acquired for themselves an illustrious reputation as persons of exceptional sanctity on the basis of their dedicated leadership, their moral qualities, and their power to work miracles. Looked upon as the founding fathers of the faith, they had won a reputation which became the bed-rock of the specifically Welsh Christian tradition, to which all subsequent religious achievement was referred and by which it was measured.[9]

3

THE AGE OF
CATHOLICISM, 1066–1509

The Early Medieval Church, 1066–1282

Christianity reached Wales during the Roman occupation, flourished during the Age of the Saints and continued on firm foundations until the arrival of the Normans. Although the term 'the Celtic Church' is fraught with controversy, it loosely describes this early period of Welsh Christianity. Can the period between the time of the arrival of the Normans and the sixteenth-century Reformation and Counter-Reformation be defined as 'the age of Catholicism'? This term also does not adequately describe the complexities of the five centuries which separate the illegal entry of the Normans into Wales and the immoral annexation of Wales by the English state through the Acts of Union of 1536 and 1542/3. The period can be divided into two phases: from the arrival of the Normans to the death of Llywelyn ap Gruffydd (Ein Llyw Olaf, Our Last Leader) in 1282, the last native prince of Wales; and the centuries of English rule before the assimilation of Wales into England marked by the Acts of Union during the Tudors.

The Anglo-Norman Conquest, 1067–1282

The centuries following the departure of the Romans saw Wales change from being an amorphous region on the western edge of the Roman Empire into a recognizable political and cultural entity. When the Normans arrived, although the people of Wales remained politically disunited, they had discovered a deeper unity because of a succession of dynastic rulers, recognisable borders, a common language, an inherited law and a shared Christian faith.

By the eleventh century, the Church in Wales was fully integrated into Latin Christendom in terms of general faith and practice, but like other parts of Europe, it had its own regional or national distinctiveness. This distinctiveness was a consequence of the 'Age of the Saints' when Wales became Christianized during the fifth and sixth centuries, followed by its comparative isolation from mainland Europe during the ninth and tenth centuries. This isolation was the consequence of the need to resist Anglo-Saxon infiltration from the east and Viking incursions from the west. The Welsh consequently turned more to their traditional links with Ireland rather than learn from England and the Continent. What kind of Church did the Normans discover when they arrived in the middle of the eleventh century?

The Welsh Church was not subordinate to Canterbury. Its leaders were independent bishops/abbots who were heads of self-contained communities which often supervised a federation of houses. Their clergy were not celibate, and often clasau were led by hereditary families. Many clas churches enjoyed vigorous and scholarly leadership, as at Llanbadarn Fawr, Llancarfan and Llandinam. Some clasau exercised responsibility for churches in a geographical area, like Tywyn for Meirionnydd, and Llanbadarn for Penweddig. Although most individual churches related to their own localized saint-founder, like Idloes, Gwynno and Tyfodwg, other churches belonged to groups or families under the names of more national saints, like Dewi, Teilo, Beuno and Tysilio. Some churches were 'owned' by lay patrons who passed on their property as an inheritance. Clerical marriage was common, and many saints/leaders were of noble descent.[1]

Although the system was far from broken, it was unacceptable to the incoming Normans, for whom the subjection of the Welsh was politically essential and ecclesiastically necessary. The system would not be repaired but replaced! A belief in racial supremacy, combined with military might, have been and remain a potent cocktail for brutal imperialism cloaked under the promise of bringing civilization or Christianity or democracy.

> The Norman conquistadores... were motivated by a selective and self-interested pursuit of their own territorial ambitions, and their grotesquely partial view of the native Welsh... the Welsh were depicted as 'a country breeding men of a bestial type'... The Welsh were barbari (barbarians), an inferior people who stood in urgent need of a sound dose of civilizing values.[2]

How could control be exercised? Norman intentions were largely motivated by greed, and they sought to transfer the wealth of Welsh churches into Norman hands. But they were also partly inspired by the need for reform. How could the new movements which were being established on the continent be introduced into Wales? The advance of the Normans and the imposition of their form of ecclesiology were neither as swift nor as thorough as they anticipated. They had not bargained either for the geography of Wales or the political astuteness and military prowess of many of the Welsh. Whereas the conquest of England was swift and completed within three years, it was over 200 years before the whole of Wales was subjected to the Norman yoke.

Twelfth-century Wales saw the emergence of two very different areas: the east, south and south-west under Norman domination was known as 'Marchia Wallia' (the March of Wales), whereas the north-west and mid-west, continuing under Welsh dynasties, was described as 'Pura Wallia' (independent Wales). In between were areas spasmodically shifting between the control of either the Anglo Normans or the Welsh rulers. The regions developed different histories.

Marchia Wallia

The key to Norman advance was the relationship between the castle, church and town. With the castle and knight came substantial colonization. Six hundred motte and bailey castles were soon erected, the majority being replaced in the twelfth century by stone castles. 'Englishries' were created in parts of Wales, and immigrants, including English, Normans, Bretons and Flemings were moved in to colonize areas like south Gower and south Pembrokeshire. Almost one hundred towns were created between 1070 and 1330, given charters by their lords or by the English king, and they became a focus of trading through markets and fairs.

The Bishop and Diocese

The Norman church arrived alongside castle, knight and immigrant peasant. The Church was a tool of conquest. The Normans discovered an ecclesiastical regime markedly different from the one they had experienced on the continent and from the one they inherited in England. Just as they were determined to master Wales politically, they similarly implanted their ecclesiastical structure. Control was exercised in several ways. The ancient system of clasau and llannau had to be eliminated. There was ruthless exploitation and most clasau were dis-endowed between 1080 and 1130. Their land and income were transferred to monastic foundations favoured by the Normans in Normandy and England. The tithes from all church communities between the Wye and the Usk were confiscated and given to monasteries in Normandy. This pattern of confiscation soon became the norm.

The abbot-bishop who headed the old pattern of connexional clasau had to be controlled. They were replaced by bishops responsible for territorial dioceses and under the jurisdiction of Canterbury. A new structure was rigorously imposed.

> ... it was in the twelfth century that the diocesan geography of
> Wales began to assume the definitive shape that it was to retain

until the twentieth century. The pioneers of the process were two remarkably forceful and enterprising bishops, Urban of Llandaff, 1107–34, and Bernard of St David's, 1115–48... By 1150, therefore,Wales had been divided into four territorial dioceses with clearly defined boundaries.[3]

Reform à la Normandy was essential. By 1107, Urban, the first Norman bishop of Llandaff, professed obedience to the primate of England. This set the pattern for the future, and by the middle of the twelfth century the bishops of all four Welsh dioceses had been pressurized into making similar professions. These new-style prelates introduced far-reaching modifications into the organization, possessions, and discipline of their sees. They replaced the earlier pattern of authority which had been based on a 'mother and daughter' affiliation, with one of jurisdiction exercised within territorially demarcated dioceses with fixed geographical boundaries. Within these boundaries came archdeaconries, deaneries and parishes. Into these parishes, tithes were introduced on a regular basis so that the clergy could be properly maintained. Although the sites of churches date to the very earliest days of Christianity, and indeed many are located in pre-Christian holy places, church buildings do not survive in Wales from before the early twelfth century. New churches were now built throughout Wales, as at Carmarthen, or re-built as at Haverfordwest, Tywyn, Meifod, Aberdaron, Llanbadarn Fawr and Beddgelert. The diocesan and parish pattern with hundreds of ancient buildings is a legacy from this catholic period, and has remained basically intact down through the centuries. Of course, there has been a transformation of context between the Middle Ages and the present. In the medieval period this was the geographical pattern and these were the church buildings central to the religious life of all the people of Wales. Now it is the inheritance, perhaps often a burden, of one section of the contemporary Christian community, the Anglican Church in Wales. Can God's people today discover, receive and share these gifts as significant for the well-being of the people of God and for the whole nation?

The contemporary exploration of sacred spaces reflects a search for 'presence, peace and stimulus' which often present an encounter with the divine.[4]

Urban created a territorial diocese along the Latin pattern and he divided the Vale of Glamorgan into small parishes. He started to build Llandaff cathedral about 1115, extended his bishopric from the Tywi to the Wye, claimed himself the inheritor of Dyfrig and Teilo, and in 1120 transferred the bones of Dyfrig from Ynys Enlli (Bardsey) to Llandaff. Bernard became bishop of St Davids in 1115, swore allegiance to Canterbury, dissolved the clas at St Davids and erected a Romanesque cathedral, the most evocative and impressive ecclesiastical building in the Wales of the Middle Ages. During his episcopate, much was made of the cult of David, and churches from Cardigan Bay to Herefordshire were dedicated to him. Bernard struggled to elevate St Davids to become the archbishopric of Wales. Gerallt Gymro (Giraldus Cambrensis, Gerald of Wales, c.1146–1223) also campaigned vigorously to have both his own position as bishop and the metropolitan status of St Davids recognized. The struggle to establish St Davids as the seat of the archbishop of Wales was argued on the grounds of the distinctiveness of the Welsh people, its tradition originating with Dewi, and its remoteness from Canterbury. It has always been Canterbury's loss that it has been so distant from St Davids, but Canterbury has always been more powerful than St Davids, and usually the biggest win in the playground. The struggle ended with Gerald's submission in 1203. Bangor had sworn allegiance to Canterbury in 1120 and the new bishopric of St Asaph followed suit in 1143.

Dedications to Celtic saints were eradicated as far as possible. The old Celtic clasau were destroyed and their endowments transferred to monasteries in England or on the Continent. This was particularly true in south-east Wales where clasau founded by Illtud at Llanilltud Fawr, and Cadog at Llancarfan were suppressed and their possessions handed over to the abbeys of Tewkesbury and Gloucester. The eradication of native Celtic traditions and their replacement by Norman and English traditions caused many to view the newly established Church as being imposed by foreigners, a suspicion which remained with many until the disestablishment of the Church in Wales in 1920 – and is still an undercurrent among some diehard 'nonconformists'.

The Benedictines

New religious movements were introduced into Wales and imposed upon the Welsh. The first monastic groups to be invited into Wales by the Norman barons were the Benedictines. Many of their churches were founded as daughter priories of English or Continental houses approved by the Normans. In the shadow of Norman castles, the Benedictines were associated with Norman overlords, their abbeys with oppressive castles and their language with the language of the conquerors. William fitz Osbern founded Wales' first Benedictine priory in Chepstow in 1071. By 1150 they had 17 houses in Wales, including Abergavenny, Kidwelly and Monmouth. The Benedictines were never fully accepted within Wales. They seemed an alien body, subject to their Anglo-Norman patrons.

> ... they remained essentially alien institutions, tied to the apron-strings of Norman lordship and recruiting exclusively from Anglo-Norman settlers in Wales and from foreign houses.[5]

Pura Wallia

The story of Wales has, however, never been straightforward. Although the Norman-English successfully stamped their power in the Marchia Wallia, most of Wales retained its independence and developed in a very different direction. These Norman colonies were only a small proportion of Wales, and Welsh patterns of landholding and law remained predominant throughout most of the country. The north-west of Wales, Gwynedd, under the leadership of Prince Owain Gwynedd (c.1100–1170) and the south-west, Deheubarth, ruled by Lord

Rhys ap Gruffydd (1132–97) succeeded in preventing the total Normanisation of Wales.

The population of Wales increased from 200,000 at the time of the arrival of the Normans to about 300,000 by the close of the thirteenth century. The proportion of people living in towns increased, both in the Norman controlled areas and in the lands of the native princes and lords. The two key Welsh princes of the thirteenth century were Llywelyn ap Iorwerth (Llywelyn Fawr, c.1173–1240) and his grandson Llywelyn ap Gruffydd (Ein Llyw Olaf, d. 1282). Welsh stone castles were built, particularly in Gwynedd, but also at places like Dolforwyn in Powys in 1273–7. This was a period of court poets (Gogynfeirdd), and they and historians, like Geoffrey of Monmouth (1090–1155), strengthened the resolve of the princes. Welsh laws codified as Cyfraith Hywel Dda (the Law of Hywel) promoted the sense of Wales being a nation distinct from the people who lived the other side of Offa's Dyke.

The life of the Church was different in the Pura Wallia from areas under Norman domination. A key family at the time of the arrival of the Normans was that of Sulien (c.1010–91) which developed a centre of learning at Llanbadarn Fawr. There were three generations of scholars. Sulien was twice bishop of St Davids and spent 13 years studying in Ireland. His son, Rhygyfarch, translated the *Hebrew Psalter* into Latin, and also described in his *Lament* (1093) the sufferings of the people of Ceredigion from the onslaught of the Normans. His *Life of St David* was written to defend the independent status of the bishopric of St Davids.

Although the ancient Welsh clasau were disbanded by the Welsh princes, as they were in the Norman March, the endowments were transferred to the establishment of houses sympathetic to the traditions of Wales. In Gwynedd, the clasau of Aberdaron, Penmon and Beddgelert were transformed into Augustinian houses. 'Gwynedd glittered then with lime-washed churches, like the firmament with the stars.'[6] Gwynedd was firmly in the mainstream of European intellectual activity.[7] In

Deheubarth, Lord Rhys transferred the income from Llandeilo to the new Premonstratensian abbey of Talyllychau. This was very different from what had happened to the clasau in the March where the endowments of Llancarfan, Llanilltud, Llandochau and Basaleg enriched monasteries in Normandy and in England. The Marcher lords had invited the Benedictines to establish their communities under the shadow of their castles and under the protection of their towns. The future was very different in Pura Wallia.

The Cistercians

The reformed monasticism of the Cistercian Order was introduced and welcomed into Wales. Although the first house, at Tintern in 1131, was introduced under Norman aegis, as an Order the Cistercians were not associated with alien conquest. They established their communities in more remote areas, emphasizing manual labour, discipline and self-renunciation. By 1201, of the 13 Cistercian houses, nine were within Pura Wallia and responded to the aspirations of the Welsh rulers.

For many Welsh people this seemed a return of the ideals of the Celtic monks. Dewi, the water-drinker, could well have been reincarnated in the self-denying ordinances of the early Cistercians. Llanddewibrefi was very close to Strata Florida (Ystrad Fflur) and not only in a geographical sense. They adopted Welsh pastoral farming and were responsible for the introduction of sheep to Wales. They identified themselves with Welsh culture and often with Welsh political aspirations. Whitland was established in 1140, and the names of Margam (1147), Neath (1147), Strata Florida (1164), Cwm Hir (1176), Llantarnam (1179), Aberconwy (1186) and Valle Crucis (1202) are among the most hallowed in the history of religion in medieval Wales. Cistercian communities were able to integrate being part of an international monastic movement with a deep sense of nationhood. They enriched the life of Wales. The monasteries, as buildings, were as impressive as Norman castles, without their militaristic imperialism. Cwm Hir, with its nave 242 feet long with 14 bays, was the longest in Wales, even longer than Canterbury. They contributed to the preservation of Welsh manuscripts. Among them is *Llawysgrif Hendregadredd*, a collection of medieval Welsh poetry assembled at Ystrad Fflur, as well as a translation of *Brut y Tywysogion*, affirming the history of independent Wales from the death of Cadwaladr in the seventh century to the death of Llywelyn in 1282. The Cistercians supported the aspirations of the Welsh princes. Llywelyn the Great was buried in the abbey at Aberconwy, and the body of Llywelyn the Last was carried by monks and laid to rest at Abbey Cwm Hir.

The End of Welsh Independence

The years 1260 to 1295 proved to be a turning point in Welsh history. Llywelyn ap Iorwerth (Llywelyn the Great, *c.*1173–1240), taking advantages of dissensions in England during the first half of the thirteenth century, had constructed a principality in Wales. His grandson, Llywelyn ap Gruffydd, was recognised as Prince of Wales by Henry III, the English king, in the Treaty of Montgomery in 1267. However, when Edward I succeeded to the English throne in 1272, he was determined to crush any Welsh aspirations of independence. He invaded Wales in 1276 and Llywelyn was forced to submit. The Treaty of Aberconwy of November 1277 stripped him of most of his gains at Montgomery. Edward built a ring of powerful castles at Builth, Aberystwyth, Rhuddlan and Flint. Llywelyn rebelled but was killed at Cilmeri on 11 December 1282. His head was severed from his body and sent to London where, crowned with ivy, it was paraded in the streets before being displayed in the Tower of London. His body was buried by the monks of Abbey Cwm Hir. This marked the close of the search for Welsh political independence and Edward was determined that this unruly people should know they were a conquered people. A bard, Bleddyn Fardd, asked the question, 'Ys terfyn byd?' (Is it the end of the world?) The death of Llywelyn and the crushing of Welsh military power was capitalised on by the Statute of Rhuddlan (or the Statute of Wales) of 1284. Llywelyn's Principality was divided into three counties, Anglesey, Caernarfonshire and Merionethshire, under the jurisdiction of the king's representative. Sheriffs and courts were established to introduce English criminal law. Wales was England's first colony. The ancient princedom of Gwynedd was annexed to become the English Principality with an English prince. Edward, son of Edward I, was crowned in 1301 at the new Caernarfon castle, symbol of English domination. The seals of Llywelyn were melted down. Y Groes Naid, believed to be a relic of the Cross and worn by the Gwynedd princes, was taken to Windsor castle, and the reputed skull of St David ended up at the Tower of London. Militarily, the Welsh were a conquered people. Politically, they were deemed non-existent. The Statute of Rhuddlan made it clear that Wales had been annexed by the English crown.

To ensure that the Gwynedd Welsh would never rise again, Edward built a ring of great castles at Caernarfon, Conwy, Harlech and Beaumaris. The economic and social instruments of English colonialism were the creation of new boroughs. They grew up in the shadow of castles, and those speaking only Welsh were ejected as foreigners. Large numbers of foreign settlers were introduced to take their place and most of the best land was reserved for these newcomers. They exercised the administrative control which had previously been fulfilled by the followers of the princes. Political and administrative doors were shut against the Welsh and power was exercised by 'men of English or marcher stock... the Welsh were believed by alien planters to be feckless, inconstant and subordinate beings, fit only for makeshift offices and hard labour. To civilize and pacify them, so it was thought, would be a great service to humanity.'[8]

The Late Medieval Church, 1283–1509

An era of 'pestilence, rebellion and renewal'. This is how Geraint H. Jenkins describes the period which follows the death of

Llywelyn ein Llyw Olaf at Cilmeri in 1282.[9] Whereas Llywelyn's death had ended Welsh political aspirations, the fourteenth century witnessed a series of economic and social disasters. The first half of the century was one of almost unmitigated catastrophe. It was a period of atrocious weather, famines and disease. The Black Death struck Europe and a third of the population of Wales died between 1347 and 1350. There were further outbreaks in 1361 and 1369. The population of Wales in 1070 had been 200,000, increasing to 300,000 by 1300, but as a result of plagues, the population fell back to 200,000 by 1370. It was 250 years before the population of Wales returned to the figure of the early fourteenth century. The implications were far-reaching. Disease and migration resulted in massive depopulation. It marked the conclusion of the feudal system. The rich took advantage of the changes and built up their estates. Society became stratified into a minority of wealthy landowners and a majority of property-less tenants and an underclass of landless paupers. It was an age of exploitation, accentuated in Wales because the exploitation was largely exercised by a foreign landowning class. Many felt resentful and cheated.

Owain Glyndŵr

Periodic unrest throughout the fourteenth century ultimately flared in the rebellion of Owain Glyndŵr. His revolt, often depicted as brief and glorious, had far-reaching implications for the future history of those yearning for independence. Glyndŵr raised the standard of revolt at Glyndyfrdwy (Corwen) on 16 September 1400 when he was proclaimed Prince of Wales. By 1403 the whole of Wales was in his hands and he inspired his followers by speaking in national terms. Parliaments were held in Machynlleth in 1404 and at Harlech in 1405. In his Pennal Programme of 1406, Glyndŵr called for an independent archbishop of St Davids, a separate ecclesiastical province, priests who could speak Welsh, and two Welsh universities, one in the north and the other in the south. He attracted the support of those who upheld the Welsh heritage. John Trevor, bishop of St Asaph, and Gruffydd Young, archdeacon of Merioneth, served as his advisors.

> At a great synod at Pennal near Machynlleth that Church adopted a sweeping policy designed to equip this new Wales... The Welsh Church was to be free of Canterbury, with its own metropolitan at St David's... Welsh clerics were to speak the language of their people, Welsh church revenues were to be devoted to Welsh needs and finally, in a clause which captured the imagination of later generations, two universities were to be created, one in the north and another in the south, to train Welshmen in the service of the new Wales.[10]

Glyndŵr was neither defeated, nor captured, nor betrayed, but disappeared from the clutches of his enemies. He has served as a national symbol. A descendant of 'y mab darogan',[11] this son of prophecy will return to fulfil the nation's dream, which remained despite the Penal Code of 1401-2. The Welsh could not buy land in England or in English towns in Wales. They could not hold major office and were prohibited from carrying arms. Only the English could garrison castles or live in Welsh towns. The English could not be convicted by a Welshman. The Welsh were second-class citizens in their own country. They were a defeated people, and if they were to survive, an identity would need to be shaped within the context of being a conquered nation. Protest was no longer possible.

Renewal

During the course of the Glyndŵr national rebellion, there were untold losses. It was a period of great destruction and some towns took centuries to recover. The ravages were by the hands of both the troops of Owain and of the English king. It took time for castles to be rebuilt and strengthened and for a pattern of settlement to be established. Wales was now a divided land with the spoils of victory shared between the Royal English Principality and the Marcher lordships, areas which became synonymous with lawlessness. The Glyndŵr rebellion accentuated the prevailing turmoil of the fourteenth century. Many took advantage of this confused situation. Leadership within the traditional feudal system was now replaced by enterprising, often ruthless gentry (uchelwyr). A new pattern of Welsh life was emerging and the new settlements and social patterns continued until the industrial revolution. The uchelwyr took advantage of more vigorous commerce. With substantial trade and greater stability, the economic base gradually widened and substantial links were forged between south Wales and the West Country and Bristol. This new pattern of power was to survive until the nineteenth century.

The Church had to adapt to this fast changing society. The old monastic houses failed to recreate themselves and, by the close of the fifteenth century, were so decayed that they were like overripe fruit ready for plucking. The Church was badly served by the higher clergy, most of which were either papal or royal appointments, and were non-Welsh and non-resident. And yet the Church discovered a new and effective role in the life of the community. The decay of the monasteries and the absence of effective authoritarian Church leadership created a vacuum which gave the opportunity for church renewal at local levels in the fifteenth century. There was also a regular pattern of church life which provided stability and security for the majority of Welsh people.

> The lives of most people in Europe in the Middle Ages were governed by their consciousness of the annual cycle of the Life and Passion of Jesus, and the interlocking cycles of the lives of the Virgin Mary and the saints. The theology of the salvation cycle gave the individual his or her sense of place in the universe, whether it was perceived by means of the deep contemplation of the pious or simply by observing the Christian festivals which marked the agricultural year on which all, pious or otherwise, depended.[12]

The adoption of the cycle of the Christian year developed during the medieval period. This pattern was shared throughout Western Christendom but had its particular national distinctiveness. It became more formalised through the introduction of the Sarum liturgy (developed at Salisbury cathedral) in 1224 by Bishop Iorwerth of St Davids and 30 years later by Bishop Thomas Wallensis. It became the standard pattern of worship for much of the British Isles. Religious celebration and secular activities were intertwined in the annual pattern of life. The era saw the upsurge of religious prose and verse, lauding the Godhead, saints and sacraments.

Recent writing[13] on the visual culture of Wales has made accessible to the general reader many of the glorious artistic expressions of medieval piety. This is also expressed in the poetry of the period. This is a sphere which demands specialist treatment[14] but examples can be found in the devotional literature created by those on pilgrimage to the statue of the Blessed Virgin Mary at Penrhys.[15] The poems of Gwilym Tew and Rhisiart ap Rhys from the fifteenth century and Lewys Morgannwg in the sixteenth century are just a few examples of the depth of religious experience common in the medieval world-view. Their work reflects a healing of body, mind and soul. A sense of wholeness is a gift because of release from sins and joy in the presence of the divine in Christ and his Blessed Mother.

The period witnessed Church rebuilding in such places as Wrexham, Mold and Cardiff. Many churches were beautified with exquisite church timber-work. Some of the finest rood-screens and rood-lofts still flourish at remote Patrisio, Llananno and Betws Newydd. The emblems of Christ's Passion were carved in wood or stone. A Jesse tree has survived in an impressive carving at Abergavenny and in remarkable glass at Llanrhaeadr-yng-Nghinmeirch. The interior walls of churches were covered with paintings. Medieval wall-paintings have recently been uncovered at Llancarfan, and the superb example of the multi-coloured Llandeilo Tal-y-bont has been moved and restored at the National History Museum at St Fagans where it attracts tens of thousands of the 'religious and not-so-religious'. The decoration was designed not only to beautify the walls, but to instruct a non-literate population with the truths of the

Bible, the liturgical year and with venerating the saints. Places and relics associated with the saints attracted pilgrims in their thousands. In a pre-literate society, emphasis was placed upon the sacraments. All over 14 years of age were expected to attend mass regularly, although most did not communicate more than once a year. For all the great milestones in the ordinary person's life – birth, rites of passage, healing of mind and soul, marriage and death – the Church conducted appropriate services and sacraments.

A highpoint in the life of most Christians was the pilgrim's holy-days/holidays. Churches were built or adapted specifically to attract and respond to the growing spiritual and secular needs of the pilgrim. The pilgrim route responded to shrines dedicated to Welsh saints and to the Blessed Virgin Mary. The pilgrims to Ynys Enlli (Bardsey) gathered for their journey at Beuno's Clynnog Fawr and made their way through Llŷn before embarking to cross perilous waters after prayers at Llanengan. Pennant Melangell attracted pilgrims to offer their prayers and offerings at the twelfth-century shrine of Melangell. Two journeys to Tyddewi (St Davids), the holiest of all Wales' holy places were equal to one to Rome. Holywell attracted the faithful to the holy waters of St Winifred's Well, and in the remote highlands of Glamorganshire, prayers were offered and candles burned at the shrine of the Virgin Mary at Penrhys.

Henry Tudor

Henry Tudor (Harri Tudur) was the first man of Welsh descent to ascend the English throne. Born at Pembroke castle and a descendant of the Tudors of Penmynydd in Anglesey, Henry defeated Richard III at Bosworth in 1485, and was hailed by the Welsh bards as the fulfilment of prophecy. Although neither he, as king, nor his Tudor successors ever set foot in Wales, he and his son Henry VIII (whose brother Arthur died before he could succeed to the throne) were to have a momentous effect on the history of Wales. Apart from a few symbolic acts, like the incorporation of the red dragon into the royal arms, Henry showed little interest in the land of his birth. Nevertheless, his accession marked a new beginning for the uchelwyr. The gentry who had been establishing their position as the powerful class during the fifteenth century rejoiced in the arrival of the Tudor dynasty, and were at the core of power and patronage in Wales for the next 300 years. The accession of the Tudors marked a new beginning for some Welsh people. Under his son Henry VIII, Wales became officially and formally integrated into England by the Acts of Union of 1536 and 1542/3, and officially and formally Protestant as a result of Henry's reformation.

The Legacy of Catholicism

How should the spirituality of the people be evaluated? Most clergy remained poor and uneducated, and the laity was illiterate. Wales was a land where most of its inhabitants were peasants locked into their piece of land, struggling to make ends meet. They lived in isolated rural communities. Their religion, like that of most Europeans, was one of symbol and ritual, as it is still for many in the twenty-first century. For most people, their religion, however badly understood and at times distorted and abused, was as necessary, inevitable, and natural a part of their universe as the air they breathed. The medieval catholic period bequeathed a legacy of ecclesiastical administration based on the diocese and the parish which provided the framework for a church capable of serving the whole nation. An even greater legacy is the sense of place and time treasured by countless churches dotted throughout the country, sacred places which remain a gift for the twenty-first century. That gift is unrecognized by the majority in today's Church, and by an even larger proportion of Wales' population. The gift remains like a saint at rest but eager to be awakened to rekindle the spirituality of new generations of seekers and searchers.

> This was when the network of parishes was completed, and the churches rebuilt in stone. The earliest survivals, mostly thirteenth

century, are protective shells, from evil spirits and from local war, but in the later years, with the country conquered but peaceful, the walls were opened up and light let in... Few churches were added to the Welsh landscape after 1500, until some three more centuries had elapsed. Until the time the chapels came, communities had the buildings they needed.[16]

Towards the end of the medieval period came the questioning minds of those seeking a reformed Catholicism, and those advocating anti-clericalism and new practices in faith, worship and ethics. Here lay the seeds of renaissance and reformation. Dynamic events taking place on continental Europe would ultimately have far-reaching effects in Wales, but although the city of Geneva was to be reformed in a lifetime, reform in Wales was a much slower and more gradual process. It would be several centuries before the radical implications of the Continental Reformation had a widespread effect on the Welsh people.

4

REAWAKENING AND REFORMING, 1509–1603

THE REAWAKENING IN the late fifteenth and sixteenth centuries is the consequence of both a rediscovery of the classics of Greece and Rome, and a thirst for new ways of expressing the place of humankind within the world of nature and God. Re-examine! Re-appraise! Be inquisitive! Return to the original sources and discover their contemporary significance. Tradition may guide but not determine. Positions and statements previously accepted as authoritative were now questioned. What is the authority of scripture, the church fathers, theological systems, the role and authority of the papacy, patterns of church government? What will be the place of the individual when people are valued as persons and not merely for being part of a system? How is the relationship explored between God and the world? How does God communicate with humankind? What is the nature of Christ, grace, sacraments, ecclesiology?

The invention of the printing press freed these questions from the confines of monastery and university, and released them into the marketplace and workplace for the new merchant classes and town guilds. Questions with both tentative and authoritative answers spread rapidly across the political divisions and classes of Europe. A new agenda had been born, an agenda which took on particular national characteristics as it crossed political frontiers.[1]

The period raised radical and dangerous questions. These questions might have been considered, discussed and then suppressed as dangerous in past generations, but now they were expressed openly, debated widely and disseminated extensively by the printing press. What was new in the story of Europe was that the sixteenth century witnessed the discovery that asking questions was no longer the priority of the elite, but that the urge to search was in the minds and spirits of all sorts and conditions of men and women. As the inherited and seemingly monolithic structures imploded, responses came in more and more radical forms – Reformed Catholics, Lutherans, Calvinists, Anglicans, Zwinglians, Anabaptists, Socinians, Hutterites – and these responses gradually impinged upon most of continental and insular Europe. It was the timing which divided the revolutionary nature of the renaissance and the reformation. From their sources in Central Europe flowed the swiftest currents in the earliest period and gradually they raced into the farthest stretches of the European continent. Eventually they flowed on to the nations on the edges of the Atlantic.[2]

Wales was one of the last of the European nations to grasp the discoveries of what began as a continental reformation, but when it finally arrived in a power, both intellectual and ecstatic, in the eighteenth and nineteenth centuries, it was to change a whole nation. The story we shall explore raises the question of why reform was so slow to arrive in Wales, and why, eventually, it was to witness such a flourishing throughout the nation.

Why was the influence of the Reformation so slow in Wales? Glanmor Williams comments that 'Wales at the beginning of the sixteenth century was far removed from the epicentres of religious upheaval and controversy. The faith was unquestionably accepted by almost all its population but was dimly apprehended. Habit rather than conviction was its mainspring;'[3] Williams points out several factors which militated against change: the geography of Wales with its inaccessible hill and moorland, the conservative and isolated pastoral communities, the absence of a capital, royal court and university, the few wealthy and cultivated households, the poverty of the Welsh Church, the smallness of the urban population and trading classes, the lack of printing presses and the scarcity of books.

Yet, events taking place in the sixteenth century dramatically changed the future story of the people of Wales. It was to prove as decisive an era as the age of the saints in the fifth and sixth centuries, and the arrival of the Normans in the eleventh. In 1485, when the Welsh Tudor family came to the English throne, Wales was a catholic country and most of its inhabitants were monoglot Welsh speakers as they had been since their emergence as a people. Decisions made during the reign of Henry VIII radically altered the status of the nation and its people. The two events which changed Welsh history were the Reformation and the Acts of Union. Both events took place within a decade of each other and changed the way the Welsh saw both themselves and their relationship with their larger neighbour. Henry, an avowed and faithful Catholic, had earned the title of 'Defender of the Faith'. The honour was granted to him by the Pope, because of his treatise 'Assertion of the Seven Sacraments' (1524), which had been written to oppose Lutheran theology. Henry's road to reform only emerged when he sought Papal permission to release him from his marriage to Catherine of Aragon. The Pope's refusal precipitated a series of events which severed the links between the throne of England and the Catholic Church. Parliament's Act of Supremacy of 1534 declared the English king 'supreme head on earth' of the Church of England. The die had been cast and England (together with Wales) was embarked on a long journey which would change its life for ever. Henry remained a catholic in theology and worship, but the nations over which he ruled were to begin a journey towards the reform and renewal of the church.[4]

During the same decade, Wales was being rapidly integrated into England by the Acts of Union (1536 and 1542/3). Amongst the changes implemented by the Acts, Wales was now divided into 13 shires, English common law displaced the native law of Hywel Dda, four circuits were established to administer English law, and the Welsh language could not be used in legal and commercial affairs. Welsh gentry, already attracted by Henry VII to the Tudor Court, now became more and more anglicised and divorced from their communities in Wales. They were achieving positions of power, wealth and prestige which tied them irrevocably to the decisions of the English monarchy. This loyalty was accentuated by the fact that the King's Welsh favourites were to receive the benefits of the dissolution of the monasteries, the closure of chantries and the purification (or desecration!) of the interiors of parish churches and their artefacts. Those who already had much, received more, and the gap widened alarmingly between the leaders of Welsh society and the common people. These absentee leaders controlled wealth and power, and abandoned their traditional language and culture. They dispensed with their communal responsibilities and began an exodus to London which has been stemmed only by the Welsh beginning to win power for themselves in the political and media capital which is twenty-first-century Cardiff Bay.

Long before the gale for reform broke with Luther and Calvin, there was a sound in the treetops in many corners of the continent. Each country has its own story, and although there were bridges linking and uniting the forms of change throughout the countries touched by reform, each nation has its distinctive story to tell because of its own peculiar social, economic, political and religious contexts. Each nation has its pre-history to the Reformation. This is as true of Wales as any other country.

Signs of Discontent

There had long been signs of discontent. Many were unhappy with the religious state of Wales. The system was creaking and on the verge of collapse. The church was maintaining a system more and more irrelevant to a thirst for a genuine relationship with God. The general condition of church life in Wales left much to be desired. While these factors do not necessarily lead to a demand for reform, they are nevertheless signs of the failure of the church to meet the spiritual needs of the people. Bishops and higher clergy were appointed, not because of their spiritual qualities, but because the King needed them for his civil service. This was true in many parts of Europe. They were lawyers rather than theologians, serving the Crown to administer law rather than meeting the needs of the people. Consequently, there was a wide gap between the church hierarchy and the common people: it was a gap in wealth, language and culture. They were absentee administrators, unable to speak the language of Wales. They could not lead or supervise the lower clergy who were poorly educated and poorly paid. In the religious orders, the friars and monks had lost the fire of enthusiasm which had motivated their early life. The people were monoglot Welsh, largely illiterate and depended on the priesthood to meet their religious needs. Glanmor Williams writes:

> As far as popular belief and devotion were in question, there was...
> a disturbing dependence on the externalities of the means of
> grace, many of which appeared to be divorced from considerations
> of morality and genuine understanding. The overwhelming
> majority of the people contented themselves with leaving it to the
> priesthood to minister the sacraments and perform the ritual on
> their behalf and put their trust in the saints. Religion consisted for
> most people of a body of traditional practices and assumptions,
> unquestionably accepted but dimly apprehended. Habit, not
> conviction, was the strongest element in their faith, as it had been
> down the centuries.[5]

Yet we should not forget that for most of Christian history – and indeed for many Christians today – the majority of the faithful have been attracted less by an understanding of faith as by an appreciation of the mystery of faith, and as such it was not the ability to read which was of prime importance. Rather, it was the majesty of the liturgical ritual, the glory of the church building, the rhythm of the ecclesiastical year, and the excitement and fun of pilgrimages which all contributed to rooting religious experience deeply into the ordinary lives of the people. However, even that rhythm is dependent upon a clergy which provides leadership by example and is present to perform the rituals of the Christian year, the annual cycles of nature and the episodes of personal and family life. With an absentee and ignorant clergy, the system collapses.

Some fifteenth-century Welsh poetry reflects a criticism of the status quo. Siôn Cent (1367–1430) called for restraint, austerity and personal devotion. A small but influential minority spread late-medieval pietism and the learning of the Renaissance. Some rejected medieval superstition but held fast to the need for the unity of the church, papal authority and the maintenance of the priesthood and the sacraments. They, however, longed for the cleansing of the Church. Richard Whitford (1470–1541), a friend of Erasmus and Thomas More, translated into English *The Imitation of Christ* by Thomas à Kempis. Sir John Price of Brecon (1502–55) became secretary of royal affairs in Wales (1540) and a member of the Council of Wales and the Marches (1541). A collector of manuscripts of Welsh interest, in 1546 he published *Yny lhyvyr hwnn*, the first Welsh printed book. It contained the Creed, the Lord's Prayer and the Ten Commandments and was directed towards people who could not read English or Latin. It also included a calendar which noted the festivals of many Welsh saints. He attacked the clergy for being responsible for the fact that 'the great part of my fellow-Welshmen are in incalculable darkness for lack of knowledge of God and His commandments'.

A different minority sided with a more radical demand for reformation. Inspired by the European Reformers, their emphasis was on the Word of God speaking through the Bible. William Salesbury (1520–84) called on his fellow countrymen to 'obtain the Scripture in your own tongue as once it existed among your happy ancestors, the ancient Britons'. Bishop Richard Davies (1501–81) was later to write in his Preface to the first Welsh New Testament in 1567: 'Therefore go forth and read. This is the book of eternal life... May God give you good will, for here you will find food for the soul, and a candle that will light you along the path that will bring you to the country of the kingdom of heaven. May God grant that, to you and to me through our Lord Jesus Christ.'

The battle of the Reformation was about the application of the new learning. Was it designed, as conservative reformers taught, to keep the Roman Church intact but purged of its corruptions? Or was it intended, as Protestant reformers argued, to bring about something newer and much more drastic, a fresh and more direct approach by the individual believer in the relationship with God?

The First Stage of the Reformation, 1527–1553

The Reformation in England and Wales was not the result of dynamic and radical Christian movements as it was with Luther in Germany, and Zwingli and Calvin in Switzerland. Henry VIII's break with Rome initiated a dramatic change in church-state relations but it did not mark a change in the theological and liturgical position of the Church of England. The English Reformation developed in two distinct phases, separated by the five-year intermission (1553–8) of Mary's reign. The first phase from 1527 to 1553 witnessed changes under Henry VIII and his son Edward VI; the second phase from 1558 to 1603, during the reign of Elizabeth, ensured that the Reformation was secured on a lasting basis. Henry, a reluctant reformer, replaced the Pope by becoming Supreme Head of the Church but retained the catholic status quo in religious matters. Anti-papal statutes were passed by parliament between 1529 and 1534, culminating in the Act of Supremacy of 1534. Commissioners were appointed in 1535 to investigate the state and value of monasteries, and in 1536 all monasteries with an annual income of less than £200 were dissolved and the property confiscated by the king. The same fate awaited chantries and the few remaining larger monasteries in 1539 with their contents taken either into the royal treasury or auctioned on the spot. Most of the proceeds enriched royal favourites and precious little came to parish churches or educational foundations. Henry's motivation was impurely political and financial.

By dissolving the monasteries he eliminated the Pope's chief supporters (although, in fact, in Wales there were only 250 monks, nuns and friars at the time) and gained for himself ready cash and new friendships and alliances from those who were granted erstwhile monastic properties. The dissolution was completed swiftly and brutally. In 1536, 24 of the 27 monasteries in Wales were dissolved. Centres of pilgrim devotion were destroyed. Two of the most famous medieval shrines were attacked: Winifred's Well at Holywell, and the shrine of the Blessed Virgin Mary at Penrhys was taken down and burnt in the garden of Thomas Cromwell in London.

There was very little opposition to changes during Henry's reign. As far as the general population was concerned, the church remained unchanged. The Six Articles of 1539 were designed to prevent the spread of Reformation doctrines and practices and there were surprisingly few changes in the everyday life of the church. The medieval rites were unaltered and continued to be conducted in Latin. The priesthood remained celibate. The only Welsh 'heretic' was Thomas Capper who denied transubstantiation and was consequently burned at the stake in Cardiff in 1542. Only two bishops adopted positive reform. Bishop Wharton of St Asaph wanted to move the see to Wrexham or Denbigh, and founded a grammar school. Bishop Barlow of St Davids wanted to move his cathedral to Carmarthen, and in 1541 set up a grammar school at Brecon.

Despite the fact that Henry remained a Catholic, he ensured that his son Edward was educated by Protestants. Only nine years old when he came to the throne in 1547, his advisors ensured that dramatic changes followed his accession. Influenced by the more radical Reformers, Edward introduced swift and unexpected changes which affected the lives of ordinary worshippers. The Six Articles of Henry were repealed. Parish churches were changed dramatically. 'Popish images'

Pentre Ifan.

The Nevern Cross.

The communion table, font and icon stand at Llanfair. When Rod and Alison Wales of Lewes, Sussex, designed the unique furnishing of the interior of Llanfair, Penrhys, they wanted to embody the history of Wales.

From Porthgain looking north. The Welsh love of the sea is reflected in the creation of the Wales Coast Path which covers 870 miles.

The Glyders. Wales is dominated by mountains. More than half its surface lies over 650 feet.

Offa's Dyke near Montgomery is Britain's longest ancient monument. The Offa's Dyke path measures 177 miles.

© Cath Morgans

Caerwent. The Apse marks what is probably the oldest Christian church in Wales, *c.*400.

Newport. St Julian's church is dedicated to local martyrs, Julius and Aaron, Wales' first known martyrs.

Caerleon. Julius and Aaron are reputed to have been martyred in the amphitheatre, probably in the 3rd century.

Caldey Island, the Latin and Ogham (6th century) inscriptions at St Illtud's Priory.

© Miara Rabearisoa

St Non's Cross (7th–9th century) near St Davids is the inspiration for the Llanfair Penrhys Cross.

© Rob Moverely

Tywyn, the Cadfan or Tywyn stone. The earliest example of written Welsh, c.8th century.

Llanwynno, St Gwynno's. A place of inspiration for pre-industrial, industrial and post-industrial Rhondda, Clydach and Cynon valleys. Guto Nyth Brân, the famous runner, is buried there.

Pontypridd, St Dyfrig's Roman Catholic Church. Dubricius, Dyfrig, a man of the Borders, born near Hereford, died on Enlli. His remains were taken to Llandaff Cathedral in 1120.

Llanilltud Fawr, Galilee chapel. The missionary-seminary of south Wales.

Icon of Dewi Sant at Tyddewi. The five icons of Dewi, Patrick, Andrew, Non and Justinian, painted and gilded by Sarah Crisp were unveiled and re-dedicated on St David's Day 2012. 'Lords, brothers, and sisters, be joyful and keep your faith and your belief, and do the little things that you have heard and seen from me.'

© Dean and Chapter of the Cathedral

St Illtud's Ilston. The 6th-century cell is built into the church tower.

Yspyty Cynfyn. With a circular wall and inbuilt standing stones, Yspyty Cyfyn is one of many Christian sanctuaries built on the site of pre-Christian holy places.

St Cadoc's Llancarfan. As in many places in Wales, the Christian faith has been practised for 1,500 years. Medieval treasures have been recently rediscovered: tales beneath the whitewash.

St Padarn's Llanbadarn Fawr. The home of Padarn, Sulien and his family, not forgetting Dafydd ap Gwilym. The new exhibition was designed by Peter Lord and opened on St Padarn's Day, 15 April 1988.

Manod, Blaenau Ffestiniog: 'Tradition' is alive and well in Manod with Archimandrite Deiniol. The doors of the iconostasis were open for a special festival. Llanfair Penrhys young people worshipped annually at the Church of the Holy Protection, and played soccer against Manod boys.

Caldey, Father Gildas at Statue of St Samson. Contemporary contemplation and mission draw on the roots of Welsh spirituality. Caldey is a place of worship for the people of Llanfair, Penrhys.

© Miara Rabearisoa

Chepstow castle. The Norman church arrived alongside castle, knight and immigrant peasant.

Saint Mary's Priory Church, Chepstow. The church was a tool of conquest.

Llandaff Cathedral. Urban, the Norman bishop of Llandaff, was the first to profess obedience to the primate of England.

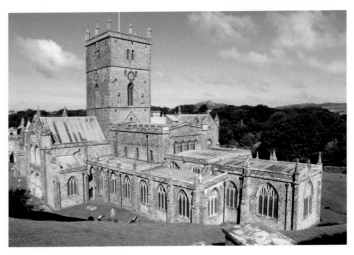

St Davids Cathedral. Bernard erected a Romanesque cathedral.

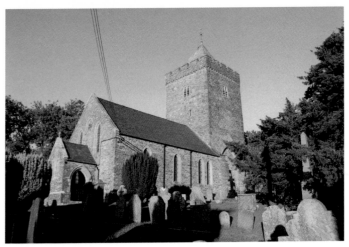

Llanddewi Brefi was very close to Ystrad Fflur – and not only in a geographical sense.

Ystrad Fflur, Strata Florida. The Cistercian cathedral-monastery of Pura Wallia. The grave of Dafydd ap Gwilym is in the neighbouring churchyard.

Cilmeri. The memorial to the death in 1282 of Llywelyn ap Gruffydd, the last native prince of Wales. Ys terfyn byd? Is it the end of the world? (Bleddyn Fardd)

Abbey Cwm Hir. The burial place of Llywelyn. Cistercians pay respects to their Last Prince.

Pennal, St Peter ad Vincula. The Pennal Letter of 1406. 'At a great synod at Pennal… that church adopted a sweeping policy designed to equip this new Wales.' The original is in the National Archives of France.

Machynlleth. Owain Glyndŵr's Parliament of 1404.

Tywyn, St Cadfan's. 'Gwynedd glittered then with lime-washed churches, like the firmament with the stars.'

Llanfair-ar-y-bryn, Llandovery. A living treasury from the medieval to the modern.

Wrexham, St Giles. 'Pistyll Rhaeadr and Wrexham steeple.' Wrexham steeple is one of the seven wonders of Wales (certainly of north Wales!).

Cardiff, St John's. A medieval tower, a Glyndŵr pub and contemporary Wales.

Pennant Melangell. The 12th-century shrine of Melangell – 'the holiest place' in the United Kingdom?

© Cath Morgans

Ynys Enlli, Bardsey Island, the burial place of 20,000 saints remains a place of pilgrimage.
© Dewi Lewis

Holywell, St Winifred's well. The faithful continue to visit the holy waters of St Winifred's well.

Llandeilo Talybont. The 12th/13th-century medieval church, originally from near Pontarddulais, has been rebuilt and redecorated (as it might have looked in 1530) at the National History Museum of Wales.

Patrisio rood screen.

Patrisio well: The finest rood screen in Wales and Patrisio's well still attract pilgrims. If Wales has been described as 'post-Christian', it is certainly not 'post-religious'.

Abergavenny, St Mary's Priory. The Jesse Tree is unique in Britain and is one of the finest medieval sculptures in the world.

Llanfair-ar-y-bryn. Crimson-flooded frame and floor from the leper window.

were obliterated and church walls whitewashed. Altars were replaced by communion tables. Images, shrines, vestments, rood-screens and lofts, candles and incense were all removed. The popular practices of venerating the saints, carrying rosaries, kneeling at mass and praying for the dead were all abolished. Reformed doctrine and worship were introduced in the Prayer Book of 1549 and in the even more radical services of the 1552 Prayer Book. The style and vocabulary of worship changed irrevocably. English Bibles were introduced into parish churches, and there were readings from the Gospel and Epistle during the service of Holy Communion. Between 1547 and 1552, William Salesbury published an English-Welsh Dictionary, a collection of Welsh proverbs and *Kynnifer llith a ban* (1551) a Welsh translation of the gospels and epistles in the 1549 Book of Common Prayer. A minority welcomed reform for a variety of reasons. The gentry had benefited from the plunder of the monasteries and churches, and this purchased their fidelity to their royal benefactor. The lay appropriation of church property strengthened the links between lay leaders and the royal house. They were in contrast to the few reforming intellectuals in places like Cardiff and Carmarthen who were influenced by Bible reading and hearing sermons. Most were uninspired by the Edwardian changes and puzzled by the new devotional and liturgical life communicated in unfamiliar English which replaced the mysterious but familiar Latin. This gave added offence to a country where the natural language was Welsh. The people of Wales feared they were being turned into English heretics, Ffydd Saeson (faith of Saxons).

The Catholic Reaction under Mary, 1553–1558

Despite the fact that Edward's religious reformation was unacceptable to the majority of Welsh people, very few had actively opposed the changes. It was not surprising that most welcomed the accession of Mary. However, the new Queen soon lost her popularity because her determination to return to the ancient catholic ways became coterminous with a fear of Papal and Spanish supremacy. In 1553, Catholic worship was restored without either Parliamentary authority or even royal proclamation. In 1554, Mary married Philip of Spain and every effort was made to eradicate Protestantism. Clergy were not allowed to marry and anti-papal legislation was repealed. Anti-heresy laws were passed and more than 300 burned at the stake in England and Wales leaving, for centuries, an indelible legacy on the consciousness of English and Welsh people. Rawlins White of Cardiff, William Nichol of Haverfordwest and Robert Ferrar, bishop of St Davids (at Carmarthen) were all burned at the stake. Mary's reign was branded by the fear of Papal Spain and by the fires of persecution. Foxe's *The Book of Martyrs* had an enormous influence on the psyche of Elizabethans. His martyrology first appeared in Latin in 1554 and was soon translated into many popular English editions. Placed alongside the Bible to be read in parish churches and in public places, *The Book of Martyrs* helped create the mind-set that patriots were of necessity Protestants.[6]

The Second Stage of the Reformation, 1558–1603

Mary was succeeded by her sister Elizabeth whose religious policy was based on the principles of the need to maintain uniformity throughout the country, and to ensure that she, as Queen, exercised control. Elizabeth steered a middle course between Catholicism and the Reformed branch of Protestantism which had emerged as a consequence of Calvin's leadership in Geneva. Elizabeth assumed the less contentious title of Supreme Governor (rather than Supreme Head) of the Church and published the Book of Common Prayer enforced by an Act of Uniformity. The dioceses were visited and the clergy took the oath of loyalty to the monarch under the Act of Supremacy. New bishops were appointed at St Asaph, St Davids and Bangor to ensure the enforcement of conformity. Of the 16 bishops appointed during Elizabeth's reign, 13 were Welshmen and many were reformers of high quality, including Richard Davies, William Morgan and Richard Vaughan.

The Translation of the Bible and Prayer Book

A central problem facing the Elizabethan bishops was how to root the life of the newly reformed church into the lives of the people. So many changes had taken place during the previous decades. The key instrument was necessarily the provision of worship in the language of the people. In medieval Catholicism, religion had been sustained through the liturgy of movement, colour and ritual and through the rhythms of the Christian season, the natural year and personal and family life. That pattern had been snapped violently during the Edwardian reforms. Most people must have been confused by the ecclesiastical see-saw movement begun by Henry and continued by his children, Edward, Mary and Elizabeth. The ordinary worshipper could not possibly grasp the reasons lying behind the despoiling of church interiors, the confusing liturgies and the changing status of the clergy. Elizabeth needed to anchor her new religious settlement in the lives of the people, and in Wales this, of necessity, meant that the congregation needed to hear the Bible and say the Prayers in their own language.

The translation of the Bible into the vernacular languages of Europe proved to be a kairos moment linguistically, culturally and religiously. The Bible was instrumental in 'saving the language' as well as 'saving the people' in many European countries. The Welsh Reformers claimed that the early Britons possessed a vernacular Bible and it was now a priority to restore a Welsh version of Scripture to the nation. Richard Davies and William Salesbury argued vigorously in favour of a translation, and in 1563 an Act of Parliament laid down that the Bible and Prayer Book should be translated into Welsh by 1567, and used in public worship in all parishes where Welsh was the normal language. Elizabeth and her advisors had no sympathy for the Welsh language but saw its value as an instrument to ensure the uniformity of the Church of England. Richard Davies, William Salesbury and Thomas Huet collaborated at the bishop's palace in Abergwili to translate the Prayer Book and the New Testament by 1567. One thousand copies were printed, enough for each of the Welsh-speaking churches in the country.

William Morgan (1545–1604) born at Tŷ Mawr, Wybrnant, produced single-handedly, while he was vicar of Llanrhaeadr-ym-Mochnant, the definitive classic translation of the Bible in 1588 – a far more significant event in the history of Wales than the defeat of the Spanish Armada. The Bible gave reality to Reformation doctrine and worship. In many parts of Europe, including neighbouring Scotland, people were reading the Bible for themselves. It is barely possible to grasp the sense of exhilaration that comes when a generation begins to discover the message of the Bible. We know the excitement when an individual discovers the Gospel. Imagine a community entering into that new world of discovery! In Wales, although this exploration began at the close of the sixteenth century, the full effect of reading the Word of God did not come until the patient educational endeavours of Griffith Jones was fanned into flame by the Methodist Reformers of the eighteenth century. The translation of the Bible kept the Welsh language alive and vigorous until the twentieth century. The William Morgan Bible provided a standard model for Welsh literature, and with the Book of Common Prayer, buttressed the sense of a separate and distinctive nationality in Wales.[7]

Nationalism and the Revision of Welsh History

Catholic recusants and Elizabethan Protestants struggled for the hearts and minds of the people of Wales. Both claimed they were the true inheritors of the ancient church of the Welsh people. In 1567, Richard Davies wrote the *Epistol at y Cembru* (Letter to the Welsh Nation), the preface to the first translation into Welsh of the New Testament. He argued that the Reformation was a return to the purity of the New Testament and the Early Church. Britain had first been converted by Joseph of Arimathea. The true faith had:

been maintained by the people of Wales intact and uncontaminated in spite of Roman persecution, the heresies of Pelagius and others, Anglo-Saxon paganism, and – most crucial of all – in face of that brand of Christianity tainted by papal superstition which Augustine of Canterbury had brought to England as the emissary of Rome.[8]

The Welsh had been dragged into the mire of papal heresy and authoritarianism. Now the people of Wales were returning to truth and light. Richard Davies' view of history appealed to his fellow-countrymen by binding the Reformation to some of the oldest themes of the history of the Welsh. Protestantism was no new heresy but was grounded in the earliest and most glorious phases of Christianity in Britain. The Reformation was not an alien English religion. On the contrary, Papism had been forced on the Welsh by their Saxon enemies. Yet God had preserved the Welsh people and their language to serve the Reformed Faith and to be a light to the nations.

An identical argument was on the lips of Roman Catholic apologists. The author of *Y Drych Cristianogawl* (possibly printed in a cave in Llandudno in 1585, and if so, the first book to be printed in Wales) argued that all earlier Christian history in Wales had been betrayed by the Reformation. He, like the Protestant historians, pointed to the introduction of Christianity by Joseph of Arimathea. He reminded his readers that King Lucius, son of Coel, had asked the Pope for missionaries to come to Britain. The first Christian emperor of Rome, Constantine, had been a Briton, received into the faith by the Pope. This great tradition was now being destroyed by the Reformation.

The Reformation is Established in Wales

It was a matter of time. Elizabeth reigned for 45 years, more than the average lifespan in the sixteenth century. The Pope had been rejected as the divinely ordained Head of the Church and the majority accepted that the monarch should choose the religion of the nation, a natural consequence of faith in the divine right

69

of kings. The emergence of the nation-state depended upon the continuity of the royal house and an accompanying unity in things political and religious: Cuius regio, eius religio (whose realm, his religion). The nation's ruler imposed her religion on her subjects. Apart from the six years of Mary's reign, English monarchs were either the Supreme Head or Supreme Governor of the Church of England. Edward, Elizabeth and James I (James VI of Scotland) ensured that the Reformers were given a monopoly of public worship, religious instruction, printed literature and ecclesiastical jurisdiction. Time, like an ever rolling stream, bears all its sons and daughters away, and in the process bore away almost all those who had remembered a pre-Elizabethan and pre-Protestant England.

Political nationalism was also a key factor. Spain was the arch enemy, the servant of the Papacy, the 'whore of Babylon'. Spanish culture and Papist religion were identified as heresy and treachery. Protestantism became identified with patriotism, independence and security, and Catholicism with disloyalty, subversion, the enemy within and external enemies. Protestantism linked Britain with other Protestant European countries (especially of the Reformed variety) and the Catholic faith was associated with the cardinal enemies of Spain and France. Elizabeth seemed victorious against the odds. Even the winds and waves served the English Protestant monarch in the destruction of the Spanish Armada. England was an elect nation.

The translation of the Bible and the Prayer Book proved to be the key to the success of the Reformation in Wales. By the end of the sixteenth century, the Reformers had grafted their ideals with patriotic instincts, and emphasized continuity with all that was earliest and best in the history of Wales. The Reformation, a renewed token of God's continuing favour, was a return to the pristine purity of Celtic Christianity. The new translation had been authorized by the restored British monarchy. The revitalization of Welsh ideals was taken to heart by the educated classes, many of whom were members of the London establishment, and merged smoothly into loyalty to the Tudor dynasty and State. Writing from a stance of superiority and power, the arguments of the Welsh Protestant Elizabethans seemed totally convincing.

5

FROM UNIFORMITY TO
PLURALISM, 1603–1689

Maintaining Uniformity: The Early Stuarts

Despite the helter-skelter of ecclesiastical change during the reigns of the Tudors, most Welsh people had not altered their religious views and practices by the close of the reign of Elizabeth. They believed and acted in similar forms to their medieval ancestors. Although they had witnessed external changes in the appearance of churches and how the liturgy was celebrated, and although they had lived through the destruction of monasteries and holy sites, external changes do not necessarily lead to a personal alteration of religious experience. In fact, they could have bred confusion and cynicism.

Although Anglicanism was approved of by the literate and upwardly-mobile, it made little popular progress. For the majority of Welsh people, life was about survival. The peasantry scratched a living from the poor soils of upland Wales. They struggled against disease, and death was an early visitant. They remained country people struggling for survival and finding their pleasures, comforts and disciplines in the norms of traditional rural life. The Welsh lived in small, isolated communities. There were few towns and communications were poor. The majority remained conservative and illiterate. There were few Welsh printed books, no universities and few centres of culture. The gentry had abandoned rural Wales for the attractions of the English Court.

And yet, slowly, patiently and inexorably, week by week, season by season, and year by year, throughout most of the reign of Elizabeth, there were regular services and readings in Welsh from the Bible and Prayer Book. Preaching was more frequent and more eloquent. The celebration of the weekly liturgy, the reading of the Scriptures, the homily or the sermon, the being together of God's people in worship was, and is, the lifeblood of the Christian community. The parish liturgy was very different from the medieval mass. Slow changes were taking place in the feelings and thoughts of regular worshippers.[1]

Printing made a difference to the lives of the more prosperous clergy and laity. There were new translations of key works. Edward James published the Welsh version of the *Book of Homilies* in 1606. In 1620 came the revised version of the William Morgan Bible and a new Prayer Book, both the work of Bishop Richard Parry and Dr John Davies of Mallwyd. Religious verses in free metres were circulated. Edmwnd Prys (1543–1623) composed *Salmau Cân* (metrical psalms) in 1621. Even more significant was the work of Vicar Prichard of Llandovery. His popular verses were published from 1658 and collected under the title *Canwyll y Cymry* (The Candle of the Welsh) in 1681. The volume was as popular in Wales as John Bunyan's *Taith y Pererin* (Pilgrim's Progress). The first cheap Welsh Bible, *Y Beibl Bach*, priced five shillings, was published in the 1630s. The seventeenth century was also a golden age for the writing of 'Anglo-Welsh' poetry with the classics of the devotional literature of George Herbert (1593–1633) and Henry Vaughan (1621–95), although their poetry/prayers would not have touched the masses of their countrymen who were unable to speak English.

The Elizabethan and Jacobean religious heritage of the Church of England was a deliberate attempt to be both Catholic and Reformed. It maintained an emphasis on a church government centred on the episcopate and dioceses, and the traditional liturgy contained much of the legacy of catholicity. Yet, when the monarch became the Supreme

73

Governor of the Church in 1559, Anglicanism had placed itself alongside other Protestant churches. It wanted the best of both worlds. Compromise may often seem a comfortable position but the *via media* can also be dangerous. Those faithful to the Papacy and the Church of Rome bitterly opposed the new church, while those exiled during the reign of Mary had experienced a more pure and radical form of church life. They were increasingly excluded by the Anglican authorities. Polarities were emerging in English religious life. The Catholic remnant was convinced that the Church of England should return to its traditional roots, while at the same time a new Puritan movement was determined to purify the national Church of its idolatry.

The Catholic Reaction

The 'old religion' maintained many adherents in Wales throughout the Elizabethan and early Stuart period. Some of the most prestigious Welsh families remained Catholic. The Somerset family of Raglan and the Morgan family of Llantarnam supported recusants in south-east Wales. The fame of St Winifred's Well at Holywell encouraged Catholics in the north-east. Nevertheless, only 15 clergy were deprived of their livings because of their refusal to accept the Elizabethan Settlement. Many fled to mainland Europe where they planned the restoration of their country to Rome. Morgan Phillips, precentor of St Davids and Owen Lewis, fellow of New College, Oxford, helped form a college in 1568 at Douai, near Calais. Their students were to be trained to return to Wales as missionaries. Another exile, Morys Clynnog, published in Milan in 1568 the first Catholic book, *Athravaeth Gristnogawl*, to be printed in Welsh.

The Papal excommunication of Elizabeth in 1570 was followed by a parliamentary statute against Catholics. The consequence was an increasingly polarized position. Hugh Owen of Plas Du in Caernarfonshire and Thomas Morgan of Monmouthshire plotted against Elizabeth, and when it failed, they fled the country to become leading Welsh conspirators against the Queen. A new generation of seminary priests returned to England and Wales to strengthen the Catholic faithful. In 1578, a new seminary was opened in Rome with Morys Clynnog as its warden. More than 200 students from Wales and the March were trained in various Catholic colleges between 1568 and 1642 but very few returned to minister in Wales.

There were secret Catholic presses near Llandudno, at Brecon and in Flintshire. Among the Welsh martyrs during the reign of Elizabeth were: Richard Gwyn, a schoolmaster from Llanidloes, who was executed at Wrexham in 1584; William Davies, a priest who was hanged for treason at Beaumaris in 1593; and John Roberts of Trawsfynydd, a Benedictine hanged, drawn and quartered at Tyburn, London, in 1610. Despite the martyrdoms and sacrifices, by 1603 the majority of the people in Wales attended the Church of England. Figures record that there were only 808 people who shunned Anglican services in 1603, compared with 212,450 who attended them.

The Emergence of Puritanism

The Puritan ethos began to crystallize in Cambridge, and from 1570 presented a serious challenge to the Elizabethan Settlement. Puritans wished to reform the Church of England with a Presbyterian form of government. They were convinced they were a chosen or elect people, and emphasized personal discipline. Even more radical were Separatists who believed that the only true Church was the congregation of saints separated from the world. Although, during the reign of Elizabeth, Puritanism was largely confined to the eastern parts of England, Wales had its morning star in John Penri of Cefn Brith, Breconshire. He became a Presbyterian while at Cambridge and wrote tracts attacking the Church of England and pleading for a preaching ministry through the medium of Welsh.

If there was one parish where a sermon was preached every
quarter, there were twenty without even that kind of provision...
The remedy, said Penry, was to secure instructive preaching in the
Welsh language, and to ensure this, there had to be a supply of
ministers so that every parish received an effective ministry. If this
could be achieved, the Christian Church in Wales would return
to that evangelical purity which it possessed before the coming of
Augustine the Monk and his Papist adulteration.[2]

John Penri joined the Separatists in London, where he
was tried at the Court of High Commission, found guilty and
hanged in May 1593. Although largely neglected and forgotten
by his Welsh contemporaries, he was later seen as a precursor
of so much which changed and identified the people of Wales.

During the reigns of James and Charles I, Puritanism
developed as a radical religious and political movement.
The Puritan understanding of the Gospel made demands
upon personal piety and advocated the transformation of
society according to Christ's Way of justice. Bold words were
accompanied by even bolder action. Tension grew within the
Church of England. Whereas James had been exposed to Scottish
Presbyterianism, Charles was a High Anglican, influenced by
Henrietta Maria, his French Catholic wife. Between 1625 and
1629 Charles' religious views became entrenched at Court and
its influence apparent in the choice of bishops. William Laud,
bishop of St Davids from 1621 to 1627 became Archbishop
of Canterbury. His views were shared by new Welsh bishops,
William Murray and Morgan Owen in Llandaff, John Owen in
St Asaph and Roger Mainwaring in St Davids.

Puritans resisted and, during the late 1620s and 1630s,
thousands migrated to New England to create a holy kingdom,
only for many to return by the 1640s to join the struggle for
a more democratic, Reformed Old England. When Charles,
short of money to fight his Scottish wars recalled Parliament,
the Puritan majority were no longer prepared to tolerate his
Personal Rule. The country was divided. The Established
Church, led by Charles and Archbishop Laud, emphasized

High Church principles and seemed to be allying church and state with Catholic Europe. Puritanism, like Elizabethan Anglicanism, became associated with patriotic nationalism in order to protect people, parliament and the true church against the Catholic papacy, France, the monarch and idolatry.

Puritanism grew in Wales during the reign of James I, particularly in the towns of Cardiff, Swansea, Wrexham and Haverfordwest. Wealthy London merchants endowed lecturers and parishes, established schools and paid for the publication of Bibles and devotional books. They wished to maintain the Reformed ethos of the Church by resisting Laudian innovations. Among the first Welsh Puritan leaders were William Wroth of Llanfaches and William Erbery of Cardiff. Both appeared before the Court of High Commission during the years 1634–8. Wroth eventually submitted and remained at Llanfaches, but Erbery was forced to resign from his living. William Wroth proceeded to 'gather' the first Congregational church in Wales at Llanfaches in 1639 and Erbery founded the second cause in Wales at Cardiff in 1640. What were the implications of the life of these new-modelled churches worshipping outside the Church of England? What now of uniformity within the realm of England and Wales? What now of the status of the Supreme Governor of the Church of England?

Henry VIII had severed Papal authority over the Church of England, but the Church retained its catholicity in theology, liturgy and ecclesiology. Henry could not have foreseen that the relationship between Church and State had embarked on a perilous journey. He and his successors could envisage no alternative to a united church in the realm. Acts of Supremacy placed the King as the Supreme Head (Henry) and Supreme Governor (Elizabeth) of the Church of England, and Acts of Uniformity ensured that the nation (England and Wales) should be obedient to the statutes of King and Church. Should the Church be Episcopal and Catholic as under Henry? Should it be Episcopal and Reformed as under Edward? Mary returned the Church to being Catholic and Papal. What of the

Elizabethan and Jacobean middle way? Charles wanted the Church to return to Catholicism. For more than a century, the struggle raged fiercely within the Church of England. What kind of Church would emerge from the struggle?

Who could have envisaged that the two small congregations meeting at Llanfaches and Cardiff would point towards a very different form of church life? Uniformity would eventually be replaced by toleration and religious pluralism, but many battles lay ahead.

The Civil War and the Commonwealth, 1639–1660

William Wroth, the old saint of Llanfaches, prayed 'that he might never hear a drum beat in order,' and according to Edward Terrel, the author of the *Broadmead Records* (1640–1688) 'he was by the Lord laid asleep before the war'. The founder of the first 'Independent... Congregational... Dissenting... Non-conformist... New England Way' church died within two years of the formation of the gathered community at Llanfaches. Wroth foresaw and feared the outbreak of war. War changes everything. Civil War divides and threatens to destroy nations, communities, churches and families. Neither England nor Wales were ever the same after war broke out in 1642. The Llanfaches congregation was the first example in Wales of worshipping Christians separating themselves from the Church of England. They probably believed their separation would be temporary and in due time they would return and help purify the parish church. Was separation inevitable? Much would depend on the attitudes of those exercising authority within the church, and those seeking freedom of worship. The year 1639 marked the tiny fissure which soon widened into a chasm between Christians who eventually came to hold diametrically opposing views of church order and social life.

The events following the formation of Llanfaches were to be paralleled in the eighteenth century by what happened to the Methodist movement. Puritanism and Methodism began as movements of renewal within the life of the Established

Church, and both trusted that the fresh impetus of the Spirit would breathe new life into the church in which they had been nurtured. It was not to be, either for Puritans or Methodists. Wroth was disciplined by the church, and Erbery forced to resign his living. There could be no turning back. A century later, Howel Harris, Daniel Rowland and William Williams experienced the failure of the ecclesiastical hierarchy to grasp the changes taking place all around them. Unity was coterminous with uniformity. Anglicanism could brook no dissent. The worlds of the mid-seventeenth and the late-eighteenth centuries were to be turned upside down. But in 1639 there were few intimations that revolutionary events were imminent.

> In the summer of 1642 an impoverished, downtrodden, and sleepy nation on the outer fringes of Europe was drawn into a civil war which few of its people had sought... Had Welshmen at the time known what the future held they would have been horrified. For many old, familiar landmarks were destroyed after 1642: following the bitter strife of civil war, Parliament was purged by the army, the king was executed, the monarchy and the House of Lords were temporarily abolished, and a republican government ruled for eleven years.[3]

On the eve of the Civil War, Wales was loyalist in its Royalism and Anglicanism. Since the days of the Tudors, the lives of Welsh gentlemen were closely intertwined with the fortunes of the monarchy. They enjoyed the status and sinecures of the Stuart Court. The Parliamentary cause was supported only in Puritan enclaves along the borders, especially near Llanfaches, Wrexham, and at the home of the Harleys of Brampton Bryan in north Herefordshire. Puritanism had also made a toehold in towns like Cardiff, Haverfordwest, Pembroke and Tenby which were linked by trade with the Puritan stronghold of Bristol. During the First English Civil War (1642–6), the Puritan cause was divided into Presbyterians eager to work out acceptable terms with the King, and Independents and more radical movements who became more and more entrenched in their opposition towards compromise. The Second English Civil War (1648–9) intensified the radicalism of those who saw Charles as 'the man of blood' incapable of loyalty to treaties and prepared to invite a Catholic army from Ireland to overthrow Parliament. Charles was executed in Whitehall on 30 January 1649. Only two Welshmen signed his death warrant, John Jones of Maesygarnedd in Merioneth and Thomas Wogan, MP for Cardigan Boroughs. Most Welsh people were horrified by the execution. Regicide was blasphemy.

Preaching the Gospel

Charles had ruled without recourse to Parliament from 1629 to 1640, but in November 1640 he was obliged to recall Parliament to raise revenue for his war with Scotland. The Long Parliament met for the first time on 3 November and was soon flooded with petitions for reform from many parts of the country. Quick off the mark was William Erbery, who was responsible for presenting two petitions, the first in December 1640 and the second in February 1641. Erbery claimed to represent reformers from the whole Principality of Wales, but especially from the county of Glamorgan, when he stated that in the 1,000 parishes of Wales, there could be found only '13 constant preachers, that preach morning & evening, or expound the catechisme every Lords day in the Welch tongue. And that in our County of Glamorgan (counted the chiefest for preaching) conteining about an 115 parishes, there are not to be found 5 constant preachers.' Parliament accepted the Petition, and Erbery and four other Puritan ministers were given freedom 'to preach in any parish where there is want of preaching'. A similar plea was made in the Petition of 1641 and permission again granted, this time to 'seven preachers of the word of God,' including William Wroth and William Erbery.[4]

As warfare intensified, the Puritan preachers, sometimes with their congregations as at Llanfaches, were forced to flee to England, some of them serving in London parishes and others acting as army chaplains. Their experience radicalised them and brought them close to the power bases in the Parliamentary cause. In 1642, Parliament established a Committee for Plundered Ministers. This Committee ejected 'scandalous or delinquent' clergymen (35 were dismissed in Glamorgan and 18 in Monmouth) and appointed 130 ministers between 1644 and 1649. The Puritan people enjoyed a new freedom to express and live Gospel values. Walter Cradock, in his sermon before Parliament in 1648, jubilantly proclaimed that the consequence of this new focus on preaching the Gospel was:

> I have observed and seen in the mountains of Wales the most
> glorious work that I ever saw in England. The gospel is run over
> the mountains between Brecknockshire and Monmouthshire as
> fire in the thatch. And who should do this? They have no ministers;
> but some of the wisest say that there are about 800 godly people
> there and they go from one to another.[5]

Petitions continued to be made to Parliament and, as a consequence, on 22 February 1650, Parliament passed 'The Act for the Better Propagation and Preaching of the Gospel in Wales'. The Act brought into existence a new political and religious regime for the whole of Wales. Forty-three commissioners were appointed for south Wales and 28 for north Wales, many of them Welsh-speaking Welshmen. The Act proposed a threefold programme which included the disciplining of ministers, their replacement by suitable servants of the Gospel, and the creation of a system of elementary education. The first part saw the removal of 'delinquent clergymen', 196 from the south and 28 from north Wales. The second part was administered by a sub-committee of 25 ministers called Approvers, who appointed 90 itinerants and lay-preachers. This government programme seemed like an answer to the prayer and plea of John Penri in the latter days of Elizabeth's reign. Of course, the scheme of encouraging itinerants was scoffed at by many. How can tinkers, tailors and blacksmiths preach without any learning? Cradock's response was to ask 'hath he the spirit, or no?' This age-old controversy has never been resolved!

The third arm of the programme saw the establishment of elementary education throughout Wales. A few grammar schools had existed for many years, but they catered only for the sons of the lesser gentry. Their education was through the medium of Latin and English. Now, for the first time, the State attempted to provide a system of primary education in Wales. Thirty-seven schools were established in south Wales and 26 in the north. Education was free and for both sexes, and schoolmasters received a salary. The most serious drawback in the programme was its insistence that education should be through the medium of English, thus reinforcing the lack of understanding of Welsh culture which had begun with the accession of the Tudors and the passing of the Acts of Union. The programme was bound ultimately to be ineffectual in a country where 90 per cent of the population remained monoglot Welsh.

The terms of the 1650 Act were for three years, and when time ran out the scheme was not continued. In its place, in March 1654, Parliament created a more London-centralised programme to apply to both England and Wales, to be administered by 'The Commission for the Approbation of Publique Preachers'. Thirty-eight Triers, including two Welshmen, Walter Cradock and Jenkin Griffith, were appointed to administer the scheme. This ambitious programme aimed at paying each clergyman an annual salary of £100, itinerants were encouraged to remain in settled livings, and rigorous standards of learning and discipline were adopted. Some very gifted ministers were appointed in Wales, including Cradock at Usk, Henry Walter at Newport, and Stephen Hughes at Meidrim in Carmarthenshire. Proposals were made by Richard Baxter, John Lewis of Glasgrug, and Dr John Ellis of Dolgellau to establish a Welsh national college for the training of able ministers. Were these not memories of the vision of Owain Glyndŵr? And also, was it a foretaste for those visionaries who established the University of Wales in the late nineteenth century? Two editions of the Welsh New Testament had been published in 1646–7 and in 1654, 6,000 copies of Cromwell's Bible were published in Welsh.[6] Nothing as ambitious had ever been attempted previously.

Cradock had exulted in the miracle that the gospel had run across the mountains like fire in thatch, and that the majority of the evangelists were not ministers, but were 'extraordinary ordinary' lay-people. More than 800 godly people between Breconshire and Monmouthshire! Cradock could not have foreseen the consequences when people have experienced the fire of the Spirit and are armed by the Scriptures in their own language. The majority of Puritans, especially Presbyterians, Independents and most Baptists, shared Cradock's orthodox Calvinism in belief, worship and morality. Despite their differences, they emphasized the unique authority of God's Word and the centrality of preaching, and argued for simpler and scriptural forms of worship, discipline and organization. They emphasized the immediate responsibility of each individual for reconciliation with God, and the obligation to make manifest the fruits of grace and election.

The Search for Toleration

Alongside the demand for an orthodox, disciplined Calvinism, other currents were racing even more fiercely. The Civil War had unleashed forces, especially within the Army, which demanded freedom of religious expression, a more egalitarian society, common ownership of property, justice for the poor and more democratic forms of government. The period saw stimulating arguments, with a demand for the publication of tracts and books. Because of the freedom of the press, sermons and lectures were given on one day, and published and read on the next. Whereas the Puritan emphasis was on the preaching of the Word of God, preachers shared many different interpretations of God's Word and there were even more colourful and dramatic responses by hearers. The result was a plethora of viewpoints. Alongside the attempt to maintain a godly and rigorous Calvinist discipline, there was the demand for freedom of interpretation. The more orthodox were disturbed to discover that once people read the Scriptures for themselves, and emphasized the immediacy of the Holy Spirit, the consequences were beyond the control of bishops, presbyters or ministers. In 1646 Milton had written 'New Presbyter is but old Priest writ large.' Many others opposed any form of external authority which tried to block the channel opened by Christ between the individual and a personal God. In Wales, the majority were like Walter Cradock and Vavasor Powell and followed the orthodox line, but others, like William Erbery and Morgan Llwyd, the most creative writer in Welsh in the seventeenth century, reached out with a tolerant spirit and advocated freedom of conscience. The new movements bursting into existence were Congregationalists led by people like Cradock, Baptists by John Miles who formed the first Baptist congregation in Wales at Ilston in 1649, radical and free-spirited Ranters in Merthyr, Seekers like Erbery, and Fifth Monarchists like Vavasor Powell, convinced of the imminent physical return of Christ. For Powell there was only one king, King Jesus! Christ would soon return and establish his kingdom. In the midst of this hurly-burly of ideas and activities, Erbery had written a far-reaching and heart-felt cry for freedom of conscience:

> That as the three chief religions in the world, are the Christians, Jews and Turks; so this Christian Common-wealth appearing so favourable to the Jews, why not to the Turks?... And if for unbelieving Jews, why not for misbelieving Christians, who in their utmost knowledge love the Truth and Peace?... why may not honest Papists have the like liberty of Conscience, in due time, amongst Protestants in England, when our Governours see good.[7]

This position was also advocated by a new movement which soon made its mark on the Welsh. George Fox's ministry had originated in the north of England about 1653, but Quakerism soon had followers in many parts of Wales. It is no accident that the widow and children of Erbery in Cardiff (after his death in 1654) and the followers of Morgan Llwyd in north Wales, should be amongst the most fervent members of the Society of Friends. They were amongst the most radical of Christians, emphasizing the inner light within all people, and abandoning traditional sacraments and social mores.

It is possible to date the creation of the two main streams within Puritanism – the emphasis on Calvinist orthodoxy, and the more radical advocacy of toleration – from the period of the Civil War and the Commonwealth. Both streams were to run more fiercely during the next two centuries and reshape Wales as a Nonconformist nation. New habits of Bible reading and household worship were formed, private meditation and the keeping of Puritan diaries followed, and the Puritan work ethic adopted. Although this was particularly true of the towns of southern and eastern England, by the close of the Civil War, Puritanism had made considerable progress in Wales. It started in the south and east of Wales, spread along the Borders and resulted in a network of Puritan congregations. Although at the Restoration the number of Puritans remained a handful, their effect on their contemporaries and the future history of Wales was to be highly significant.

Restoration, Uniformity, Persecution, 1660–1689[8]

For royalists, the young Charles had succeeded his father in 1649 and reigned as king in exile. They anticipated that his return, in 1660, would restore the indissoluble relationship between Church and State. Most Welsh people welcomed the king's restoration of Anglican Orders and rejoiced in the abandonment of the heavy-handed moralism and sabbatarianism of the Puritans. They willingly returned to the familiarity of the Church of bishop and Prayer Book. The Rule of the Saints had ended with a whimper. Erbery died in 1654, Llwyd and Cradock in 1659, and Powell was imprisoned from 1660 (except for a brief respite in 1667/8) until his death in 1670.

The merry monarch would restore merry England. The country was ruled by a king by divine right, supreme governor of the Church of England. But would Charles govern a 'middle-way' church like Elizabeth and James, or restore the Laudian church of his father? Charles soon revealed his colours. Discussions took place between Anglicans and Presbyterians at the Savoy Chapel in the Strand in 1661. Could both be held within the national Church? There was no compromise and the King and his Royalist Parliament passed the Act of Uniformity in April 1662. All ministers were ordered to declare in front of his congregation before the feast of St Bartholomew on 24 August 1662 his 'unfeigned assent and consent to every thing contained and prescribed... in the book of common prayer' and to 'the form and order of making, ordaining, and consecrating of bishops, priests, and deacons.'[9] The penalty for refusal was to lose one's position. Two thousand ministers did not comply and were ejected from the Church of England.

Laws (the Clarendon Code) were passed between 1661 and 1673 insisting that only those taking Anglican Communion could hold public office and attend universities. Dissenters were prevented from worshipping in public, and their ministers forbidden residence within five miles of their previously held churches. Nonconformists worshipped in secret, 'in barns, forests, fields, simple houses in the back alleys of towns, and anywhere except in churches.'[10] A hollow bureau in Llanidloes, a secret room at Ysgafell, and the story of Cae'r Fendith (The Field of Blessing) near Newtown are tangible reminders in Montgomeryshire of the days when dissenting preachers were hidden when the authorities called to persecute.

Although the Act of Uniformity aimed at enforcing obedience on the people of England and Wales, it failed dismally in its purpose. Persecution fanned the flames of Dissent. The Commonwealth had created determined Dissenters. Prevented by their convictions from conforming to an Episcopal, Prayer Book, Established Church, foundations were laid for religious pluralism. Enforced conformity drove Puritans out of the Church. In 1660 and 1661, 93 Welsh clergymen lost their

livings, followed by a further 25 in 1662. In 1638 William
Erbery had been the only cleric in Wales to be ejected for his
nonconformity. The Commonwealth had left its legacy.

Puritans were not the only Dissenters. Worse persecution
was inflicted on Roman Catholics and Quakers. The image of
Catholicism had been shaped by John Foxe's *Book of Martyrs*
and memories of the Spanish Armada, the Gunpowder Plot,
and Irish armies, all of which created a popular anti-Roman
mythology. This image was touched with realism because
Charles proved to be a crypto-catholic who was received into
the Catholic Church on his deathbed. The religious census
of 1676 revealed 541 recusants in Monmouthshire alone,
served by 15 priests and supported by the Somerset family of
Raglan. In 1678, the Jesuit College founded in 1622 at Cwm in
Llanrothal in Herefordshire was ransacked, and in 1679, five
priests, Philip Evans and John Lloyd at Cardiff, David Lewis at
Usk, Charles Meehan at Ruthin, and John Kemble at Hereford,
were barbarously executed. This marked an acceleration of the
slow decay of Catholicism in Wales, a decline not halted until
Irish immigration during the mid-nineteenth century.

A similar fate befell Quakers, hated both by Anglicans and
Nonconformists as religious heretics and as people turning the
world upside down. Quakerism had spread rapidly in Welsh-
speaking areas, particularly in Merioneth, Montgomery and
Radnor.

A special Quaker Act was passed in 1662, and remorseless
persecution continued until it was so unbearable that from
1682 onwards many fled to America, especially to the Quaker
haven of Pennsylvania. Two thousand left during the last
two decades of the seventeenth century, including 900 from
Merionethshire, particularly around the area of Dolgellau.

The bishops and Anglican gentry exercised irresistible
power which eventually proved disastrous for the Church of
England. Lay impropriators owned a great deal of church land
and revenue, and were responsible for clerical appointments.

> Poverty was also the root cause of most of the familiar weaknesses of the established church – absenteeism, non-residence, pluralism, nepotism, and neglect... no real attempt was made to eradicate abuses within the church or to reform its anomalies... some bishops preferred to rest their idle bones on the plush ermine of the House of Lords rather than venture into one of the barren corners of the land.[11]

Geraint H. Jenkins suggests that the situation differed between the two northern and the two southern dioceses. Bangor and St Asaph were well served by cathedral dignitaries of learning and distinction. Humphrey Humphreys of Bangor (1689–1701) was an assiduous bishop who was concerned about reform and supported the Society for the Promotion of Christian Knowledge. On the contrary, Llandaff had no Welsh-speaking bishop for 200 years. In St Davids and Llandaff, many were appointed whose sole concern was their own advancement. Ministry was a career and not a vocation. Curates, particularly badly treated, were the lowest in the pecking order.

The Act of Toleration was passed in May 1689, soon after the accession of William and Mary. Only Trinitarian Protestant ministers were allowed to conduct worship, and freedom of worship was not granted to Catholics and Unitarians. Although the Act recognized the existence of Nonconformists, it imposed severe restrictions on where they could worship, what kinds of professions they could take up, and they were refused entry to university. Consequently, Nonconformist ministers formed their own academies. When Samuel Jones lost his living at Llangynwyd in 1662, he opened an academy in his farmhouse in Brynllywarch, beginning a tradition of nurturing Dissenters which has survived into the twenty-first century. Dissenters were also obliged to pay rates and tithes, increasing their grudges against the Established Church. Although free to build their own meeting houses, they were treated as second-class citizens, a stigma continuing until the repeal of the Test and Corporation Acts in 1828.

Although Nonconformists did not enjoy full rights of

citizenship for over 200 years, the Code meant that Dissenters were legally 'tolerated'. The die had been cast and Wales (and England) was no longer forced to subscribe to the straitjacket restriction of the enforcement of one church for one nation. Although, by the end of the seventeenth century, Nonconformists remained a minority within Wales, they became increasingly significant and influential as the next century progressed.

> The archbishop of Canterbury's religious census of 1676 suggests that no more than one in twenty of the population of Wales attended Nonconformist services in that year. Although these were few, these were the people who laid the foundations of Welsh Nonconformist culture, a culture which would play a central role in the history of Wales in subsequent generations.[12]

The 1689 Toleration Act gave permission for Nonconformists to build places of worship. They took full advantage of the Act and by 1697 chapels had been built at Pencader, Cefnarthen, Capel Isaac and Henllan Amgoed in Carmarthenshire, Tredustan in Breconshire, Maesyronnen in Radnorshire, Penmain and Llanwenarth in Monmouthshire. By 1715 there were 70 Nonconformist chapels in Wales, mostly in Carmarthen, Glamorgan and Monmouth. The best preserved and typical is Maesyronnen, registered in 1697. This was a completely different situation from 1639 when the first Dissenting Church had been founded in Llanfaches. This minority of Dissenters were to change the face of Wales and lay the foundations of a radical, egalitarian society.

> This small minority of second-class citizens, Dissenters who rejected the State Church, numbered perhaps 5 per cent of a population of around 350,000. Independents and Baptists mostly, half of them were in the south-east, in Monmouth, Glamorgan and Brecon... And after the great storms had passed, there they were in the land of Poor Taffy and his squires, a clutch of chapels, schools, slowly growing communities, with a memory of a time which broke kings, of their state schools, and of that Welsh national college which the Triers had proposed. Into the service of

the Word, indeed, many of them moved, into academies and the printing press, to create in themselves and in the communities they were shaping in the American colonies, an alternative society with an Atlantic dimension.[13]

6

LITERACY AND REVIVAL, 1689–1770

The Revolution in Literacy

Wales began to be transformed when its people learned to read. They learned to read in their own language. They learned to read the Bible of William Morgan. A biblically literate people eventually changed society. The eighteenth century witnessed the seeds of the future transformation of Wales. Wales was the first nation to create an indigenous literate working class. The language of this working class was Welsh, the traditional language of its people. And this working class read the Bible. The English language had been the instrument of power, commerce, political and social advancement since the Acts of Union had effectively absorbed the nation of Wales into its larger, stronger neighbour. Reading the Bible in Welsh prevented what would have been the inevitable extinction of the Welsh language and culture.

Griffith Jones, born at Pant-yr-efail, Penboyr, Carmarthenshire, through his passion for the human spirit, his organising abilities and his perseverance, taught the people of Wales to read the Bible translated by William Morgan of Tŷ Mawr, Wybrnant. Within two generations, Wales was a biblically literate nation. Parallel with this educational revolution, the people of Wales created its own indigenous religious tradition. The sixteenth-century European Reformation finally arrived with the mid-eighteenth-century Evangelical Revival which created Calvinistic Methodism, reinvigorated the older Dissenting traditions and the Church of England, and laid the foundations by which Wales became a nation of Nonconformists in the nineteenth and early twentieth centuries.

The Wales of the nineteenth century was dramatically different from the Wales of the early eighteenth century. Many factors contributed to the monumental changes and it is possible to over-emphasize the effect of the Methodist revival on the people of Wales. In fact, Nigel Yates argues that:

> Methodism in Wales was an outcome of the pastoral revival of the Established Church, a revival which had emphasized the basic education of the laity by the parish clergy, so that they could read the Bible and knew the catechism, and the formation of religious societies of devout lay people for self-examination, Bible reading, prayer and thanksgiving, and using hymns. Howell Harris... was nourished on Anglican classics of spirituality... Griffith Jones... was never a Methodist... but was responsible for the conversion experiences of the two early leaders, not only Howell Harris, but Daniel Rowland... His circulating schools provided many recruits for Methodist societies.[1]

This is a salutary antidote to the 'Methodist interpretation of Welsh history' which is often similar to the way the newly-converted explain their transformation. Memory becomes flawed. The post-Restoration Established Church was castigated by Methodists for being dominated by an English absentee hierarchical clergy and an anglicised gentry. The patent weaknesses of the Church of England were reflected in its poverty at parish level, and in the pluralism, nepotism and non-residence of its clergy. Ignorance and neglect were widespread. The unholy alliance between State and squire had even more deleterious consequences with the Hanoverian appointment of alien, absentee bishops. Methodists also described Dissenters as intellectuals, shrunken in numbers and zeal. Dissenters were responsible for the spread of rationalism and deism. Dissenting was a 'head-religion', cold, antagonistic to enthusiasm, self-interested and unappealing to the people of

Wales. William Williams, Pantycelyn, described the situation as 'When Wales then lay in some dark and deadly sleep, with neither Presbyter nor priest nor prelate awake; in the murky pitch-black night'. [2]

Pantycelyn's description was by no means accurate. The legacy of Puritanism had created a growing insistence on individual accountability, personal devotion and an emphasis on a religion which was more immediate, inward and heartfelt. Edward Samuel described the situation very differently from Pantycelyn. 'To God be the thanks that the Light of the Gospel now shines as brightly in Wales as almost any other country, there are more edifying, godly books more frequently printed, and no doubt now better preachers in our midst than existed in any age for a Thousand Years.'[3] Anglicans and Dissenters cooperated in evangelising the poor on social, political and religious grounds. Bibles, Prayer Books, Catechisms and other devotional literature were published. Thomas Gouge, a London clergyman, founded The Welsh Trust in 1674 to teach devotional literature to children through the medium of English. Between 1674 and 1681, the year of Gouge's death, 3,000 children attended the Trust's schools. Stephen Hughes persuaded the Trust to provide Welsh religious texts. Eight thousand copies of the New Testament were published in 1678, and a further 10,000 in 1690, as well as editions of the works of John Bunyan, Rhys Prichard, and William Perkins. In 1678 alone, the Trust was responsible for distributing 5,185 Welsh books. The Society for the Promotion of Christian Knowledge (SPCK) was founded in London in 1698 and flourished particularly in west Wales through the support of Sir John Phillips and Sir Humphrey Mackworth. By 1715, 68 schools had been established and a further 28 between 1715 and 1727. Almost half the schools were established in Carmarthenshire and Pembrokeshire. The work of the charitable trusts created a spate of energetic publishing. Between 1660 and 1730, at least 545 books were published in Wales – 406 between 1700 and 1730, compared with 108 between 1546 and 1660. There were six major editions of the Welsh Bible, running to a total of 44,000 copies.

Griffith Jones and the Circulating Schools

Out of these movements came the astonishing work of Griffith Jones (1683–1761). He was the key figure in the movement towards national literacy. A farmer's son from Penboyr in the Teifi valley, he was presented by Sir John Phillips with the living of Llanddowror in 1716. Griffith Jones married Margaret, the sister of John Phillips in 1719. Jones had been a supporter of the work of the SPCK but doubted the validity of its emphasis on teaching through the medium of English. He was aware that the natural language of the majority of the people was Welsh, and that the key to their grasping the Gospel was by learning to read the Bible in Welsh.

Griffith Jones inaugurated his scheme of Circulating Schools in 1734. He trained his prospective tutors at Llanddowror before sending them to various parishes to teach children and adults. A school remained in a parish for three months before the tutors moved on to another location. To suit the convenience of the students, classes were usually held during the autumn and winter. His concern was to provide for his pupils the means of salvation. Children and adults were taught the catechism, to sing the psalms and to learn how to pray. Jones produced annual reports, *Welch Piety*. By 1761, the year of Jones' death, 3,325 schools had been held at 1,600 places located in all Welsh counties except Flintshire. About 250,000 people had attended these schools, over half the population of Wales. The schools continued successfully until the death of his patron, Bridget Bevan, in 1779. Over a period of 50 years, 70,000 Welsh Bibles had been provided by the SPCK. Griffith's efficiency was remarkable. His annual reports show that he was an excellent bookkeeper and used his income wisely.

The seminal and remarkable work of Griffith Jones cannot

be overestimated. The Welsh working-class was now literate, a basic tool of human development. They were literate in their own language, and the instrument of their education was the Bible. They learned to read and express themselves in the language and thought-forms of the Bible. This new community would soon question received assumptions and ultimately create a national self-confidence which helped shape the future of Wales.

> His efforts led to a fundamental transformation of the life of Wales.
> By the second half of the eighteenth century, Wales was one of
> the few countries with a literate majority. Griffith Jones's schools
> aroused interest outside Wales, and do so still; Catherine, empress
> of Russia, commissioned a report on them in 1764 and they were
> suggested as a model by UNESCO in 1995... as the Welsh became
> increasingly literate, they were prepared for the immense social
> changes which they were soon to encounter, thus ensuring that
> their experience of industrialization, although traumatic, would
> not be as traumatic as that of peoples who had not received such
> preparation.[4]

The Methodist/Evangelical Revival

Part of the legacy of Puritanism both within a 'reforming Anglicanism' and in Nonconformity was an emphasis on a more personal religious experience. The work of Griffith Jones resulted in a biblically literate society. The dual emphases of a personal faith and the knowledge of Scripture paved the way for the evangelical revival of the eighteenth century. Two hundred years had elapsed from the outset of the Reformation and there had been a century of Puritan preaching. Family prayers and private devotion had become a common feature of domestic piety. Bible reading and theological discussion were now a reality of Christian life. The schools of the Welsh Trust and the SPCK, and particularly the Circulating Schools of Griffith Jones, are linked historically and geographically with the seminal areas of the Methodist Revival. The schools proved to be the cradle for spiritual renewal.

The Methodist Revival began as a movement within the Church of England. Its early leaders, although influenced by Puritan piety, were not nonconformists. Howel Harris (1714–73), Daniel Rowland (c.1711–90) and William Williams (1717–91) were young, rural Welsh speakers. They experienced the crisis of the despair of sin and guilt, followed by a transforming sense of forgiveness and salvation. They were convinced that it was through dramatic conversion that God saved sinners from eternal damnation. The gift of being in a personal relationship with the living Christ was not the consequence of slow, careful catechising or regular participation in the sacraments. The need for personal conversion lay at the heart of the Christian experience. The call to repent was central to Christian preaching.

The Methodist preachers emphasized personal responsibility. Decisions were of eternal significance. Life hinged on making a decision for Christ and against the Devil, because life's journey ended either in heaven or in hell. The heavy mortality rates caused by outbreaks of severe epidemics of typhus in 1727 and 1731 intensified the fears of hell. An apocalyptic battle was fought between the powers of light and darkness. The call to renounce sin and accept Jesus created a religion of immediacy. The power of preaching was the key instrument of conversion to melt the stubborn heart.

Howel Harris was a seminal figure in early Welsh Methodism. His conversion in 1735, three years before the conversion of John and Charles Wesley, marks the origin of the Welsh revival. Harris, born in Trefeca and educated at the Dissenting Academy at Llwynllwyd, was converted after hearing sermons on Easter and Whit Sundays at St Gwendoline's Church, Talgarth, and personal contemplation at Llangasty.

> Harris himself gives a precise date to his conversion, namely Whit Sunday 1735, and he remembers it for the rest of his days, 25 May, just as he remembers Easter Sunday, when his heart was 'strangely warmed within him' for the first time, and just as he remembers

the eighteenth of June when his forgiveness was sealed with the divine words 'I change not.'[5]

After inviting others to his home for Bible reading and prayer, he began to preach in the open air. He formed societies or seiadau to strengthen the faith of the new converts. After being rejected for ordination, he consulted Griffith Jones who advised caution. In 1737 he began working with Daniel Rowland, and among their early converts were Howel Davies (1716–70), the apostle of Pembrokeshire, and William Williams. In 1739, Harris and George Whitfield, the leader of the Calvinist wing of Methodism, travelled to London to meet John and Charles Wesley, the Countess of Huntingdon and the Moravians. Harris' following years were spent in preaching, and organising seiadau. However, in 1750, at the Association meeting at Llanidloes, a split took place in the Methodist movement, and Rowland and Harris went their separate ways. In July, at Llantrisant, Harris was expelled from Methodism for heresy because of his theological emphasis on the death of God on the Cross (Patripassianism), and because of questions about his relationship with Madam Sidney Griffith, the 'prophetess' of Cefn Amlwch in Llŷn. Harris retreated from the main Methodist movement and concentrated on his work at Trefeca where he established a Christian community, known as *y teulu* (the family). By 1755 there were 102 members of the *teulu*, founded on a rigorous life of devotion. Harris was eventually reconciled with the main Methodist movement after a second revival took place at Llangeitho in 1762, but played no further significant part in the wider Methodist movement.

Daniel Rowland, born at Bwlch-llan near Tregaron, Cardiganshire, was ordained a priest in 1735 but was not given preferment because of his Methodism. He remained as the curate at Llangeitho until he was deprived of his ministry in 1762, at the time of the second revival. Converted under the ministry of Griffith Jones, he met Howel Harris with whom he cooperated for many years. Rowland's ministry, focused on Llangeitho, served as a magnet for the Methodist people. Llangeitho became a national preaching centre and thousands attended the monthly communion services. The revival of 1762 was an extraordinary experience, inspired by Daniel Rowland's preaching and the hymns of William Williams. Pantycelyn's first anthology, *Caniadau*, sold 1,200 copies in a few months. The extreme enthusiasm of this second Revival disturbed the Church authorities and Rowland was deprived of his curacy. As a consequence, Rowland's followers built a chapel which now became the centre of his ministry. Llangeitho has been described as the Mecca of Calvinistic Methodism. Pilgrims would travel by boat from Llŷn in order to be present at Sunday communion at Llangeitho.

> At the quarterly meeting held at Llangeitho that year [1783], [Thomas] Charles observed 'about twenty clergymen, and between sixty and eighty preachers'; he heard Daniel Rowland preach twice, 'and also three clergymen, as well as several of the preachers... The preaching started on Saturday, and went on until ten o'clock on Wednesday morning.'[6]

Harris and Rowland were joined by William Williams.[7] Born at Cefncoed, a small farm at Llanfair-ar-y-bryn, Carmarthenshire, he later lived at Pantycelyn, the original home of his mother. His father was a Dissenter and in order to prepare his son for training as a doctor, Williams was sent to the Dissenting Academy at Llwynllwyd, Llanigon, Breconshire (where Harris had been educated). It was in Talgarth churchyard in 1737 or 1738 that he heard Howel Harris preach and experienced conversion. Ordained a deacon in 1740, he served for three years at Llanwrtyd where Theophilus Evans took him on as curate. The relationship must have been extremely uneasy because Evans was 'one of Methodism's bitterest enemies, who on one occasion, from the pulpit at Llanwrtyd, denounced the new revivalists as false prophets and hot-headed fools'.[8] Williams became an assistant to Daniel Rowland in 1743. The Watford Sasiwn had decided that he should leave his curacy and support Rowland in organising seiadau in Radnorshire, Montgomeryshire and Cardiganshire. It is no surprise that the bishop refused to ordain him a priest because of his organising of seiadau.[9] An itinerant preacher and the chief superintendent of seiadau, Pantycelyn was a writer of prose, poetry and supreme hymns. Williams wrote more than 800 hymns and has retained his popularity to such an extent that 88 have been included in *Caneuon Ffydd* (2001), the new ecumenical hymnbook. The effect of the hymns of Pantycelyn was electrifying. Thousands of his contemporaries were touched by their power and their influence had an unparalleled effect on the nation.

The bishops closed the doors to the three pre-eminent leaders of Methodism. The decisions of the bishops reflected the age-old conundrum of how to maintain discipline and orthodoxy while the winds of the Spirit are blowing in fresh and uncomfortable ways. How was the Church to maintain its coherence while these unorthodox young men were challenging the foundations of episcopal discipline? Calvinistic Methodism emphasized the centrality of preaching which brought the convert to the point of decision, and created an organised structure to enable the convert to grow in the way of holiness. The newly converted could recount their experience, be supported in the way of righteousness and prevented from back-sliding. The average Methodist society (seiat) numbered between 15 and 25 members. The first permanent seiat was held in 1737 at Y Wernos, a farmhouse in the parish of Llandyfalle, Breconshire. Their growth mushroomed.

> By 1750, 428 societies had been established, 346 [81 per cent] of which were situated in the six counties of south Wales. Societies tended to cluster together in local fellowship and prospered best in areas such as Trefeca, Llangeitho-Tregaron, Llanddowror and the vale of Glamorgan, where guidance and leadership were strong. There were fifty-one societies in Montgomery and Radnor, but in the five counties of north Wales... only thirty-one societies had been founded.[10]

The Methodist leaders were conscious of the need to supervise these close-knit seiadau which could easily become separatist groups. The seiat has much in common with Puritan conventicles which also attempted to reform Anglicanism as a 'church within the Church'. They too had been forced out of the Church of England. Twenty Methodist leaders, including Harris and Williams, and chaired by Daniel Rowland, met in a 'sasiwn' in 1742 at Dugoedydd, a farmhouse in the upper Tywi valley, to discuss the organisation of Methodist societies. The following year they met again at Watford, near Caerphilly, where George Whitfield presided at the first joint Anglo-Welsh Association of Calvinistic Methodists. The burden of these early leaders was to bring new life into the established Church. They regarded schism as abhorrent, and it was only with the second generation of leaders that Methodism moved inexorably towards separation and the creation of a new denomination. That was to happen formally in 1811 when the first ministers were ordained.

The evangelical revival in Wales was dominated by Calvinistic Methodists. Wesleyan Methodism made little inroads into Wales in the eighteenth century. Although John Wesley visited Wales 50 times, because he saw the Welsh language as a barrier to the mission, his influence was restricted to the English-speaking regions of south Pembrokeshire, east Breconshire and around Cardiff. By the time of Wesley's death in 1791, there were only 600 Wesleyans in Wales. Growth in Methodism was to await the work of Edward Jones of Bathafarn and Thomas Coke of Brecon at the close of the century.

Responses and Reactions to Methodism

Despite the fact that the earlier Methodist leaders conformed to the Articles of the Church and held their meetings outside church hours, Anglican critics were fearful of what they saw as excessive and sacrilegious enthusiasm. Pryce Davies accused Howel Harris of 'fanaticism and hypocrisy'. Griffith Jones judged Harris and Rowland as guilty of 'enthusiastical and incredible fooleries' and censured Harris as being 'obstinately erroneous and conceited'. Many Anglican clergy were as committed as were the Methodists to deepen the Christian experience of their people, but were desperately unhappy with the emotional vagaries of Methodism. When Methodists ordained their own ministers in 1811, a committed body of Evangelicals remained within the Church of England and were to exercise a profound influence during the nineteenth century.

Many Dissenting preachers rejoiced in the new vitality entering the church. Henry Davies of Blaengwrach established the first nonconformist cause in the Rhondda at Cymmer, Porth, in 1743 and invited Howel Harris to Glamorgan. Edmund Jones, the 'Old Prophet' of Pontypool, served congregationalism for 69 years, and was a staunch supporter of the Methodists. Lewis Rees, educated by Henry Davies, built a chapel (Yr Hen Gapel) in Llanbrynmair and prepared the way for Howel Harris to preach in north Wales. Philip Pugh of Llwynpiod supported Daniel Rowland and prepared his defence against the accusations of his bishop that he was preaching irregularly. Dafydd Jones, the drover from Caeo, wrote his own hymns and also translated the hymns of Isaac Watts. Another congregational hymn-writer was Morgan Rhys of Cil-y-cwm, an itinerant teacher with the circulating schools. Dafydd William of Llandeilo-fach, also a schoolmaster and a friend of the Methodists, wrote very popular hymns. The swift growth of Independents and Baptists during the last quarter of the eighteenth century owes a great deal to the evangelical revival. Edmund Jones estimated that there were 106 Congregationalist and Baptist churches in Wales in 1742, 88 of which were concentrated in the six counties of south Wales. Independents increased their number of churches to 100 in 1775, while Baptist membership grew from 1,601 in 1760 to 5,786 in 1790. They were being prepared for the spectacular growth in the nineteenth century.

Radical thinkers moved in a very different direction from the Revivalists. Teachers and students at the Dissenting Academy in Carmarthen (the largest town in Wales until the late eighteenth century) were appalled by the blind emotionalism of the Methodists, and advocated the place of reason in their exploration of faith. Thomas Perrot, who in 1718 became the second principal, moved the college in an increasingly liberal direction. There was a gradual journey through Arminianism to Unitarianism. The first Unitarian congregation in Wales was founded in 1733 at Llwynrhydowen, near Llandysul. Many congregations were converted to this more rationalist faith in the area on the border between Carmarthenshire and Cardiganshire. An eminent and influential rational thinker was Richard Price (1723–91) of Llangeinor. Trained for the Presbyterian ministry, his pilgrim's progress led him to a religion based upon reason and nature. A philosopher and a mathematician, he is best remembered as a champion of liberty. He defended the American and French Revolutions, received an honorary doctorate from Yale in 1781, and was invited by the American Congress to serve as its financial adviser. David Williams (1738–1816) of Waunwaelod, near Caerffili, was educated at the Carmarthen Academy. After serving as a minister at Highgate, Middlesex, and opening a boarding school in Chelsea, he and Benjamin Franklin founded the Thirteen Club. He wrote a 'liturgy for universalists', which won praise from Voltaire, Rousseau and Frederick the Great. He was formally invited to France to advise on its new Constitution. Edward Williams or Iolo Morganwg (1747–1826), of Flemingstone, has been described as 'one of the ablest and most versatile men ever born in Wales'.[11] A leading Unitarian, amongst the many achievements of this 'Bard of Liberty' was his holding the first Gorsedd ceremony at Primrose Hill in London in 1792. At the Carmarthen eisteddfod of 1819, he made the Gorsedd an integral part of eisteddfod proceedings. He and Richard Price were associated with the Gwyneddigion, a society of Welsh patriots founded in London in 1770. Thomas Evans, Tomos Glyn Cothi (1764–1833) of Gwernogle, Carmarthenshire, became the Unitarian minister of the Old Meeting House in Aberdare. Probably it was because of his sympathy for the French Revolution that he was imprisoned in Carmarthen in 1803.

> Thus there were two distinct streams in the religious history of eighteenth-century Wales. While the majority were attracted to revivalist zeal (zeal which represented a reaction against the Age of Reason), a small minority sought to modify religious doctrines in the light of reason. And in the long term, the few who rejected traditional dogma were to be at least as influential as those who adhered to it.[12]

The people of Wales would soon face the most revolutionary changes in their history. After 1770, industrialization, coupled with the rapid growth and movement of population, would change completely the physical and spiritual contours of Welsh society. How would the people of Wales face such a radical transformation? Would biblically literate farm labourers be able to cope with the challenges of urbanized society? Many other questions were part of a future unchartered agenda. Would Calvinistic Methodists remain within the Church of England, throw in their lot with the Nonconformists, or create a new denomination? Dissent was also at a crossroads. Many were inspired by the Revival, but others were moved by rationalism and romanticism. Would Dissent become more 'evangelical' or 'rationalist'? Would both streams continue to flow in the nineteenth century? Would the old wineskins be sturdy and flexible enough to cope with radical change? Would the Church be ready to face as great a challenge as any it had faced throughout its history? Were the people of Wales prepared for a new age?

7

FROM DISSENT TO
NONCONFORMITY, 1770–1851

A New Wales

The new age arrived at revolutionary speed. In 1770, the people of Wales remained tied to the land as they had been for centuries. Their lives were controlled by wealthy landowners and they were obliged to be faithful to the parish church dominated by clergy and squires. Most spoke only Welsh, while power was exercised by English speakers. Few towns existed, apart from Carmarthen, Wales' largest town for many centuries, and Swansea, prosperous through its combination of heavy industry and its fashionable seaside resort.

Early signs of eighteenth-century industrialisation included weaving cloth in the Severn valley, spinning cotton in Holywell and Mold, shaping pottery in Buckley, smelting iron in Bersham, and extracting copper from Parys Mountain in Anglesey for smelting in Holywell and in 'Copperopolis' Swansea. However, no-one could have envisaged the revolutionary industrialization which began during the final decades of that century. War with France between 1793 and 1815 created an insatiable demand for iron products, and the areas at the heads of the south Wales valleys were soon developed and ruthlessly exploited. The first phase of the industrial revolution (1780–1850) was dominated by iron when the population of Wales more than doubled. The iron-dominated communities of the south Wales valleys stretched from Blaenavon through Butetown (Rhymni),

Dowlais and Hirwaun to Llanelli, with new towns perched on what had been bare uninhabited moorland. By 1851, Wales was the first country in the world in which more people were employed in industry than in agriculture. In 1780, there was not a single town with more than 5,000 people, but by 1851 there were 18 such towns, with Merthyr the uncrowned capital with a population of nearly 47,000. The second phase (beginning about 1850) was the era of coal, when the population doubled again to reach 2,523,500 by 1914. Three major industrial belts formed: the south Wales coalfield, the north-east coalfield and the slate communities of the north-west.

People were on the move in a way unprecedented in Welsh history. They migrated from country to town, leaving the oppression, poverty and hunger of rural life for the new world of iron and coal, many of them armed with a confidence shaped by a literate nonconformist background. The first half-century saw the move from west and mid Wales to Glamorgan and Monmouth. By 1851 almost 40 per cent of the population of Wales was focused on these two counties, while the rural counties experienced massive depopulation. In the second half of the century the migration came largely from England, creating long-term repercussions for Welsh society. This new melting pot was composed of Welsh speakers, English-speaking Welsh, and people from England and further afield. A vibrant new society of young, healthy, energetic industrial workers and their families burst into existence with explosive suddenness. Wales was the world's first industrial nation and, in this frontier-world, the Welsh landscape and society changed irrevocably. The century bore witness to innovative technology, ambitious entrepreneurship and the amassing of great wealth by a minority of industrial masters. It also created a society with a massive maldistribution of wealth, with industrial communities suffering deprivation, disease and early death.

Unrest and Protest

What was the reaction of people to these radical changes? The decade between 1834 and 1845 was amongst the most troubled in the history of Wales. A succession of violent struggles between master and worker saw the rich man in his palace and the poor man determined to batter down his gate. The Merthyr Rising of 1831 was 'the most ferocious and bloody event in the history of industrial Britain'.[1] The people of Merthyr, a stronghold of radical Unitarians, were inflamed by the decision of the ironmaster, William Crawshay, to lower wages. Huge crowds gathered in the centre of town where they were confronted by 80 men of the Argyll and Sutherland Highlanders. Twenty members of the crowd were shot dead outside the Castle Hotel, the red flag was raised (possibly for the first time in these islands) and the town remained in the control of the rioters/protesters for almost a week. In the trial that followed, Lewis Lewis (Lewsyn yr Heliwr) was exiled to Australia for life, and Richard Lewis (Dic Penderyn) was hanged at Cardiff Gaol on 31 July 1831. Dic Penderyn is revered as Wales' first working-class martyr, with memorials to him in the Merthyr of his arrest, Cardiff of his hanging and Aberavon of his burial.

The defeat of the protest was answered by the formation of a miners' union. The employers, however, acting swiftly and ruthlessly, dismissed 4,000 miners and the Union collapsed within months. The crushing of peaceful protest and working-class organisation led to violent action. The Scotch Cattle, as anonymous protesters were dubbed, were particularly active in the Monmouthshire valleys. Was it the only action possible when negotiation was ruled out? Social unrest was further fomented by the Poor Law Amendment Act of 1834. Workhouses were established throughout the country, families were forcibly separated and the poor treated as criminals. The Chartist movement attempted political change through peaceful and democratic protest and inspired two major episodes of unrest in Wales. At Llanidloes, in April 1839, three London policemen were besieged in the Trewythen Hotel and during 'pum diwrnod o ryddid' (its five days of freedom), the town was controlled by local Chartists.[2] In south Wales, in November of the same year, thousands led by John Frost and Zephaniah Williams marched down the valleys to Newport. Soldiers waited for them at the Westgate Hotel; 20 Chartists were killed and three leaders exiled to Australia.

Protest was not confined to the industrial areas. South-west Wales witnessed the Rebecca Rioters, who took their inspiration from a verse in scripture: 'And they blessed Rebekah and said unto her, Let thy seed possess the gates of those which hate thee' (Genesis 24: 60). Men, dressed as women, attacked tollgates. The first was destroyed at Efailwen (on the borders of Carmarthenshire and Pembrokeshire) on 13 May 1839 and although the violence was focussed on tollgates, the underlying grievances lay in deep-seated poverty, insecurity and fear of the workhouse.

A pioneer who defies any attempt at categorization is Robert Owen (1771–1858). Born and buried in Newtown, his economic and social activities were focused in Manchester, New Lanark in Scotland, and New Harmony in Indiana. His schemes for social reconstruction (which he termed socialism) marked him as a forerunner of the cooperative movement and of trade unions. His religious views were inspired by his conviction that the 'Power which governs and pervades the universe has evidently so formed man, that he must progressively pass from a state of ignorance to intelligence.'[3]

Wales in 1851 had changed dramatically during the past half-century. Technological progress in the rural and industrial worlds had provided the engines for revolutionary changes. Within this world, dominated by extremes of wealth and poverty, the response was of both protest and suppression. How would the churches respond to such momentous change?

The Church of England

The shortcomings of Anglicanism predated nineteenth-century industrialization. The Acts of Uniformity (1662) and Toleration (1689) had reconfirmed the supremacy of the Church of England but, at the same time, had acknowledged that the spiritual yearnings of all the people in England and Wales could not be encompassed within one uniform Christian body. The place of the Dissenter was now legally recognised. The Evangelical Reawakening of the eighteenth century deepened the Anglican dilemma. The Church was unable to respond positively to Methodism. Yet, despite its failings, by the close of the eighteenth century, the Anglican Church commanded the adherence of the majority of Welsh people. The pendulum was to swing dramatically during the next half-century.

By the time of the religious census of 1851, only nine per cent of worshipping Welsh people attended the parish church. Wales had chosen to reject the Church of England and had become Nonconformist. What were the issues which caused people to become deeply dissatisfied with the Established Church? Bishops were invariably absentees from their dioceses. Most parish clergy were poverty-stricken and dependent for their livings on English-speaking squires. Their main duty seemed to be that of serving as chaplains to landowning families. Many benefices were in lay hands and their income had been passed on to English colleges and schools. Monoglot Englishmen were often appointed to Welsh livings. Many ordinands had little training, coming straight from grammar schools which provided them with little instruction either in divinity or Welsh.

These problems were exaggerated by the industrial revolution. The population increase was phenomenal and the Church found itself incapable of meeting the needs of rapidly burgeoning communities. In 1831, of the 853 parishes in Wales, half were in the diocese of St Davids. Parish boundaries could not be altered and some of the churches were in the most remote locations. The worst problems were in the diocese of Llandaff where in the huge parishes of Bedwellty, Mynyddislwyn and Ystradyfodwg, all experiencing rapid increases in population, the few scattered medieval churches were invariably in the wrong places. People physically and spiritually left behind the old mother church, *Yr Hen Fam*.[4]

The mid-nineteenth century witnessed the beginning of renewal in the Church of England. The Ecclesiastical Commission was founded in 1836 and, between 1834 and 1840, a series of bills was passed to reform the Church. The Ecclesiastical Commissioners were given authority to subdivide large parishes, to increase and equalize clergy stipends, to construct new churches, renovate older ones, and provide houses for the clergy. Tithes were to be paid in money rather than in kind. The Royal Commission of 1910 calculated that £3½ million had been spent between 1840 and 1906 in the restoration and extension of church properties. Bishops encouraged services to be held in Welsh.

Further developments took place in the field of education. Schools were established, and by 1833, when the government first made contributions to schools, there were already 150 National schools in Wales compared with only 15 British or Nonconformist schools. The foundation stone of St David's, Lampeter, was laid in 1822 and the first ordinands received in 1827.[5] The college was founded by Thomas Burgess, bishop of St Davids, a great patron of Welsh cultural activities. Anglican concern for improved education led to the call for a royal commission into the state of education in Wales.[6] The Education Report of 1847 served as a wake-up call to all concerned about the nurture of the people of Wales. The Report was the consequence of fear of social unrest because of the Rebecca riots, Chartism in mid and south Wales, industrial strikes, and the widespread protests which led to the European revolutions of 1848. The Report, known as the Blue Books, however, caused even further bitterness in the relationship between the Anglican establishment and Nonconformity, a bitterness which continued into the twentieth century.

The Welsh become Nonconformist

The Church is not often noted for responding appropriately and swiftly in periods of radical economic and social change, but the first half of the nineteenth century witnessed a startling and positive response in the ministry and mission of churches in Wales The change is put clearly by Gwyn Alf Williams:

> When the Methodists finally withdrew from the Church under persecution in 1811, Nonconformists, old and new, by then accounted for some 15 to 20 per cent of the population. By the first religious census of 1851 they outnumbered Anglicans on average by five to one; in many places the ratio was seven and even ten to one... A people which around 1790 was still officially Tory and Anglican, over little more than a generation became a largely Nonconformist people of increasingly radical temper. It is one of the most remarkable cultural transformations in the history of any people.[7]

The Religious Census of 1851

The Registrar-General ordered that a census be made of accommodation (sittings) and attendance in every place of worship in England and Wales on the last Sunday of March (Palm Sunday) 1851. Although there were weaknesses in the process (some churches were not listed, workhouses and gaols were ignored, and individuals worshipping twice were counted twice), the census reflected a very accurate picture of the contrast between an England which remained largely Anglican, and Nonconformist Wales. While England provided seating for 51.4 per cent of the population, Wales provided for 75 per cent of its population. There were major contrasts between industrial and rural areas. London had the least provision, with places for only 24 per cent of its population. The lowest provision in Wales was in Merthyr with 58 per cent, but the highest were in Machynlleth and Dolgellau, with 124 per cent and 116 per cent respectively.

In Wales there were 976,490 attendances out of a population of 1,163,139. This would suggest that almost everyone who was fit and able worshipped that Sunday. Eighty per cent were in chapels and 20 per cent in parish churches. Analysing the statistics is, however, not straightforward. Most churches offered two and some had three services every Sunday. How many worshipped twice, perhaps even three times? If only those at the largest service are counted, the number of worshippers was 480,000, 40 per cent of the population. This does not mean that 60 per cent were absent that Sunday but it does provide an indisputable figure. The figures suggest that at least half the population were in worship. The stark contrast is between Anglicans and Nonconformists. If England and Wales are looked at together, 47 per cent were in Church and 49 per cent in chapel. In Wales, only nine per cent were in Church and 87 per cent in Nonconformist chapels. Anglicans were strongest in rural, English-speaking areas, while Nonconformity flourished particularly with Welsh speakers, both in rural and industrialised areas. Of those worshipping, 25 per cent were Calvinistic Methodist, 23 per cent Independents, 21 per cent Anglicans, 18 per cent Baptists and 13 per cent Wesleyans.

> Indeed, the first half of the nineteenth century was a period of remarkable growth for all the Nonconformist denominations in Wales. By 1851 there were 2,813 chapels in the country, the result of a building programme which is among the most striking happenings in Welsh history. Between 1801 and 1851, it is estimated that a chapel was completed in Wales every eight days.[8]

How had Wales become Nonconformist so rapidly?

A Nonconformist Nation

By the 1770s, there were two forms of Nonconformists. The old dissenting traditions of Independents and Baptists had experienced persecution, resistance, Civil War, further persecution and ultimately a limited degree of toleration in 1689. They continued to suffer the ignominy of being a hated minority, prevented from holding political or social power. Quakers, also an early dissenting community, had been persecuted almost out of existence, with large numbers, especially from mid Wales, fleeing to America for religious freedom. Some Independents and Presbyterians had moved, by way of Arminianism to Unitarianism.

The 'newer' Nonconformists were Methodists, both Calvinist and Wesleyan. They had remained within the Church of England throughout the eighteenth century, until reluctantly they formed their own churches. When New Methodism allied itself with Old Dissent and grasped the opportunities provided in the newly developing industrialised communities, Wales became a Nonconformist people. The chapel followed the forge and the pit and those who worked at the forge or in the pit became chapel people.

Migrants moved into the new industrial communities, thirsted to worship and read the Bible, and did not seek permission from any central body. They created individual causes, often beginning in the 'long room' of the pub, using cottages for Sunday schools and eventually building places of worship. The number of chapels proliferated during the first half-century. A daughter chapel was usually supported by a mother chapel which had probably only recently herself come into birth. Unrestricted by parish structures, independent of endowments and sustained only by voluntary contributions, they created buildings of significance and risked massive personal debt. Almost every industrial village soon had chapels of the four main Nonconformist varieties. The leaders were from similar working-class backgrounds as their congregations. Most ministers were Welsh-speaking men, trained in Welsh Dissenting Academies, steeped in Welsh culture and eminently capable of translating their Christian experience into the ordinary, everyday life of their communities.

Leadership within the chapels was shared between the minister and laypeople (almost invariably laymen). In the *sêt fawr, y sgwâr* (the big seat or the square) sat the elder (Presbyterian), deacon (Congregationalist and Baptist) and circuit leader (Methodist) exercising leadership with skill and dedication. Men of different social classes: miners, engineers,

Cardiff. The memorial to Rawlins White. Remembered and forgotten in a premier Cardiff departmental store.

Haverfordwest. The memorial to William Nichol in a main street in Haverfordwest (left).

Carmarthen. The memorial to Robert Ferrar in the centre of Carmarthen town.

Llanrhaedr-ym-Mochnant. William Morgan translated the Bible while serving as Vicar of St Dogfan's from 1578 to 1595.

© Cath Morgans

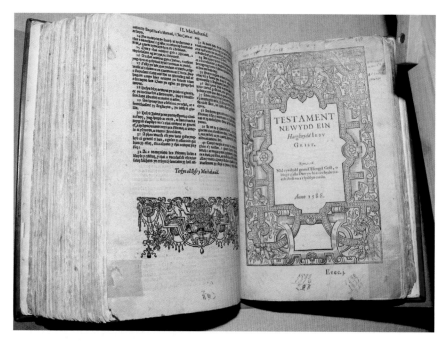

Beibl William Morgan, Tŷ Mawr, Wybrnant.

Tŷ Mawr, the birthplace of William Morgan, in the company of Gerwyn Edwards, 'Wil Tŷ Mawr', curator of the house and one who helped re-open the church of Saint Tudclud, Penmachno, a treasury of ancient stones and contemporary mission. Closed in 1997 and declared redundant in 1998, with the will of the local village community it reopened in 2009 for the burial of a young local soldier killed in Afghanistan. It was the first church in the Church in Wales to be reopened from a redundant state. Monthly services are being held in the church. It is open to visitors on most days, and there is a self-service coffee shop and small shop in the church.

Wrexham. The relics of Richard Gwyn at the Cathedral of Our Lady of Sorrows. Richard Gwyn was born in Llanidloes and martyred in Wrexham in 1584. The Catholic church in Llanidloes is dedicated to Our Lady and Saint Richard Gwyn.

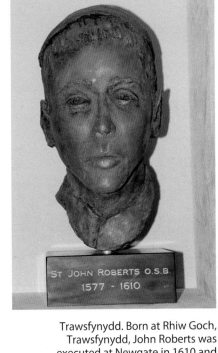

Trawsfynydd. Born at Rhiw Goch, Trawsfynydd, John Roberts was executed at Newgate in 1610 and canonised in 1970.

Usk. The parish of SS David Lewis and Francis Xavier. David Lewis, a Jesuit, 'Father of the poor' was hanged in Usk in 1679 and also canonised in 1970.

Cefn Brith, Epynt. The birthplace of John Penri, Puritan martyr. Hanged in London in 1593, he was later described as 'the morning star of Protestant Nonconformity in Wales'. John Williams, the resident farmer wisely commented: 'They executed John Penri in 1593 – they were too late! The Bible had been translated in 1588.'

Llanfaches. Founded in 1639, this was the first 'new-modelled church' in Wales.

Ilston. The first Baptist congregation in Wales.

Brynmawr, Dolgellau. The home of Rowland Ellis, a Quaker leader who because of religious persecution, emigrated to Pennsylvania in 1686. The town he founded is called Brynmawr, as is the famous women's college. Taken from *Mae'r Gân yn y Galon*.
© Friends in Wales

Llanidloes. Bureau at Trinity Church. The hollow bureau dates to the period of persecution of Nonconformists, 1662–89.

Brynllywarch. Samuel Jones was one of the 2,000 ejected in 1662. He founded the first dissenting academy in Wales in his farmhouse.

Maesyronnen. Worship in the oldest and best preserved Nonconformist chapel in Wales. Probably a converted Elizabethan barn, a church has worshipped there since 1697 but the cause dates much earlier. It is reputed that Oliver Cromwell worshipped with the community.

Llanwenarth. One of the oldest Baptist chapels. In many historic causes, tradition combines with contemporary mission.

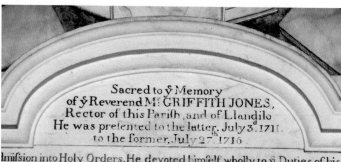

Llanddowror. Griffith Jones was vicar of Llanddowror. His innovative circulating schools led the Welsh to become one of the first literate nations.

Sacred to ẙ Memory
of ẙ Reverend M: GRIFFITH JONES,
Rector of this Parish, and of Llandilo
He was presented to the latter, July 3ᵈ. 1711.
to the former, July 27ᵗʰ 1716.

lmission into Holy Orders, He devoted himself wholly to ẙ Duties of his
u'd faithfully & conscientiously to discharge throughout the Course of
us of the Importance of the Vocation, wherewith he was call'd,
is time & Attention to that one great Concern, which came upon
rches. In his Preaching, He inculcated ẙ plainest & most obvious Duti
e enforc'd upon the minds of his Hearers with a truly Christian Z
nteresting a manner, that none could depart unaffected or unc
Instructor from ẙ Pulpit, only His own Example added Weight

Trefeca, the home of Y Teulu (The Family), Howel Harris' experiment in Christian community.

Llangeitho, the 'Mecca' of early Calvinistic Methodism. Daniel Rowland was curate until he was deprived of his ministry in 1762, the time of the second revival (left).

Llandovery. The memorial to Vicar Prichard inside St Dingad's church, Llandingad. His *Canwyll y Cymry* (1658 onwards) was as popular in Wales as *Pilgrim's Progress*.

Pantycelyn, home of William Williams, preacher, superintendent of seiadau and above all, 'y pêr ganiedydd, the sweet singer of Wales'. Cecil and Aled Williams and Hefin Jones are the 6th, 7th and 8th descendants.

Llandyfalle. Y Wernos was the home of first Methodist seiat in 1737 and the house in which Howel Harris met his future wife, Anne Williams of The Skreen, Erwood.
© Alan Griffin

Dugoedydd. The meeting-place of the first association (sasiwn) in 1742. Daniel Rowland chaired the meeting of 20 Methodist leaders, including Howel Harris and William Williams.

Carmarthen. The dissenting academy, 'the Presby', home of radical Christianity. The building is now the home of the Carmarthen Evangelical Church. A strange irony of history.
© Rev. Tom Evans

Llwynrhydowen. The first Unitarian congregation founded in 1733. A new chapel was built in 1879 after the congregation was locked out of the original chapel by the local landowner after the General Election of 1868. The radical minister at the time was the Rev. Gwilym Marles (William Thomas) who was an ancestor of Dylan Marlais Thomas and the church historian Horton Marlais Davies. In July 2015 the original chapel was reopened for community purposes.

Cardiff, the Dic Penderyn Memorial remembers Wales' first working-class martyr: arrested in Merthyr, hanged in Cardiff, buried in Aberavon.

Llanidloes, the Trewythen Hotel. 'Pum diwrnod o ryddid, Five days of freedom' marks the Chartist uprising in 1839.

Newport. Twenty Chartists were shot by soldiers during the Newport Rising at the Westgate Hotel in 1839.

Efailwen Memorial. 'And they blessed Rebekah.' The tollgate at Efailwen was destroyed by the hosts of Rebecca in 1839.

St David's, Lampeter, opened in 1827 to train ordinands for the Church of England. The College is now a constituent member of University of Wales Trinity Saint David.

© Rev. Tom Evans

Lampeter, Chapel of St David's. Rowland Williams of Halkyn 'established the right of freedom of enquiry for the clergy of the Church of England'.

Carmarthen, Trinity College. A Church of England institution, the college opened as the South Wales and Monmouthshire Training College in 1848. The college is also a constituent member of University of Wales Trinity Saint David.

© Rev. Tom Evans

Bangor Normal College was opened by Nonconformists in 1858 with the support of the British and Foreign School Society. It is now part of Bangor University.

Llanidloes, the National School, supported by the Church of England, opened in 1845. It is now the local rugby club.

Trefeglwys. The British School opened in 1865. The British and Foreign School Society was supported by Nonconformists. It is now a private home.

Swansea. Bethesda chapel holds the grave of Christmas Evans, the leading Baptist preacher of his generation. The chapel closed in 1994.

Llanfaes. The grave of John Elias. 'A hyper-Calvinist,' John Elias was the force behind the Confession of Faith (1824) of the Calvinistic Methodists. To his enemies he was known as the 'Pope of Anglesey'.

Bala, Capel Tegid. Thomas Charles, one of the heroes of Calvinistic Methodism is also linked with the formation of the Sunday school movement and the British and Foreign Bible Society (BFBS).

Abergynolwyn. The birthplace of Mary Jones whose walk to Bala in 1800 at the age of 15 helped inspire the formation of the BFBS. Llanycil, near Bala, is the home of a permanent exhibition centre: 'Byd Mary Jones World' opened in 2014.

Pontrobert. Hen Gapel John Hughes, the home of the Rev. John Hughes and his wife Ruth, was the 'spiritual home' of Ann Griffiths, and since 1995 has been a Centre for Christian Unity and Renewal, guided by Nia Rhosier.

Soar y Mynydd founded by Ebenezer Richard (the father of Henry Richard) in 1822. 'Between clarity of light with hints of crimson came Duw Cariad Yw' (God is Love).

doctors, teachers, were all members of the leaders' meeting. Sunday schools met the needs of all ages, for both women and men, and provided training for lay leadership. Worship was centred on preaching, and their chapel buildings were centred on the high pulpit, beneath which were the communion table and the big seat. Preaching was biblical, direct and persuasive, speaking to the needs of earnest men and women. John Elias (1774–1841), the 'Pope of Anglesey', was the force behind the Calvinistic Methodist 'Confession of Faith' in 1823. Christmas Evans (1766–1838), born near Llandysul, helped transform the Baptist tradition by his powerful preaching. He visited each of the Welsh counties on an annual and sometimes bi-annual preaching tour. William Williams (1781–1840), another great preaching itinerant was ordained a Congregationalist minister at Y Wern (Minera, near Wrexham) and founded many new chapels in the north-east as well as ministering in Liverpool.

Calvinistic Methodism grew particularly in communities where there were circulating schools. The formation of Sunday schools is often linked with the name of Thomas Charles (1755–1814), whose education at Llanddowror must have influenced his commitment to all-age literacy. Thomas Charles is associated with Bala, to which Mary Jones had walked from Llanfihangel-y-Pennant in 1800 to buy a Bible. Tradition points out that because of the encounter between this young woman and the renowned church leader, Charles planted the seed which developed into the British and Foreign Bible Society.

Bala is roughly equidistant between Llanfihangel-y-Pennant in the west and Llanfihangel-yng-Ngwynfa in the east. Just as Mary Jones' walk to Bala has been formative in Welshwomen's and Welshmen's search for the treasury that is Scripture, the hymns of Ann Griffiths (1776–1805) of Dolwar Fach have also left an invaluable heritage. Ann became a Calvinistic Methodist in 1796–7 during a period of revival in the area. She loved to go to Bala on the Sacrament Sundays and had a momentous conversation with Thomas Charles. Her hymns reflect her deep religious experience and are shaped by her knowledge of scripture. Her 70 hymns were created orally and were 'recorded' by her friend John Hughes and his wife Ruth. It is remarkable that Thomas Charles should have created such an indelible influence on both Mary Jones and Ann Griffiths.

> She [Ann] is commonly acknowledged as the greatest woman poet in the long literary history of Wales. Even in translation it is possible to see that she is the most profound and passionate woman hymn-writer in the history of Britain as a whole.[9]

Between 1790 and 1810 Methodism began to extricate itself from the Church of England, emerge as a church, and ally itself with Dissent. This was partly a reaction to their vilification as revolutionaries by Anglicans who associated Methodists with radical Dissenters. They began to register their meeting houses and, by 1810, 150 Methodist churches had been built. They needed their own recognised leadership to preach and celebrate the sacraments. By 1800, only a dozen Anglican clergymen were deemed acceptable to the Methodist movement, and Anglican clergy themselves became increasingly reluctant to welcome Methodists to the communion table. Thomas Charles had no desire to break away from the Established Church, he was content to subscribe to the Articles of the Church of England and found sectarianism abhorrent. It was not until 1811 that he felt forced to consider separation from Anglicanism when he ordained nine men to the ministry at Bala and a further 13 at Llandeilo. Effectively, this meant that Methodists were now Nonconformist.

> In the year of secession and the ordination of ministers Methodism ceased to be an evangelical wing of the Church and became a new nonconformist denomination. It grew to become the strongest of denominations among dissenters in Wales... In 1811, however, Methodist clergy were forced to choose, either to continue their support to the Church as in the past or withdraw from it.[10]

They were Nonconformists of a very different background from traditional Dissenters. They had broken reluctantly from the centralized Church of England and their structure and theology were subject to an equally centralised leadership and discipline. For Thomas Jones of Denbigh, the Articles of the Church of England were satisfactory, but after his death in 1820, they were superseded in 1823 by the Confession of Faith, bound by High Calvinist doctrines, and inspired by the leadership of John Elias of Anglesey.

The first Wesleyan societies came into existence as a result of John Wesley's preaching journeys, but his influence was comparatively minimal in most of Wales. By 1770, there were only half a dozen societies and they were in anglicised Wales. In 1780, Edward Jones of Bathafarn (a farm in the Vale of Clwyd) was converted to Wesleyan Methodism while working in a woollen mill near Manchester, and when he returned to Wales he founded the first Welsh-speaking cause at Rhuthun. Thomas Coke (1747–1814) of Brecon, the superintendent of the Methodist Episcopal Church of America and the 'father' of Methodist missions, took a resolution to the Wesleyan Methodist Conference in London on 8 August 1800 to establish a mission to the Welsh. The growth was remarkable, and there were 100 congregations in existence by 1810, and 293 chapels and 11,839 members by 1858.

The Temperance Movement[11]

The myth of the English village portrays a comfortable relationship between the parish church, the village green and the homely inn. Industrialised Wales, in particular, presented a very different picture from this idyll. In rural areas, drunkenness became a serious problem, and in the new industrialised communities it became a pandemic. In the early nineteenth century, water was often unsafe, and beer was cheap. Industrialisation brought heavy, dangerous work, while young migrant workers arriving at the iron and coal areas were anxious to escape the moral restrictions of their rural backgrounds. Following the Beer Act of 1830, there was a huge increase in the number of drinking places. The number of licences in west Wales increased from 158 to 1,226 between 1830 and 1832, and the Dowlais ironworks were surrounded by 200 taverns.

Over-indulgence was the concern of employers who needed sober workmen, working-class wives who saw their husband's wages dissipated on drink, and chapel people who upheld the need for personal discipline. The temperance movement began in America in the 1820s. The British and Foreign Temperance Society was formed in London in 1831 and the Manchester Welsh formed a branch in October 1831. The first branch in Wales of the BFTS began in Swansea in 1833. By 1835 there were 25 temperance societies in Wales. Valiant attempts were made to advocate temperance, but often they were doomed to failure. The demon drink was too powerful. For example, members of the Ebbw Vale temperance society were allowed to drink two pints of beer a day. It was soon discovered that many members 'saved' up their pints to drink 14 on Saturday![12] This led to the formation of a movement for total abstinence and the Cardiff Total Abstinence Society was formed in October 1836. Both organisations attempted to deliver their message attractively. They created ceremonial orders organised in an almost military campaign. They provided alternative recreation in the form of coffee taverns, temperance hotels, libraries and literary societies. Later in the century they grasped the attractiveness of community singing, and in 1854 the *Gymanfa Ddirwestol* (Temperance Singing Festival) of Gwent and Morgannwg was formed in Merthyr to encourage congregational singing.

From the 1840s onwards, church and chapel cooperated in propagating the temperance movement which took on the characteristics of a moral and religious crusade. This was partly a reaction to the protest movements of Rebecca and Chartism and a response to the shock of the Blue Books. This united front held firm until the 1860s when the mood changed and the denominations parted company. Calvinist Methodists remained firm in their opposition to alcohol, but the other

Nonconformists and Anglicans varied in the intensity of their opposition.

Revivals and Nurture[13]

The Methodist revival of the eighteenth century challenged the Church of England, reinvigorated traditional dissent and helped form the two new denominations of Calvinistic and Wesleyan Methodism. Opinions differ widely on the significance of revivals in the religious life of Wales. For some, the growth of Nonconformity in the nineteenth century was the result of a series of evangelical revivals. Revivalist preaching, ecstatic prophesying and miraculous forms of healing guaranteed the blessing of God. Natural disasters, plagues and epidemics were signs of God's punishment on an immoral society. Revivals were the life-blood of the church, producing spirit-filled and born-again Christians. Once one revival had passed, there would be prayers for, and an expectancy of another revival. The revival was the 'natural' – or should one say 'supernatural' – prerequisite of Welsh religious life?

Revivals took place in almost every decade of the first 60 years of the nineteenth century. Revivals broke out in Beddgelert between 1817 and 1822, in Caeo in 1828, from where it spread to Swansea, Neath and Merthyr, and in Anglesey and Caernarfon in 1831–2. The Bala awakening continued from 1837 to 1842, and a major revival took place in south-east Wales in 1849. The year 1858/9 witnessed a powerful revival which had begun in America, but broke out in Tre'r-ddôl in Cardiganshire and spread particularly to Aberdare where 19 chapels were opened between 1859 and 1862. Revivals were often associated with particular social, political and economic forces. Different incidents seemed to trigger, or at least be associated with, the outbreak of a revival. This was the period of post-war depression, bad harvests, outbreaks of cholera, the enclosure acts, the sinking of the *Rothesay Castle* in 1831, Chartist riots and industrial unrest in 1849, strikes and falling wages in 1859. Revivalist preachers used these events as forewarnings of the wrath to come. Gwyn Davies describes Wales as 'the land of revivals'. The outpouring of the Holy Spirit is the life-blood of the Church:

> The Spirit is always present with Christ's people, but at times he is 'poured out' upon them. The result is a revolution in the life of the church: Christians are awakened and filled with new zeal and confidence, and the reality of the Christian faith is demonstrated to society at large, leading to an increase in the number of those turning to Christ. Periods of revival have been a marked feature of Christianity in Wales. It is largely through these revivals that the faith has exercised such an extensive influence over the nation.[14]

There is an alternative view. Revivalism has been described as an attempt to recreate the religion of the past and to avoid contemporary challenges. Temperance and revivalism were seen as a panacea to the ills of society. Did church leaders fail to understand the nature of protest and associate it only with the dangers of revolution? In fact, major changes were taking place in Welsh society because of the mission of the churches. The centuries following the Reformation had witnessed the emergence of Puritanism, the growth of literacy and a maturing self-confidence. These changes took place gradually within the context of a rural Welsh-speaking Wales. Literate, self-confident Nonconformists moved in the nineteenth century from their strongholds in Carmarthen, Pembroke and Cardigan to find work. Bringing their religion with them, they helped create a new kind of community centred on pit and chapel. From these twin centres emerged workmen's halls, libraries and a radical politics determined to transform society. Nonconformity captured the excitement of the age and, by 1851, Nonconformity had won the allegiance of three-quarters of the nation's population.

8

FROM NONCONFORMITY TO CONFORMITY, 1851–1903

THE ZENITH OF Nonconformity was as early as 1859. Having tripled in size during the first half of the century, its strength and authority had been created and exercised by working people. They streamed into the industrialized areas, particularly from west and mid Wales, bringing their religion, language and culture. In 1867, Henry Richard (1812–88)[1] of Tregaron, Congregationalist minister, 'apostle of peace' and MP for Merthyr, claimed that Wales was 'now a nation of Nonconformists'. Dissent flourished and expanded throughout the century, although in diminishing proportion to the rapidly increasing population. The four major Nonconformist denominations (Calvinistic Methodists, Congregationalists, Baptists and Wesleyans) boasted 352,249 communicants in 1882, with strength anchored in effective all-age Sunday schools, an educated ministry, and nonconformist values of sabbatarianism and temperance accepted as social norms.

Chapels were the bastions of Welsh culture. The heroes of the pulpit were lauded superstars. Nonconformity's creative energy was phenomenal, especially in industrialized Wales. The Temperance crusade rallied the denominations to cooperate together. Industrialists patronised local culture by encouraging libraries, reading rooms, choirs, bands, orchestras and eisteddfodau. A series of Revivals attracted fresh blood into the life of the churches. The press was dominated by denominational literature. The London journals had limited circulation compared with Nonconformist periodicals. The Baptists' *Seren Cymru* (1851), the Congregationalists' *Y Tyst Cymreig* (1867), the Calvinistic Methodists' *Y Goleuad* (1869), the Wesleyans' *Y Gwyliedydd* (1877) and the Anglican *Y Llan a'r Dywysogaeth* (1881) published local and national news, shared theological and ecclesiological views and also gave leadership on political and social issues. A similar success story can be told of Welsh musical life. Hymn-singing in four parts and the use of tonic sol-fa was developed by the Methodist, John Roberts (Ieuan Gwyllt) and the Independent, Edward Stephens (Tanymarian).[2] It developed all the more rapidly after the 1859 Revival. Cymanfaoedd Canu (Singing Festivals) flourished, as did choral societies, the most famous of which was Y Côr Mawr of Aberdare, particularly after it won first prize at Crystal Palace in 1872 and 1873. As well as the singing of home-grown hymns, the music of Handel, Haydn, Mendelssohn and Mozart became the common fare of the Welsh choral world, and gave their names to countless little Welsh boys! Wales was the Land of Song.

However, rapid social change meant that Nonconformity's success was relatively short-lived. The challenges facing late-nineteenth-century religion in Wales were highly complex. Did success itself play a part in unravelling the prime role played by religion in the community? 'Chapel' provided Welsh cultural life with its music, drama, poetry, choral festivals and eisteddfodau. Chapel became coterminous with Welsh cultural life. What did going to chapel come to mean for many people? Was there uncertainty about the role of popular religion? Was the purpose of chapel to be the custodian of Welsh culture or to serve as a community responsive to the call of God? Could it play both roles? It is a perennial dilemma. The Christian faith emerged from Jerusalem, Greece and Rome, and western Christianity is shaped by its relationship to at least three seminal cultures.

Foreign Mission

A remarkable consequence of nineteenth-century Nonconformity was the emergence of foreign mission in the life of all denominations. Thomas Coke (1747–1814) the Wesleyan Methodist from Brecon, was Wesley's 'bishop' to American Methodism; he made 18 crossings of the Atlantic and died on his way to India. The London Missionary Society was founded in 1795. Its first missionary was John Davies (1772–1855). Born in Llanfihangel-yng-Ngwynfa, he worshipped alongside John Hughes, Pontrobert (with whom he held a voluminous correspondence) and Ann Griffiths, the great hymn-writer, before serving in Tahiti for 55 years. Other LMS missionaries were David Jones (1797–1841) and Thomas Bevan (1796–1819), who both left Neuaddlwyd in Cardiganshire to become the first missionaries in Madagascar. The story of the tragic deaths of Bevan, his wife and child, and of Jones' wife and child reflect the spirit of self-sacrifice which motivated so much of early missionary endeavours. David Jones was joined by David Johns (1796–1843) and David Griffiths (1792–1863) who laid the foundations for the strongest protestant church in Madagascar. Other Welsh heroes of the mission field were Griffith John of Glandŵr, Swansea (1831–1912), who spent 50 years in China, establishing churches and schools, a home for lepers and a theological college, as well as translating the New Testament into Wen-li and Mandarin. Timothy Richard (1845–1919) of Ffaldybrenin, Carmarthenshire, was sent by the Baptist Missionary Society to China where he served as 'a scholar, teacher author, philanthropist, missionary statesman, mandarin and adviser to the court... Indeed, he enjoyed greater power than any Welshman in history, apart from David Lloyd George. He was honoured by the Chinese with membership of the Order of the Double Dragon.'[3] Robert Jermain Thomas (1840–66), of Rhayader and Llanover, martyred as he attempted a second journey to Korea, is recognised as the founder of protestant mission to that country. Perhaps the most remarkable field of mission for the people of Wales was initiated by the Calvinistic Methodists in north-east India. The work was inaugurated by Thomas Jones (1810–49) who left Berriew in Montgomeryshire in 1840 and laid the foundations of the church in the Khasia hills. He gave the Khasi language a written form and was the first to publish books in that language, including Matthew's gospel which Jones translated. The work spread to the Lushai hills (Mizoram) and continued for 150 years with fruitful ministries in the areas of education, church planting and in health-care.[4] The ministry of thousands of Welshmen and Welshwomen over a period of more than two centuries has produced mature and energetic churches in many parts of the world. In the twenty-first century those countries are sending missionaries to Wales.

The Church of England

The foundations for the renewal of the Church of England had been laid with the establishment of the Ecclesiastical Commission in 1836 and by the passing of a series of parliamentary bills to reform the church. Particularly decisive action came through the leadership of Alfred Ollivant (1798–1882)[5] who was appointed bishop of Llandaff in 1849. Soon after his appointment he received a letter describing the need for radical reform, from Thomas Williams, archdeacon of Llandaff. Ollivant responded by creating the Llandaff Church Extension Society, a society supported by the patronage of the Marquis of Bute, Lords Tredegar, Windsor and Dynevor, the Bruce and Gwynn families of Neath, the Vivians' of Swansea and the Phillips' of Newport. Between 1831 and 1906, 827 new churches and large numbers of parsonages and schools were built in Wales. The policy was to form a church followed by a school. Ollivant's work was developed by Bishop Lewis (1883–1905) who instigated a further 201 new projects. The witness of the Church was becoming much more vibrant. Between 1850 and 1910, the number of clergy increased from 700 to 1,543, the number of parishes to 1,014 and the number of churches to 1,527. Communicants doubled during the same period.

The decade between 1856 and 1866 also saw a renewed commitment to social and pastoral work. The clergy provided soup kitchens in Merthyr and clothing clubs at St Mary's, Cardiff, during the severe winter of 1860. Relief funds were raised during the pit disasters at Cymmer, Porth, in 1856 and 1861. Sunday schools and adult classes proliferated. More than a thousand National schools had been opened by 1870. Colleges for the training of teachers were opened in Carmarthen in 1848 and in Bangor in 1856.

In the 1830s the 'Oxford Movement' came into existence, determined to recapture the Catholic tradition within the Church of England. High churchmen interpreted the parliamentary reforms as an assault by the state on the authority of the church. In September 1833, they set out their beliefs in the first of what was to be a long series of tracts, thus earning for themselves the name of Tractarians. One of the early leaders, alongside Newman, Keble and Froude, was Isaac Williams (1802–65), born in Aberystwyth, who wrote Tract 80 on 'Reserve in Communicating Religious Knowledge' which lost him the election to the chair of poetry at Oxford (1842). 'The new church and parish of Llangorwen near Aberystwyth, opened in 1841, were the first in Wales where the ideals of the Oxford Movement were put into practice. The moving spirit behind it was a layman, Matthew Davies Williams, the elder brother of Isaac Williams.'[6] In 1847, the church at Llangasty Tal-y-llyn was transformed according to Tractarian principles by another layman, Robert Raikes (a descendant of Robert Raikes, the founder of Sunday schools). Howel Harris had experienced a converting experience in this church during the previous century. It was not until much later in the century that the ritualistic aspects of the Oxford Movement took root in Wales. Amongst the early pioneers were Evan Lewis who came in 1859 to Aberdare, which provided the first home of St

Michael's theological college in 1892. In 1903 it was decided to relocate to Llandaff, close to the cathedral. 'Here St Michael's flourished, and moved in a somewhat more Anglo-Catholic direction under the influence of Timothy Rees, a future bishop of Llandaff.'[7] In 1872, Arthur Jones arrived at St Mary's, Cardiff, and F.W. Puller at Roath. Through them the Anglo-Catholic position strengthened, particularly in the diocese of Llandaff. The closing half-century witnessed a bitter internal struggle between the evangelical and Oxford Movement wings of the church.

There was, however, an even bitterer external struggle with Nonconformists over the issue of tithes and of disestablishment. The combination of the worsening depression in farming and the fact that most landowners were Anglican and their tenants were Nonconformist led to protests against the payment of tithes. Farmers at Llanarmon-yn Iâl in Denbighshire 'formed themselves in 1886 into a local Anti-Tithe League and declared that they would not pay any of their tithes.'[8] They had been encouraged by the journalism of Thomas Gee, editor of *Baner ac Amserau Cymru*, and the political prowess of men like T.E. Ellis and David Lloyd George. The farmers prevented animals which had been confiscated by bailiffs being sold in 'distraint sales'. Protests grew in number and in intensity in 'the tithe war'. Eight were brought to trial at Ruthin Assizes in February 1888 and found guilty of assault and riot. They became known as 'The Llangwm Tithe Martyrs'. Protests continued until 1891, by which time the 'Land Question' became focused on the question of land-ownership, whereas the bitter antagonism between Chapel and Church concentrated on the necessity of the disestablishment of the Church of England.

While Church and Chapel were involved in this internecine struggle, both seemed to be oblivious to the consequences of major social and political changes which would ultimately challenge the essence of being Christian and the fabric of church life.

The Challenge of Language: Immigration

The Reformation arrived in Wales when the fruits of literary programmes and the Evangelical Revival combined to create a people who read the Bible in their own language, and shared their Christian experience in conventicles / seiadau / class meetings. The Bible, worship, hymns and prayers took on new vitality when the medium was the language of the people. But, what happens when the language complexion of the nation alters? What are the consequences of a shifting language frontier?

The 1801 census revealed that of Wales' 587,245 inhabitants, probably 470,000 spoke Welsh. The second half of the nineteenth century witnessed a dramatic cultural revolution. The first generation of industrial dwellers had been largely Welsh speakers from rural Wales. They were now joined by English speakers from the neighbouring counties of England. Nineteenth-century Wales saw a higher proportion of inner migration and immigration than any country in the world, except the United States. A new society was rapidly being formed. South-east Wales, where the majority of Welsh people now lived, was dramatically reshaped. It was a society with a cross-fertilization of languages and cultures. In 1901, the population of Wales was 1,864,896 over the age of three, of whom 929,824 spoke Welsh. While the number speaking Welsh had almost doubled, the population as a whole had almost quadrupled. Those with a command of English had increased nine-fold. The linguistic frontier had moved westwards. Between 1881 and 1891, 63 per cent of the immigrants into Glamorgan came from England. The percentage of Welsh speakers in Rhondda dropped from 61 per cent in 1881 to 50 per cent in 1911 and to 42 per cent in 1921.

There was also a devastating shift in attitude towards the language. English was admired as the language of progress, science, business, management and of getting on in the world. Welsh was depicted as the language of religion and the arts but not the language through which you earned a living. Within a generation, people who had spoken only Welsh ensured that their children learned English to give them a future. Within decades following 1881, monolingual Welsh-speaking families became bilingual, on route to becoming monolingual English speakers. All the pressures were against the use of Welsh. Within Welsh-speaking chapels in the central and eastern valleys of Glamorgan and throughout Monmouthshire, the language divide between the generations was stark. Older people responded to the wholeness of worship while the younger people enjoyed the hymns! The cause for the decline in the language was partly caused by the sheer numbers of English people crossing the border and finding work and a new life in the industrialized south-east. But there was an even more significant reason. The people of Wales were losing confidence in their own language.

Brad y Llyfrau Gleision
(Treason of the Blue Books)

William Williams of Llanpumpsaint inadvertently changed the course of Welsh history. On 10 March 1846, Williams, MP for Coventry and a London businessman, proposed that parliament set up a government commission into the state of education in Wales. A prominent radical, his concern was for working-class children to learn English. His proposal emerged from a long background. Wales was feared as a hotbed of protest. The Rebecca Commission of 1844 had reported that it was 'the existence of the Welsh language which hindered the Law and the Established Church from civilizing the Welsh... the wildness of the Welsh could be tamed by steeping them in an English education.' Westminster was oblivious to the fact that two-thirds of the population of Wales spoke only Welsh, and that a Welsh-language culture was flourishing in both rural and industrial communities. Their value judgments were blinded by an obsession with English language and culture. For them, the Welsh language was a primitive, inferior patois.

The government responded with a three-man commission. Although R.R.W. Lingen, Jellynger Symons and Vaughan Johnson had no knowledge of Welsh, nonconformity or elementary education, to a large extent their evidence was accurate. They travelled widely and worked diligently to present a report of 1,252 pages in three blue-covered volumes by April 1847. The report presented a detailed picture of the inadequacy of elementary education. The few National (Anglican) and British (Nonconformist) schools were insufficient to meet the needs of the population. Schools were badly funded and teachers had little training. To make matters worse, Welsh-speaking children were obliged to learn through the medium of English, a language many teachers barely understood. However, some of the premises drawn from the Report caused a furious response. The commissioners blamed the lack of educational attainment on a combination of the use of the Welsh language and on Nonconformity.

> The racial theories of the period probably encouraged them to denounce the Welsh as backward and barbaric. The Welsh took particular offence at being portrayed as dirty, lazy, feckless and mendacious, with their wives and mothers depicted as slatterns. They resented the commissioners' insistence that the survival of Welsh and the concomitant strength of Nonconformity were the cause of Welsh barbarity.[9]

Although less than ten pages were devoted to these libels, these pages attracted the London journals which subsequently vilified the people of Wales. Welsh patriots were furious and condemned what they regarded as the treachery of Welsh clergymen who had given evidence to the three commissioners. R.J. Derfel's play of 1854, *Brad y Llyfrau Gleision* ('Treason of the Blue Books'), did much to popularize opposition to the Report. By using the word 'treason', Derfel evoked the Welsh myth of the 'Treason of the Long Knives', the myth of the murder of British chiefs invited to a Saxon banquet. The Church of England was depicted as the enemy within. Although many Welsh Anglicans also attacked the Report, the damage had been done and a furious Nonconformist reaction intensified throughout the century.

Among the long-term repercussions of the Blue Books of 1847 were that many Welsh leaders became convinced that the Welsh language was outdated and stood in the way of progress. The remedy was to modernise and anglicise. The government saw English as the language of progress and commerce. Some middle-class Welsh people saw the relationship between the languages in a similar way. The 1870 Education Act introduced elementary education throughout Wales, but the language of education was English and there were sanctions against the use of Welsh. Welsh should die quietly. The *Western Mail* described Welsh speakers as narrow-minded. 'Forward-thinking people' knew that Welsh did not pay! The Welsh Intermediate Act of 1889, which brought higher-level education throughout Wales to both sexes, concentrated on the English language. The way forward was through the medium of English. A highly educated and articulate middle class emerged from the grammar schools, but in the process the Welsh language was jettisoned.[10]

At the Swansea National Eisteddfod in 1863, Bishop Thirlwall of St Davids urged everyone to learn English and keep Welsh as an attraction for tourists. Kilsby Jones (1813– 89), the eccentric and influential Nonconformist preacher, told his congregations, 'Be faithful to Welsh on Sunday... but when Monday morning comes, I advise you to learn English, for that is the language of trade and the language of the most adventurous people on earth.' The English press ridiculed Welsh and advocated the English language as the way of progress for the British people. Welsh could be left to preachers, romantics and yesterday. English was the language of tomorrow, progress, industry and commerce. The formation of 'English causes' helped to accelerate the decline. The Wesleyans had already formed English circuits in the eighteenth century; Baptists established the 'English Assembly of Monmouthshire' in 1857, and Calvinistic Methodists and Independents established English causes in the latter half of the nineteenth century.

The denominations' future needed to be safeguarded by their alliance with the language of progress. The consequence was an increasingly segregated society. Communities already divided between the Church of England and various kinds of Nonconformists now splintered into linguistically divided churches. As the struggle increased for a place in the diminishing market, so did rivalry between the churches. The church became 'capel ni', our chapel. Most towns could offer a choice of at least eight chapels, for Welsh and English speakers of the major four denominations. The size of these chapels was often competitive. Small unpretentious dissenting places of worship were rapidly replaced by larger and more ornate chapels, with grander pipe-organs usually in the most prominent position. By 1905, there were 1,229 Nonconformist places of worship in Glamorgan alone – a threefold increase since 1851. The seamless Body of Christ was barely recognizable within the market forces of nineteenth-century Welsh religion.

The Challenge of Conformity

For the first 50 years of the nineteenth century, extraordinary ordinary people, migrants into the industrialized communities, had created new chapels through their own efforts (one every eight days for 50 years!) and provided their own leadership. The second half of the century witnessed chapel leadership shift away from the artisan to the pit manager and under-manager, to the craftsman, tradesman and shopkeeper. As a reaction to the calumnies of the Blue Books, and inspired by Victorian 'Samuel Smiles' aspirations of self-improvement, the middle classes were determined to prove themselves hard-working, educated, temperate and upholders of the Sabbath. There was a gradual rupture between the chapel and the pub. Nonconformity gradually morphed into conformity. The radical surge ebbed. A social hierarchy was emerging, and when the respectable exercised authority, social cohesion was undermined.

As the pace of industrialisation accelerated, Nonconformity

found it impossible to keep up with the dramatic changes of a world of entrepreneurial greed, accompanied by an inevitable horrific squandering of human life. Passive acceptance of the status quo was no longer acceptable. An eternal reward in heaven was not enough. The new key words were justice, equality and radical change. Industrial tensions inevitably led to confrontation. Agendas progressed on parallel lines: the agenda of pulpit, big-seat and pew; the agenda of coal face, pit-wheel, pub, club and streets. The chapel was being left behind. Chapel discussed in the language of Welsh, the issues of relationships between chapel and chapel, and chapel and church. Chapel was concerned about temperance and disestablishment. Chapel celebrated its life in the singing festival, eisteddfodau and penny readings.

Organised religion failed to give social leadership to the new industrial communities. The new middle class, dominant in the *sêt fawr* and insensitive to radical social problems, allied itself with the emerging Liberal Party at Westminster and in local county councils. The Nonconformist agenda was one of seeking their rights vis-à-vis the Established Church, rather than the rights of working people. A focus of their concern was the disestablishment of the Church of England rather than the problems of injustice and inequality in a polarized, industrialised society. Their striving for a respectable sobriety led to the passing of the Sunday closing of public houses in 1881, a decision which served to increasingly divide chapel people from the pub/club people of Wales for a century. Professor Glanmor Williams argues, from the novels of Daniel Owen of Mold, that the seeds of conforming Nonconformity would inevitably lead to a disastrous harvest. Nonconformity really became conformity. Respectability and social acceptance were the hallmarks of religion. Owen was convinced that the quality of religion had begun to decline by the close of the nineteenth century. The golden age of the pulpit had passed and elders were lacking in character and conviction. Keeping up appearances was what was important. This was critical for those engaged in trade and industry. Owen realized that the standards of morality were impossible for most people to keep; and often those of the greatest moral rectitude were people who found it difficult to accept and forgive.

> The result was a heavy emphasis on outward respectability with a scrupulous concern for all the negative virtues: to refrain from drink, swearing, gambling, adultery, in short from all earthly and carnal temptations. More precisely, it was essential not to be seen to be indulging in any of these vices... He [Jones the policeman] like Captain Trevor, had no illusions about the overriding force of the 'eleventh' commandment, 'Thou shalt not be found out'.[11]

The Challenge of Nationhood

Late Victorian and Edwardian Wales exuded optimism. The confident Welsh saw themselves as world leaders in industrial muscle, commercial enterprise, Liberal politics and the rapidity of social progress. Britain ruled the waves and coloured the world map red. This imperial greatness was partly the consequence of a seemingly unlimited supply of Welsh coal. Welsh national consciousness trumpeted a new flourishing in the late nineteenth century. Confidence in being Welsh saw the creation of new national institutions: the Football Association of Wales in Wrexham in 1876, the National Eisteddfod in 1880, the Welsh Rugby Union in Neath in 1881, the University of Wales in 1893, the National Museum in Cardiff and the National Library in Aberystwyth, both in 1907. The Welsh National Agricultural Society and the Royal Commission on Ancient and Historical Monuments of Wales were formed in Aberystwyth in 1904 and 1908 respectively. Cardiff became a city in 1905.

At the same time there was an abortive attempt to reflect this optimistic self-confidence in political self-determination. Cymru Fydd (the Wales that will be) was formed in London in 1886 and soon spread throughout Wales. Among its aims were the disestablishment of the Church of England, land and educational reforms and Welsh Home Rule. In the early 1890s, Lloyd George became its prominent leader but attempts to develop Cymru Fydd into a political movement were destroyed by the perennial bogeymen which haunted Welsh consciousness. At a catastrophic meeting in Newport in January 1896, Robert Bird, a Cardiff Wesleyan alderman, rebuffed Lloyd George's appeal for national unity with the following words:

> There are, from Swansea to Newport, thousands of Englishmen, as true Liberals as yourselves... who will never submit to the domination of Welsh ideas.[12]

This sentiment was to be repeated ad nauseam on innumerable occasions throughout the twentieth century. The churches were as divided as political parties in their attitude towards self-government. The sentiments and phobias of Robert Bird have always had a strong following, and it has been comparatively straightforward to exacerbate the natural divisions within Wales by creating a spurious alienation between Welsh and English speakers, 'gogs' (northerners) and 'hwntws' (those far away over there – in the south) and reminding mid Walians that they are always the forgotten people. At the time of Cymru Fydd, the churches of Wales were incapable of speaking with a common mind. It would take more than a century before the churches, political parties, and national sentiment united to fulfil the vision of Welsh political self-determination.

The Challenge of a New Politics

It was not coincidental that the pre-eminence of Nonconformity coincided with the ascendancy of Liberalism. The Reform Acts of 1867 and 1884 resulted in the replacement of the Tory landowners' and squires' monopoly of power by the Liberal Party. In 1885, Liberals won 30 of the 34 seats in Wales, and in 1889 they triumphed in the newly-formed county councils. Liberalism and Nonconformity were on the march together. One of the signs of this new relationship was the passing in

1881 of the first law designed to serve only the people of Wales. This law prevented the sale of alcohol on Sundays throughout Wales with the exception of Monmouthshire (it was extended to that county in 1921). Emerging imperialistic Nonconformity revelled in the demise of Toryism and the emergence of the Golden Age of Liberalism. They shared optimism, an emphasis on education, and opportunities for the economic entrepreneur.

That optimism was not shared by the majority of working families. The south Wales coalfield, in particular, experienced a deepening conflict between those who lived in mansions built *from* coal, and those who lived in terraces built *above* coal. Mining families lived in constant jeopardy day after day. In Rhondda alone, catastrophic explosions took place in 1856 in Cymmer when 114 men were killed, in Ferndale in 1867 and 1869 when 178 and 53 died, in Penygraig in 1880 (101), in Maerdy in 1885 (82), Tylorstown in 1896 (57) and Wattstown in 1905 (119). Named catastrophes account for only 17 per cent of those killed in colliery accidents. Adding insult to injury was the erratic wage system shaped by the sliding scale by which wages were changed according to the sale-price of coal. Absentee plutocrats continued to prosper while the miners' families starved.

Nonconformity failed to grasp that the Liberal search for conciliation between master and worker was no longer reflecting the anger and frustration of the south Wales workers. Liberal compromise gave way to head-on conflict. The new leaders of the working miners discussed in English the need to confront injustice and inequality in their experience of everyday life. Political and lodge meetings were held in English, and the political and industrial leadership shifted from the like of William Abraham (Mabon, 1842–1922), Liberal, chapel deacon and eisteddfodwr, to Keir Hardie, a Christian Socialist. The South Wales Miners' Federation (the Fed), created in 1898, affiliated itself with the Miners' Federation of Great Britain in 1899 and the Labour Party in

1908. Power soon fell into the hands of young radical leaders who agitated for a minimum wage and saw the struggle in the coalfields as class warfare. The breach was widening between the life within the chapel and the life of work and leisure. The success of the Fed led to its domination of much of Welsh life for almost a century. The Fed (and its successor, the National Union of Mineworkers) died at the same time as industrialized Wales. The lack of a creative relationship between the churches and the ideas represented by either Cymru Fydd or the South Wales Miners' Federation had profound repercussions on the history of twentieth-century Wales.

The Challenge of a New Theology

The latter half of the nineteenth century witnessed major challenges to the understanding of faith. Scientific exploration, especially through geology and biology, and the new criticism of the Bible, were issues which had to be faced. It seems that most church leaders in Wales were indifferent to the new learning emerging from Europe. Tudur Jones asserts that Calvinism had lost its momentum and did not reinvigorate itself to face the new challenges. He points out that the crisis imposed by the new learning 'was postponed in Wales because thinkers were reluctant to get to grips with difficult and complex matters... the intelligentsia had not fully realized the seriousness of the scientific attack. Certainly, it hardly affected any of those who attended the prayer meetings... The Higher Criticism was slow to make its mark in Wales.' [13]

Some welcomed the new learning. Among them was Rowland Williams (1817–70), born at Halkyn, Flintshire, who in 1850 was appointed professor of Hebrew and vice-principal at St David's, Lampeter. In 1854 he preached at Cambridge a sermon on 'Rational Goodness', and in 1860 he expressed the latest biblical scholarship in his contribution to 'Essays and Reviews', a collection of essays advocating free inquiry in religious matters. 'He was now vicar of Broad Chalke in Wiltshire, and he was prosecuted for heresy by the tractarian bishop of Salisbury, Walter Kerr Hamilton... Condemned on three charges in the Court of Arches, Williams won his appeal to the Privy Council and established the right of freedom of enquiry for the clergy of the Church of England.'[14] Other notable scholars were Lewis Edwards and his son, Thomas Charles Edwards. Lewis Edwards (1803–87), of Penllwyn (Capel Bangor, Aberystwyth), who had married the granddaughter of Thomas Charles, established the theological college at Bala in 1837 for the training of Calvinistic Methodist ministers. During his principalship of 50 years and his establishment of the quarterly magazine, *Y Traethodydd*, he shared the latest information in theological, philosophical and scientific fields.

> Edwards held to the moderate Calvinism which had been preached
> by the Calvinistic Methodist fathers, enshrined in the hymns of
> William Williams, Pantycelyn, defended in the sophisticated works
> of Thomas Jones of Denbigh and given creedal expression in the
> 1823 Confession of Faith... Edwards put forward a way of doing
> theology which went beyond the rather sterile dualisms of the
> past.[15]

Thomas Charles Edwards (1837–1900) the first principal of the University College of Wales in Aberystwyth (1872) succeeded his father at Bala in 1891 and was a preacher, teacher and biblical commentator. His address on 'Religious Thought in Wales' (1888)[16] given to the Pan-Presbyterian Council in London expressed his hope that theological challenges were being met, and narrow fundamentalism was being replaced. His ground-breaking theology expressed particularly in *The God-Man* of 1895, expressed:

> The need of the day was for a sound understanding of Christ's
> incarnate life, that he had shared humanity in the depths with the
> whole of the human race. The movement was away from Christ's
> vicarious death in place of the elect, forensically understood, to a
> deep life-giving union with the whole of humankind but activated
> in the believer through the specific ministrations of the Holy Spirit.[17]

'The principal [T.C. Edwards] knew that the world was changing all around.'[18] It remained to be seen whether the churches in Wales would be able to create fresh theological approaches which would satisfy the enquiring minds of new generations in the twentieth century.

9

CONFORMITY BEGINS TO
CRUMBLE, 1903–1945

The Brink of the Twentieth Century

The new confident Wales was creating its own history. The transformation of the south and north-east as the result of rapid industrialization and the influx of immigrants produced completely new expressions of being Welsh. Two-thirds of all Welsh people lived in the south-east of the country. This imbalanced demography reflected three startlingly different communities and lifestyles. 'American Wales,' centred on Newport, Cardiff, Penarth and Barry, reflected a cosmopolitan and commercial life. 'Welsh Wales,' having emerged with dramatic swiftness in the southern mining valleys was a vibrant new style of being Welsh, but at the same time experienced a slow erosion of its rural, Welsh-speaking, Nonconformist foundation. The Valleys created a new fierce form of Anglo-Welshness with its own dialect of Wenglish. Y Fro Gymraeg stretched throughout most of Wales, from Sir Fôn to Sir Gaerfyrddin (Anglesey to Carmarthenshire), despite the sapping of much of its population towards the world of commerce and relative prosperity. For much of the twentieth century, it maintained its Welsh-speaking, Nonconformist culture. In addition to the threefold pattern, from the unique slate communities of Caernarfonshire and Merionethshire there emerged an eminently creative and radical industrial Welsh-speaking culture. Pembrokeshire, that little England beyond

Wales, and parts of the Marches continued with an ambivalent approach to their cultural and historical mores. Should mid-Walians look downriver to Hereford, Shrewsbury and Oswestry, or cross the hills to Aberystwyth and Machynlleth?

Nonconformity was convinced it was in the vanguard of the new emergent Wales. There seemed a divine inevitability about the future progress of triumphalist Nonconformity. Wales was the natural land of Revivalism and the locus of progressive religion. Their theology and ecclesiology reflected the triumphant liberal optimism of the Late Victorian and Edwardian period. Individualistic faith, believing itself stripped of the debilitating and suffocating superstition of catholic sacerdotalism and priest-ridden structures, was the creative source of the inevitable triumph of Nonconformist religion. Many battles had been won. The State Church, once identified with political authority and the ruling classes, was now a minority church and the ally of a minority political party. Chapels were built where people lived, and ministers were well paid, well housed and well educated. Their congregations were literate. Nonconformity was the natural product of an inevitable evolution of religion which had progressed from papal superstition through the state religion of the Church of England into the clear light of Nonconformity. Only one question remained. Which particular brand of Nonconformity conformed most to the will of God? Each denomination smugly knew the answer to that question. At the turn of the century, the Revival of 1904/5 seemed to be the harbinger of a sequence of divinely inspired events which would usher in the victory of the Kingdom of God. Welsh Nonconformity was in the vanguard of the new world order. The arrival of the twentieth century was like the dawn of the millennium.

The Revival of 1904/5

Surely nothing could go wrong? A form of religion which had been continually renewed by a series of revivals throughout the eighteenth and nineteenth centuries was once more re-charged by the Welsh Revival of 1904/5. God's promises would not fail because prayers had been offered incessantly for another revival. Celtic romanticists might wait for Arthur to return from his cave, nationalists anticipate that Glyndŵr would escape from his hiding place, but the faithful godly were promised that the next Revival was only a matter of waiting for God's time. The Revival broke out suddenly in 1904. Calvinistic Methodists in south Cardiganshire held prayer meetings, seeking to recapture the spirit of the 1859 Revival. Joseph Jenkins, the minister of Tabernacle, New Quay, was one of the early leaders, but the name particularly associated with the Revival is Evan Roberts (1878–1951). While training for ministry at Newcastle Emlyn, he had a conversion experience at Blaenannerch, near Cardigan, and when, in October 1904, he returned to his home chapel, Moriah, Loughor, he held revivalist meetings. From there he toured the south Wales valleys and by January 1905, more than 34,000 had been converted. His revival meetings were very different from those experienced in the past. It can be justifiably called 'a young people's revival' with its emphasis on extempore prayer and the singing of revivalist hymns which were led particularly by a group of young women.[1] The services rejected formalism and advocated short addresses rather than long sermons. Its theology was focused on the unbounding love of God and the need for a total response. Evan Roberts led missions to Liverpool and to north Wales but with limited success, at least in comparison with the response engendered in the south. There were 7,370 converts in north Wales, whereas by March 1905 there had been 76,566 converts in the south.

As in previous periods, the revival was encouraged by social conditions. The winter of 1904/5 has been described as the winter of discontent. There were low wages, non-unionism caused divisions within the mining community, and there were outbreaks of cholera and typhoid in Aberdare. The Revival itself evoked both favourable and critical contemporary responses. For some, the Revival was a remarkable outpouring of the Holy Spirit. The leadership of young men and women helped erode the hierarchical and patriarchal structure of chapel authority. For others, however, it was a retreat into emotionalism. The Revival created a narrow view of the work of the Holy Spirit with a corresponding inability to recognise the varied ways in which God is at work in the world. Although many were backsliders once the heat of the movement had cooled, many lives were permanently changed and through them, the experience influenced later generations. Was the 1904 Revival the last of its kind? Although many have prayed for a similar outpouring of the Spirit, the style of the 1904 Revival may have marked the end of a particular form of communal religious experience which depended upon a society steeped in Scripture and receptive to a particular form of charismatic leadership.[2]

Nonconformity

The statistics of Welsh Nonconformity just before the outbreak of war are quite remarkable.[3] In 1914, the Calvinistic Methodists claimed 185,000 communicants, 335,000 adherents and 178,000 Sunday school members; Congregationalists had 160,000 members and 145,000 in Sunday schools; the Baptists 125,000 members and 140,000 in Sunday schools and the Wesleyans 41,422 members (with no corresponding figures for Sunday scholars). Their combined membership was 535,000 with a further half million either adherents or in Sunday schools. Almost half the total population of Wales belonged to one of the four major Nonconformist denominations. The majority worshipped and learned through the medium of Welsh. Language and Dissent bolstered each other. Added to the 'big four' were smaller protestant traditions like the Society of Friends, Unitarians, a variety of Methodists, Brethren, Scotch Baptists, Apostolics, Salvation Army and the Presbyterian Church of England. Nonconformity seemed impregnable. Churches and chapels were found in almost every community in Wales. Many had been built or re-built during the previous 50 years and were the most prestigious buildings in most communities. Chapels belonged to a people who had made great sacrifices to build and pay for them. Their personal and communal debts were often not paid off until the turn of the century, frequently on the silver jubilee of the opening of the building. They were a source of considerable pride.

> At least two thirds of the Welsh-speaking Welsh were church members; the equivalent figure among the English-speaking Welsh was a third at most... They were served by 4,000 ministers and priests; they could draw upon the assistance of 25,000 deacons, elders and wardens; 11,000 sermons were preached in them every Sunday; their Sunday schools were attended by almost half the population; at least two million meetings were held annually in their vestries and halls; their members bought countless commentaries, hymn books and religious periodicals.[4]

The journey from rural Wales to a world of terrace houses, pavements, gas, electricity and the accompanying benefits of hospitals, schools, pubs, sport and theatres seemed like crossing from the wilderness into a Promised Land. Their new chapels, and sometimes their communities, were given the names of 'Holy Land' communities. The new mining village of Tylorstown, founded only in 1876, within 20 years had its Ebenezer, Libanus, Sion, Horeb, Bethany, Moriah and Beulah. These new immigrants were changing their society.

However, there were dangerous undercurrents to crossing the Jordan. The massive immigration of English speakers into south-east Wales, coupled with the insistence that teaching and learning must be through the medium of English, undermined the apparently indissoluble link between Nonconformity and the Welsh language. Dissent was also anchored into what proved outworn social values in the abortive defence of the Sabbath and the advocating of total abstinence. Equally anachronistic was the political obsession with disestablishment as a tool to undermine the Church of England. By the close of the nineteenth century, Nonconformity had become trapped in its own success by becoming 'conformist and establishment'. It failed to grasp far greater challenges and opportunities. Working men and their families were now concerned about earning a decent standard of living and struggling for a more just and equitable society.

The vacuum created by the ambivalence of Liberalism and its handmaiden, Nonconformity, was filled by the advent of socialism. The key figure in south Wales was Keir Hardie (1856–1915), miners' leader and one of the two MPs for Merthyr.

> Hardie certainly hit the right note with the working class of south Wales. His combination of Christianity's eschatological ideal with the challenge that it should be realized in the present, not only persuaded many working men that Socialism would lift them out of their bondage, but that through it Christianity would finally find a true embodiment.[5]

Socialism was presented as the expression of the Christian way. The Sermon on the Mount was advocated as the credo which enabled cooperation to replace selfish individualism. The coming of God's Kingdom entailed the sharing of the earth's natural resources rather than the accumulation of personal wealth. Robert Pope notes five key leaders of the early dissemination of Christian-socialist opinions. Silyn Roberts, Calvinist minister in Tanygrisiau, was certain that 'love of God and of neighbour were more important than creeds', and adopted socialism along with contemporary biblical scholarship. John 'Gwili' Jenkins was a tutor at the Gwynfryn Academy, Ammanford. The foundation of his liberal theology was that life in all its fullness belonged to 'every man regardless of his birth right'. T.E. Nicholas, 'Niclas y Glais', combined commitment to Socialist principles with his Welsh identity. Another central figure was John Morgan Jones who ministered at Hope Calvinistic Methodist chapel in Merthyr from 1898 to 1935 (apart from a brief stay in Bangor). A fifth was D. Tudwal Evans, a Welsh Baptist in Newport. He claimed that 'Jesus could not be the Saviour of the World without being a Socialist because the world was imprisoned in the clutches of SELF... If we follow Jesus faithfully we can be nothing less than Socialists.'[6]

For a minority of ministers, the labour movement was the fulfilment of the religion of Jesus. It presented the solidarity of being human and expressed the necessity of working together for the fulfilment of God's purposes. This view was, however, not that of the majority of church leaders. Many were vehemently anti-socialist. Socialism was described as a 'virus', socialists were 'infidels', while Bodringallt (Rhondda) Welsh Independent chapel threatened excommunication on any who attended political meetings on a Sunday.

When the Labour Party began to present a credible political alternative to the Liberals, ministers were fearful that their chapels would be split on political lines. Nonconformity, which had been identified with Liberalism, now found itself in no man's land. Manual workers were attracted by socialism, while the middle classes remained faithful to the Liberal Party. Rather than taking sides, ministers tended to withdraw from political issues. They were in a no-win situation. The labour movement seemed to be fulfilling a prophetic message of righteousness, while the chapels were withdrawing from the implications of what should have been their principles. It took the bloody confrontations in Tonypandy in 1910 and Llanelli in 1911 to convince some Nonconformists to take seriously the political consequences of social injustice and poverty. As a result of the work of Daniel Lleufer Thomas, the interdenominational Welsh School of Social Service was formed in 1911. Inspired by those of a liberal theology, it began under the auspices of Independents and Baptists but was soon extended to include all the denominations in Wales, except the Roman Catholics. An alternative stance was presented by the Cardiff Conference of 1911, which attempted to maintain the centrality of the Liberal Party in Welsh political life by inviting Lloyd George as its key speaker.

Society increasingly followed secular values. The churches failed to grasp the implications of new advances in scientific, literary and biblical criticism. A division was opening up in

Welsh industrial society, a breach particularly noticeable where the English language was advancing. In 1908, even in Welsh-speaking Caernarfon, a local newspaper surveying church and chapel worshippers, reported that only one in eight of the population attended. By 1914 all the main denominations were recording decreases in membership, with 26,000 having left since the peak of the Revival. What was to follow accentuated the crisis. The terrors of the First World War and the betrayal of the working classes after their return from the Front made Nonconformity appear increasingly irrelevant, both to those who were politically conscious and to those who sought a panacea in escapist materialism. A day of reckoning was at hand.

The Church of England

By 1914, the Church of England was beginning to recover from the doldrums of the nineteenth century. There were 155,000 communicants and 196,000 in Sunday schools. For many, Anglicanism seemed to present a more coherent system of doctrine, liturgy and discipleship than did its Nonconformist rivals. On the other hand, its political energy, like that of the Dissenters, was focused on defending its position as the established Church of England.

The act of disestablishment was the culmination of a long struggle by Nonconformists. There were four phases[7] to the long struggle: the first phase began during the mid-nineteenth century as a consequence of the so-called treachery of the Blue Books; the second phase around the year 1868 with the newly-extended urban franchise; the third phase in 1887, when disestablishment was officially enshrined in Liberal Party policy, and the final phase in the much-changed world of the twentieth century. Nonconformists were increasingly bitter about their payment of tithes to the Church of England and the necessity of obeying Anglican marriage laws and burial rights. They were determined to destroy what they regarded as the oppression of clergy and gentry. However, the 'victory' took so long in coming that it seemed almost irrelevant in an increasingly secularized society.

> In 1910, an immensely detailed, multi-volume statistical analysis of religion was published by the Disestablishment Commission. This revealed that the Church was indeed in a commanding position, with 25.9 per cent of the churchgoing population being Anglican communicants, making them the largest single religious body in Wales. The older interdenominational rivalries seemed increasingly out of place in the new century, and theological matters paled before the formidable agenda of pressing economic and social concerns.[8]

The Liberal government proposed a Royal Commission in 1906, a Disestablishment Bill in 1912, and an Act of Parliament in 1914, although the outbreak of the First World War prevented the Act from being implemented until 1920. The battle was fierce, expressed particularly by the antipathy between Lloyd George and Bishop Alfred George Edwards of St Asaph, who became the first archbishop of Wales in 1920. For Nonconformists, the Church of England epitomised the Establishment, dominated by an anglicised aristocracy which was divorced from the majority of the people of Wales. On the other hand, Anglicans were convinced that they were the inheritors of an ancient Welsh Christianity forged out of the traditions of Dewi and Augustine. This animosity diverted the energies of both protagonists from the real contemporary challenges. As a consequence, many moderate Christians felt it necessary to abandon this in-fighting between two forms of irrelevant conformity.

The Roman Catholic Church

Even as late as 1914, Roman Catholicism remained a minority religion within Wales. In 1851 there were only 20 Roman Catholic churches in Wales, almost half of which were in rural Monmouthshire. In 1850, the diocese of Newport was founded, based on Hereford, and in the same year, the diocese of Menevia was created with Shrewsbury as its centre.

However, the second half of the nineteenth century witnessed the immigration of tens of thousands of Catholic Irish into urbanized south Wales. The twentieth century was to witness a major shift in church demography.

The First World War

From 1885 to 1918, the life of Wales was dominated by the Liberal, Nonconformist middle-class. Controlling national and local politics, they shared a common ideology shaped by an emphasis on individual freedom. This emphasis was reinforced by the Revival's insistence that salvation was the consequence of personal decision. Liberal Welsh Nonconformity, in the person of David Lloyd George, seemed to be at the heart of power in Westminster. Those exercising authority wield the power of myth. Henry Tudor had fulfilled the prophecy of the Red Dragon by restoring the ancient lost kingdom of Britain. Lloyd George was now purifying that kingdom with nonconforming vigour. Both dreams turned into nightmares.

Europe took leave of its senses in 1914. Nations which had prided themselves as bringing civilization to 'the dark continent' now revealed that their imperialism was unleashing the dogs of war. Barbarism seethed beneath a veneer of civilization and the First World War destroyed their liberal optimism. The dream of inevitable progress had been a dangerous illusion. Religion had seemed to be an integral part of the onward march of humanity. Hundreds of thousands of young Welsh men, encouraged by their churches, made their way with blind optimism into the trenches of France and Belgium where they were confronted by a similarly blind and optimistic generation of young Germans. It was not quiet on the western front. Peace came only with the silence of death. Generals, politicians, priests and ministers preached a mixture of false idealism and a cynical jingoism, and presented their young followers with death and despair. Faith died in mud.

Nonconformity was at the forefront of the call to serve and save King and Empire. Your country needed you; your country, uniquely blessed by God, needed you. Urged on by ministers like the two most popular Calvinistic Methodist preachers in Wales, Thomas Charles Williams of Menai Bridge and John Williams of Brynsiencyn, young men obeyed the call to be dutiful to King and God.

> In order to encourage volunteers, it was necessary to foster the belief that a man's supreme duty and virtue was to kill Germans and to die for the Empire. This was a credo alien to the beliefs which the majority of Welsh people claimed to profess. Among Nonconformists, military life was held in deep distrust.[9]

When Lloyd George became Minister of Munitions in 1915, this call took on the added zeal of the necessity to liberate the small nation of Belgium. Germans were depicted as the ultimate enemy, and the war defined as a crusade against barbarians. Even conscription in January 1916, anathema to liberally-minded Nonconformists, was seen now to be the duty of his majesty's subjects. The First World War, the first industrialized war in history, extinguished faith in the goodness of both God and humankind. The image of God was obliterated.

Official records reveal that 272,924 men (21.52 per cent of the male population) served during the war, and 35,000 of these were killed. Many faithful chaplains acted with great courage and served as fine examples of muscular Christianity. Although there had been a long tradition of peace-making amongst Nonconformists (Henry Richard was and still is known as the 'apostle of peace') and in 1913 the Union of Welsh Independents had passed a resolution against warfare, few opposed the war and those who did were usually vilified. Many suffered considerably for their Christian pacifist principles.[10] George M.Ll. Davies (1880–1949) was imprisoned as a conscientious objector. He was elected as Christian Pacifist MP for the University of Wales in 1923–4. During the 1930s he worked with the unemployed at the Maes-yr-Haf Settlement in Trealaw, Rhondda. Others were Lewis Valentine, a Baptist who served in the Medical Corps and later became a founder of

Plaid Cymru; Puleston Jones, a Calvinistic Methodist minister, the 'blind preacher' and one of the founders of Oxford's Dafydd ap Gwilym Society, and Thomas Rees, Principal of Bala-Bangor Independent College and editor-in-chief of *Y Geiriadur Beiblaidd* (Dictionary of the Bible). Others opposed the war because of their Socialist politics. The poet Gwenallt (David James Jones, 1899–1968), one of the founders of Cymdeithas y Cymod (The Fellowship of Reconciliation), was imprisoned as a conscientious objector for his Marxist views. He was later to return to Christianity. Arthur Horner, later president of the South Wales Miners' Federation, was imprisoned for his involvement in the Easter Rising in Ireland.

One of the consequences of the First World War was the obliteration of the long-standing relationship between Nonconformity and the Liberal Party. It marked the end of liberal political and social optimism and killed the religious instinct. A generation of men was lost and a generation of women was bereaved. The atrocities of the war became etched in the collective memory. Men returned from the abominations of the war to reject the jingoistic and duplicitous promise that this was the war to end all wars. They returned with another promise in their ears: they would return to a land fit for heroes. What life could they now anticipate?

The Inter-War Years: The Years of the Locust

The long Depression following the First World War destroyed the 'new nation' which had been created by industrialization and shaped by Nonconformity. Industrial growth went into reverse with catastrophic consequences, and by the end of the 1930s the people and landscape of Wales were on the road to ruinous post-industrialization. Wales, a land to which people had migrated for work and relative prosperity, was now a land from which people fled. The choice was stark. Wither on the dole and remain at home, or escape into the England of fresher fields and new pastures.

Wales' de-industrialization was the result of its dependence on one industry. Many south Wales communities, born of iron and coal, died with the demise of iron and coal. The population of Wales, which had increased rapidly throughout 200 years, fell into a steep decline because of mass emigration, particularly of the younger and more enterprising. A generation was forced to abandon its homeland. One of the consequences of these years of the locust was that the Liberal Party was jettisoned. In the 1880s, the people of Wales replaced their hereditary allegiance to the Tories by supporting the vision and aspirations of the Liberals. During the 1920s, Wales became a stronghold of the Labour Party. It seemed that the policies of Conservative and Liberal had produced the catastrophe of the war and the vain promises of a brave new world for returning heroes. The new Labour movement seemed to epitomise the struggle for justice for working people.

The Depression destroyed much of Welsh life. Young men had fought the war to end all wars. They had struggled to create a land fit for heroes. They returned to the dole. They were now as disposable on the streets of Rhondda as they had been in the trenches of Western Europe. Wales lost 390,000 of its people between 1925 and 1939, and did not recover its 1925 figure until 1973. Many fled to the English Midlands, to Slough and Dagenham. 'Not dead but gone to Slough', wrote Gwyn Thomas, the Rhondda novelist. The valleys of south Wales were redundant and obsolete. They had served their purpose and could be abandoned. Coal and wealth had been sucked out and the residue left to moulder. Those remaining in Valley communities barely survived. Unemployment was on a scale unknown in western society. Unemployment reached 27.2 per cent in 1930 and 42.8 per cent by 1932. At Dowlais in 1939, 73 per cent were unemployed.

> [The] Political and Economic Planning Authority (PEP) proposed that the whole population [of Merthyr] be shipped out to the river Usk... the same solution would have to be applied to Ebbw Vale, Abertillery, Blaenavon, Bargoed, Mountain Ash and a score of other places, where something like 40 per cent of the Welsh had

until recently lived. The central core of the population of Wales had become redundant.[11]

The destruction of the coal communities was paralleled by a steep decline in their flourishing culture. The story of the erosion of the Welsh language had begun during the latter half of the nineteenth century. The causes are complex but include the denigration of Welsh as a peasant language incapable of meeting the new challenges of industrialization. Changes in educational policies emphasized teaching through the medium of English, and a new generation of English speakers had grown up encouraged by their Welsh-speaking parents to reject their language for the sake of catchwords like 'progress, modernisation, work and prosperity'. The immigration of English speakers during the last decades of the nineteenth century and the emigration of Welsh speakers during the 1920s and 1930s almost marked the death knell of Welsh as a living language and culture. The number of Welsh speakers dipped steeply from 50 per cent of the population in 1891 to 40 per cent in 1911, 28 per cent in 1951 and 18.9 per cent in 1981. Between 1921 and 1951, the number of Welsh speakers in the Rhondda fell from 69,000 to 31,000. The destiny of Nonconformity was closely intertwined with the state of the Welsh language. They had marched forward together during the nineteenth century and it seemed they were destined to expire together by the close of the twentieth century.

Nonconformity: Internal Debates

What happened to Nonconformity during these years of the locust? Its alliance with traditional Liberalism had left it incapable of the radical change necessary to place itself alongside the new poor. Many in the Labour and trades union movement saw chapel people as bourgeoisie, reactionary and otherworldly. Many brought up in Nonconformist families, for a variety of reasons, abandoned their tradition: Saunders Lewis became a Catholic; Caradog Evans vilified Nonconformity in his short stories; Rhys Davies, the novelist, Idris Davies the poet, and Tom Jones, the politician, just drifted away.[12]

The churches were aware of the crisis. 'By the 1920s the main themes of theological liberalism were advanced as embodying the central message of Christianity. The same familiar images were emphasized: the Fatherhood of God, brotherhood of man and the ethical task of the Kingdom.'[13] This 'liberal theology' inspired the creation of 'Urdd y Deyrnas' (the order of the Kingdom), an organisation enabling young people to explore the social implications of the Gospel. The movement was inspired by the leadership of Herbert Morgan, Baptist and director of extra-mural studies at the university in Aberystwyth; Miall Edwards of Memorial College Brecon and a pre-eminent theologian; and John Morgan Jones, who became principal of Bala-Bangor Independent College in 1926. Their pamphlets on social issues reveal that their central convictions included 'replacing competition with the ideal of cooperation, and having the development of character as the desired goal.'[14]

Denominational committees discussed why working-class men were leaving the chapels. In 1919, Calvinistic Methodism began to explore its own life. Could the church respond to the inevitable changes of post-war society? A variety of committees explored denominational history, doctrine, church order, ministerial education, worship, mission, and social questions. In 1933, after considerable heat and some light, by Act of Parliament and by Royal Assent, the denomination emerged with two titles, the Calvinistic Methodist Church and the Presbyterian Church of Wales. It reaffirmed its orthodoxy. At the heart of the debate was whether to reform the 'Cyffes Ffydd', the 1823 statement of faith which was part of the church's constitution. Should it be reformulated in the light of biblical and theological scholarship? A decade of inevitable strife followed between the more liberal and the more conservative. A commentary on the Pentateuch, rejecting Mosaic authorship, caused a huge furore, as did the publication of *Y Geiriadur*

Beiblaidd (The Dictionary of the Bible) in 1926. Debates were continuing when, in 1928, an explosive figure emerged on the scene and a series of events took place which radically changed the tone of the debate.

Tom Nefyn Williams (1895–1958)[15] was inducted to the pastorate of Ebenezer Calvinistic Methodist Chapel, Tumble, in 1926, the year of the General Strike. He initiated a housing campaign and explored innovative liturgical practice when, for example, he placed lumps of coal on the communion table. Four elders resigned and Presbytery referred the case to Association in 1927. Accused of heresy, in 1929 he resigned from the pastorate at Tumble and was suspended from the ministry. He and his congregation were locked out from the chapel on the morning of Sunday, 7 October. Although Tom Nefyn's followers formed an independent cause, Llain y Delyn, he returned to north Wales and was reinstated in 1932 as a Calvinistic Methodist minister. Meanwhile, Calvinistic Methodists continued their debates until July 1933 when a Parliamentary Act confirmed the theological position of 1919. Much movement and considerable expenditure had enabled the church to stand still.

Similar theological debates raged amongst the other Nonconformist denominations. The debate within Congregationalism saw 'liberalism' represented by Miall Edwards and Oliver Stephens, while the classic orthodoxy of Karl Barth was introduced through the writing of Vernon Lewis and J.E. Daniel. At the same time a much more conservative theological position was advocated in the ministries of R.B. Jones of Porth and Nantlais Williams of Ammanford. Their annual conferences at Llandrindod were described as the Welsh Keswick. They emphasized biblical inerrancy, the omniscience and omnipotence of Christ, the substitutionary theory of the atonement and the return of Christ. Both the secularism of the world and the worldliness of the church were castigated. Although their ministries attempted to recapture the fervour of the Revivals, after the death of R.B. Jones, the Llandrindod

Conference declined and inner tensions split the conservative witness.

Witness in the World

While Nonconformity debated theology, it was becoming increasingly divorced from the issues which concerned the majority of Welsh people. Although the *Titanic* was sinking, the band played on and the deckchairs were endlessly shuffled. The church did debate the principles of a fairer society, but they rarely faced the practical consequences of injustice and inequality. While churches thought, prayed and discussed, the new socialist leaders tackled the issues of work and unemployment, and in the process created an alternative secular society. English became the language of economic and political action.

The miners' lodges shaped workers' solidarity and provided workmen's halls for libraries, study-courses, billiards, dancing and cinemas. New cultural forms emerged to replace the chapel. What had been relatively unified communities in the nineteenth century now divided themselves into 'chapel people' and 'club people'. Although there was often a mutual respect, they were moving in diametrically opposite directions. Chapels could not compete with the new leisure world of sport, pub and club, cinema, the dance hall and Sunday excursions.

Most chapels saw the new movement as a threat. Ministers and their congregations feared social unrest and the call for radical political change. For them, the socialist creed was humanist and materialistic. The unrest and riots of 1910–11 caused the chapels to withdraw from political action. Because of the fear that congregations would split between traditional Liberals and new Socialists, it was safer to withdraw from political debate. The consequence was that the churches were seen as unworldly, and they lost the loyalty of the workers. The lodge meeting and the deacons' meeting debated different agendas in what were the same communities, but they may as well have been different worlds. The 'left' in society organised

the Red Sunday protests of 3 February 1935 against the means
test, and responded to the fascist onslaught during the Spanish
Civil War, in which 174 from Wales fought on the republican
side, 33 of whom were killed.

Most chapels became increasingly detached from this
political world. A notable exception was Rex Barker in his
imaginative and practical work at the Methodist Central Hall
in Tonypandy. Another was Leon Atkin whose ministry at the
Methodist Central Hall in Bargoed proved to be too radical
for his colleagues and consequently he served at St Paul's
Congregational Church in Swansea. Quaker settlements at
Maesyrhaf and Brynmawr were other attempts to be alongside
the unemployed and provide practical solutions to the crisis.
Alban Davies exercised a pioneering ministry at Bethesda
Independent chapel, Ton Pentre. Involved with two deputations
to prime ministers, Ramsay MacDonald in 1935 and Neville
Chamberlain in 1937, Davies recognized how divorced they
were from empathizing with the crisis. It led him to becoming
a Welsh nationalist. All of these ministers could be defined as
belonging to a liberal tradition. Those who were concerned in
preserving orthodoxy seemed not to notice what was going on
in the streets around them.

> Religion, indeed God himself, was seen to be on the side of privilege
> and the ruling class. By the late 1920s Welsh Nonconformity,
> which had prided itself so long on having retained the loyalty of
> working men and their families, seemed no longer to have anything
> constructive to contribute to the social and political debate in
> Wales.[16]

The Church of England / The Church in Wales

The late Victorian and Edwardian periods had been dominated
by the bitter debate over the disestablishment and the
disendowment of the Church of England in Wales. By the time
the Act became law in 1920, the issue had become irrelevant
to the majority of Welsh people. It proved a trivial issue

compared with the catastrophic upheaval of the First World War. The Act, however, ultimately was to transform Welsh Anglicanism. When the Welsh Church Act came into operation on 31 March 1920, Anglicanism became one more independent denomination within the rainbow of Welsh church life. The new-ancient church was released from being the Established Church dominated by the supervising restrictions of Canterbury. On 7 April 1920, the bishops chose A.G. Edwards[17] (bishop of St Asaph) as the first archbishop of Wales (1920–1934). The Church in Wales possessed the glorious heritage of Wales' parish churches as well as the four ancient cathedrals at Bangor, St Asaph, Llandaff and St Davids. Two new dioceses were created, Monmouth in 1921, and Swansea and Brecon in 1923. Although the Church began to adapt itself to the new challenges, the bench of bishops unfortunately reinforced the impression that they belonged to a superior anti-Welsh hierarchy, distanced from Nonconformity and remote from the life of the majority of the people of Wales:

> ... the disestablished Church in Wales remained hierarchical in nature, aristocratically inclined and still very ambivalent about its status. As late as 1935 its Governing Body comprised six barons, ten baronets, five knights, eleven titled ladies, three sons of peers, two generals, one vice-admiral, one brigadier-general, sixteen colonels and an assortment of majors, captains and members of the gentry many of whom would arrive in their chauffeur-driven Rolls Royces for the annual three-day meeting at Llandrindod. There was something rather inappropriate about this gathering when in the industrial valleys not thirty-five miles to the south, men, women and children in their tens of thousands were afflicted by unemployment, deprivation and considerable hunger.[18]

Within this context, the appointment in 1931 of Timothy Rees (1874–1939) as bishop of Llandaff came as a revelation. A member of the Community of the Resurrection at Mirfield, Timothy Rees has been described as a catholic evangelical with a passion to root the Gospel in everyday life. His high church ecclesiology was balanced by an ecumenical openness and a passionate social concern. His early death in 1939 robbed Anglicanism and Wales of a positive ministry which might have drawn together warring and competitive Christian traditions. Nevertheless, Anglicanism was continuing to strengthen at the expense of Nonconformity. The number of Easter communicants had increased from 159,957 in 1920, to 193,668 in 1939. Disestablishment in 1920 had seemed like a tragic loss of status, but in fact it was laying the seeds for the renewal of the church.

The Roman Catholic Church[19]

In 1916 the Cardiff Province was established, comprising the Metropolitan Archdiocese of Cardiff (which includes Herefordshire) with the diocese of Menevia as a suffragan see. On 13 April 1921, Francis Mostyn was enthroned as archbishop of Cardiff and metropolitan of Wales. The Roman Catholic Church felt it was coming home after a very long absence. During the first 25 years of the twentieth century, the number of Catholics in the archdiocese of Cardiff increased from 59,640 to 84,100 and in Menevia from 9,881 to 21,675. The increases were the consequence of a combination of natural birth rate, immigration and conversions from other Christian traditions. These included Saunders Lewis, T. Charles Edwards, great-grandson of Lewis Edwards, a foremost Calvinistic Methodist theologian, and Catherine Daniel, daughter of a Congregationalist minister and married to J.E. Daniel, the Congregational theologian. Both Francis Mostyn and Bishop Francis Vaughan of Menevia were convinced that the Roman Catholic Church alone reflected the one, holy, catholic and apostolic church. Anglicanism and Nonconformity were equally schismatic. For Michael McGrath, who became archbishop in 1939, association with non-Catholics was anathema. The hierarchy were equally opposed to socialism which they described as an expression of the anti-Christ. The divisions within Wales were seen particularly clearly in the opposing positions taken during the Spanish Civil War. For intellectuals the matter came to a head in 1943 during the election for the parliamentary seat of the University of Wales, when W.J. Gruffydd, professor of Welsh at Cardiff, stood as a Liberal, and defeated Saunders Lewis, the Roman Catholic, who was the Nationalist candidate. Two styles of Catholicism existed during the inter-war period. The minority were the descendants of old Welsh Catholic families and the new intellectual converts. The vast majority were either Irish immigrants or the descendants of immigrants. The Catholic working class lived in the cities of south Wales and were often amongst the most impoverished in society. Although both Mostyn and Vaughan stood alongside their parishioners, they made no suggestions on how to create a more just political order.

The Second World War

It was a cruel irony that the scourge of unemployment was temporarily solved by the onset of the Second World War. Although the war did not have the same devastating effect as the war of 1914–18, 15,000 Welsh men and women were killed in the armed services. Severe air raids destroyed much of the centre of Swansea and parts of Cardiff with considerable loss of life. Wales was also affected by the arrival of 200,000 evacuees during the first two years of the war.

Opposition to the war was maintained by Cymdeithas y Cymod which had been founded in 1914. In 1942 the Union of Welsh Independents called for the beginning of peace negotiations. Opposition to the war was also supported by many within Plaid Cymru and a dozen were imprisoned. Conscientious objectors were dismissed from their posts in Cardiff and Swansea. A long-term effect on the story of Welsh culture was the confiscation of seven valleys and the eviction of 219 people who farmed on Mynydd Epynt. By 1945, ten per cent of the surface of Wales was held by the War Office. During the post-war years, there were designs on land in Preseli, Tregaron and Trawsfynydd. The land of Wales was becoming militarized.

When the troops had arrived home from the First World War, they had been burdened by an experience of disillusionment. They were greeted with the reward of unemployment, and the only release for many was to emigrate from their home country. These were not the experiences of those returning in 1945. Most were convinced they had fought a righteous struggle against the barbarism of the concentration camps of Europe and the death camps of Indo-China. For them, the war had been a battle for civilization. They were also rewarded with the optimism of a new start with the radical Labour government of Clement Attlee. There were hopes of the creation of a new society. Would the church have a role to play?

10

REACHING THE MILLENNIUM, 1945–2015

The New Context

Victory in Europe Day (8 May 1945) and Victory over Japan Day (15 August 1945) marked the conclusion of terrifying worldwide hostilities. The immediate post-war period showed no signs of the imminent Cold War and the threatening clouds of nuclear holocaust. Now that the war was over, there was work to be done, girded by the optimism of a new start with the radical Labour government of Clement Attlee. Key utilities and industries were nationalized – they belong to the people now! – and there was popular thanksgiving over the establishment of National Insurance, the Industrial Injuries Act, National Assistance and the National Health Service. For most Welsh people the changes were doubly welcomed because at the helm were two Welsh Labour politicians, James Griffiths and Aneurin Bevan. Justice and equality heralded a victorious new beginning for Britain, Wales and visionary socialism. Full employment was maintained, the Welsh industrial base began to diversify and a political consensus was shaped.

The Labour Party dominated Welsh local government for decades. Two diverting streams emerged. One, inspired by Aneurin Bevan, a miner, MP for Ebbw Vale and architect of the NHS, was fiercely centralist, pro-British and opposed to any suggestion of a separatist Wales. Another more devolutionist stream emerged, led by three Welsh MPs, D.R. Grenfell, MP for Gower, son of a miner and a Welsh Independent; Bill Mainwaring, MP for Rhondda East, a miner and a conscientious objector during the First World War; and Jim Griffiths, MP for Llanelli, son of a colliery blacksmith and also a Welsh Independent. Two issues, reflected in the opposing positions of Bevan and Griffiths were to be of significance throughout the rest of the century. The first was the debate on the nature of being Welsh and the place of the ancient language in an increasingly cosmopolitan society. The second was the issue of devolution and self-government.

A Distinctive Language and Culture

A line of cultural continuity, shaped by the Welsh language, had existed from the origins of the nation until the twentieth century. By the post-war period, questions were being asked on whether that continuity had been snapped. Would the language still be spoken in the twenty-first century? Decline in the use of the Welsh language was rapid and appeared inexorable. It seemed certain that Welsh would pass into oblivion. 'Everyone speaks English! Who needs a superfluous language and a redundant culture?' Many Welsh people swallowed whole the English argument for a universal language, as long as it was English!

With the drowning of valleys, the growth of nationalized forests and the militarization of large swathes of land, Wales was being transformed into the combination of a gigantic national park for leisure activities and an area for military exercises. With unemployed Welsh emigrating and second-home owning English immigrating, Wales would soon enjoy the dubious status of being the home for the tired and retired.

> 'We are fortunate in our neighbours,' said a woman from Liverpool who had settled in Llanfair Mathafarn Eithaf; 'they are nearly all from Merseyside.'[1]

The struggle for Welsh self-determination and the preservation of the Welsh culture travelled along a similar

Brecon. The Congregational Memorial College was a successor to dissenting academies. The college at Brecon served from 1839 to 1959 (this building was opened in 1869). It reflected Nonconformity in its heyday. It is now divided into flats.

The Plough Chapel, Brecon. Conformist Nonconformity seemed very different from its origins at Maesyronnen.

Tregaron. Henry Richard. 'Wales is now a nation of Nonconformists… I have always been mindful of three things: Not to forget the language of my country; and the people and cause of my country; and to neglect no opportunity of defending the character and promoting the interests of my country… My hope for the abatement of the war system lies in the permanent conviction of the people, rather than the policies of cabinets or the discussions of parliaments.'

THE REVD. DR. THOMAS COKE,
BORN IN THIS TOWN ON THE 28TH SEPTEMBER, 1747
WAS BAPTIZED IN THIS CHURCH.
HE WAS MAYOR OF BRECON IN 1770.
BECAME A CURATE AT SOUTH PETHERTON, SOMERSET.
WHILST THERE HE MET THE REVD. JOHN WESLEY
BECAME A SUPPORTER OF THE METHODIST MOVEMENT
AGEING JOHN WESLEY ADVISED HIM TO
GO PREACH THE GOSPEL TO ALL THE WORLD.
HE BECAME FOUNDER OF
METHODIST EPISCOPAL CHURCH OF U.S.A.
AND
METHODIST OVERSEAS MISSIONS.

Aberdare. Griffith Rhys Jones, 'Caradog' born in Trecynon, conducted Y Côr Mawr which won first prize at Crystal Palace in 1872 and 1873 (above left).

Neuaddlwyd: Dr Thomas Phillips, minister of Neuaddlwyd chapel and academy, inspired Thomas Bevan and David Jones to become missionaries in Madagascar (above right).

St Mary's Brecon. The memorial to Thomas Coke, born in Brecon and the 'father' of Methodist missions.

Jerusalem, Yr Efail, Berriew. Thomas Jones of Berriew was the first Calvinistic Methodist missionary to the Khasia Hills in India. In the photo is Hans Schmeinck, a faithful and courageous member of the church. He arrived in Wales after the Second World War as a German prisoner of war.

Bethel, Sketty, Swansea. Griffith John of Glandwr, Swansea, served as missionary in China for 50 years.

Llanover. Robert Jermain Thomas was born in Rhaeadr, nurtured in Llanover and martyred in Korea. Hanover Chapel is now a place of pilgrimage for Korean Christians.

Ffaldybrenin. Timothy Richard, born in Tanyresgair, served in China and received the honour of the 'Order of the Double Dragon'.

© Tom Evans

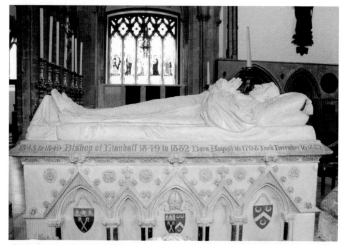

Llandaff Cathedral. Bishop Alfred Ollivant created the Llandaff Church Extension Society and inspired the renewal of Anglicanism in the diocese.

Llangorwen. The Oxford Movement arrived in Wales at Llangorwen near Aberystwyth. The stone altar was the first in Wales since the Reformation.

Cardiff. St Michael's first opened in Aberdare in 1892 before moving to Llandaff in 1907. From 2016 it will continue as the St Michael's Conference Centre as a key element in the Church in Wales' new St Padarn theological institution.

Aberystwyth. Established in 1872, University College of Wales, Aberystwyth with the University Colleges of Cardiff and Bangor, became a founder member of the University of Wales in 1893. One of the dreams of Owain Glyndŵr was fulfilled.

Penllwyn (Capel Bangor). Lewis Edwards of Penllwyn established a theological college at Bala in 1837 for the training of Calvinistic Methodist ministers. His is one of the most influential of Welsh families. He married Jane Charles, granddaughter of Thomas Charles.

Aberystwyth University. The son of Lewis Edwards, Thomas Charles Edwards was the first Principal of the University College of Wales, Aberystwyth (1872–91), before succeeding his father as Principal of Bala College.

Blaenannerch. While training for the ministry of the Calvinistic Methodists, Evan Roberts was converted at a 'convention' at Blaenannerch in 1904. Mair Davies shares the story with hundreds of visitors.

Llanfaes, Anglesey. One of the most popular of Calvinistic ministers, John Williams, Brynsiencyn, became honorary chaplain to the Welsh Division during the First World War. He was regarded as Lloyd George's greatest recruiting officer in Wales.

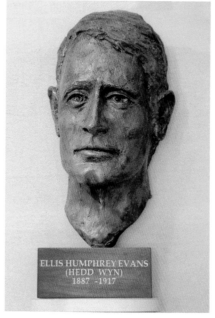

Trawsfynydd. Hedd Wyn, Ellis Humphrey Evans, a shepherd from Trawsfynydd, was killed at Pilkem Ridge, a month after sailing to France. His poem 'Yr Arwr' (The Hero) won the chair at the Birkenhead National Eisteddfod of 1917. The chair was draped in black.

Tylorstown. Memorial to the pit disaster of 1896 when 57 men and boys were killed. There are hundreds of similar memorials throughout Wales, including The Guardian at Six Bells, and the Welsh National Memorial at Senghenydd which was unveiled on 14 October 2013.

Tylorstown. Soup kitchen at Horeb Welsh Baptist Chapel, Tylorstown, 1926. Has anything changed? There is now a food bank in Tylorstown.

Llain y Delyn, Tumble. The followers of Thomas Williams (Tom Nefyn) obtained the financial assistance of the Society of Friends to build a 'society house' in Tumble.

Ton Pentre, Bethesda. Alban Davies exercised a pioneering ministry at Bethesda, Capel yr Annibynwyr, Ton Pentre from 1925 until his death in 1972. In his funeral the Rev. Emrys Jones of Treherbert stated 'an oak tree has to fall before you can measure its length'. The chapel seated 1,000 and closed in 1996.

Trealaw. Maesyrhaf was one of the first 'Quaker settlements' in south Wales. It was started in 1926 by Emma and William Noble who moved from Swindon. They were supported by the Maes-yr-Haf Committee which usually met in Oxford, chaired by A.D. Lindsay, Master of Balliol College.

Llanuwchlyn: Michael and Michael D. Jones, father and son, both served as principals of the Independent College at Bala. It was the vision and leadership of Michael D. which led to the foundation of the Welsh colony in Patagonia in 1865.

Tredegar. The stones were erected to celebrate the life of Aneurin Bevan at a spot where he addressed his constituents. The three outer stones represent Rhymney, Tredegar and Ebbw Vale. The visions of Jones and Bevan are both needed to create a healed and coherent national community.

St Asaph Cathedral.
A.G. Edwards, bishop of
St Asaph, was the first
archbishop of the Church
in Wales from 1920–34. The
west window at St Asaph
is dedicated to Archbishop
Edwards.

Cardiff. The Metropolitan
Cathedral of St David
was built between 1882
and 1887. St David's was
declared the Cathedral
Church of the new
Archdiocese of Cardiff
on 12 March 1920. The
cathedral contains a shrine
to our Lady of Penrhys.

Cofiwch Dryweryn. The village of Capel Celyn was drowned in 1965 to provide water for the city of Liverpool.

Epynt. Babell Calvinistic Methodist Chapel closed in 1940 when the land was confiscated and the people evicted. The government demanded the land for military training. It is still used for that purpose. Iorwerth Peate records an 82-year-old lady of Hirllwyn Farm, saying to him, 'It is the end of the world here.' Remember the elegy of Bleddyn Fardd, 'Ys terfyn byd.'

© Alan Griffin

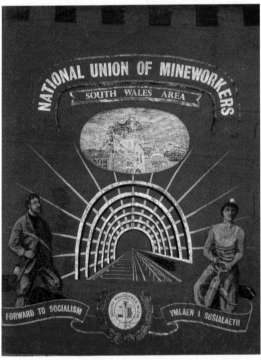

South Wales Miners' banner, 'Forward to a better tomorrow.'

© South Wales Miners' Library, Swansea

Maerdy. On 5 March 1985, led by the Tylorstown and Maerdy Colliery Band, the miners walked from the village of Maerdy to the colliery. The pit remained open until 1990.

© Tylorstown Band

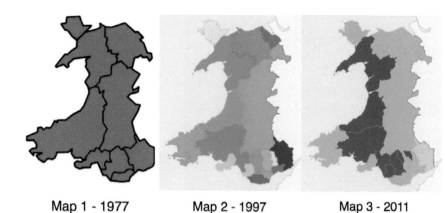

Map 1 - 1977   Map 2 - 1997   Map 3 - 2011

The first referendum of 1979 was either 'Devolution or Demolition Day'. On 1 March 1979 every county voted in favour of 'our common Britishness' (map 1). The second referendum of 1997. The 'Yes' vote was spearheaded by Ron Davies, the Secretary of State for Wales, and a joint campaign with the Liberal Democrats and Plaid Cymru led to a positive vote, by the smallest of margins (map 2).

The third referendum took place in 2011 for 'further powers for the Cynulliad/ Assembly'. Every county, except Monmouthshire (and that failed by only 1 per cent) had voted a resounding 'Yes' to the Assembly (map 3).

Y Senedd was opened in 2006. 'The Senedd is not just a building for Members, it is your building. It is the main public building of the National Assembly, the main centre for democracy and devolution in Wales' (www.assembly.wales).

Swansea. The first cinemas to open in Wales on a Sunday were in Swansea. The Plaza, opened in 1935, was the largest cinema in Wales. It closed in 1965. It was replaced by the Odeon Centre which was itself demolished in 2015. There were no victors.

© Dewi Lewis

Tylorstown. The Duke of York Hotel is the last pub open in Tylorstown. The Tylors, Queens, Jubilee and Bridgend have all long gone. The Sunday Closing Act of 1881 was repealed by the Licensing Act of 1961. Local authorities held plebiscites until the last area, Dwyfor, capitulated in 1996.

Does it have to be either... or...?

Morriston. Tabernacl Morrison opened in 1872. Built to seat 1,450, it cost £18,000 and has been described as 'the cathedral of Welsh Nonconformity'.

Swansea. The Liberty Stadium is the home of Swansea City Football Club and the Ospreys regional rugby team.

Can it be both... and...?

Cardiff. Tabernacl, the Hayes, is a Baptist chapel, built 1821 and rebuilt in 1865. Tabernacl maintains a Welsh-speaking presence in the centre of Wales' capital city.

Cardiff. St David's Dewi Sant Shopping Centre. 'When you can't decide what to get them, get them everything.'

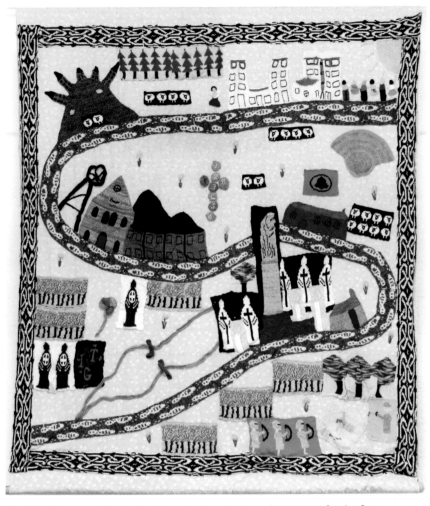

The Llanfair banner. Created by Anne Lord and Janet Jukes in 1993 for the first anniversary of the opening of Llanfair. It explores and celebrates the story of Penrhys.

Soar y Mynydd.

Our Lady of Penrhys.

The Guardian of the Valleys.

Llanfair-ar-y-bryn, Llandovery.

And so we came to the end of our journey. Between clarity of light with hints of crimson came Duw Cariad Yw – God is Love. Here was the prayerful beseeching of Our Lady of Penrhys. Here was the Nameless One of Six Bells calling out that every name must be remembered. Duw Cariad Yw – God is Love. Câr Di – You are to love. Our journey had ended, or had it only just begun?

route during the twentieth century. How and when did the fightback begin? Was it through the founding of Urdd Gobaith Cymru (the Welsh League of Youth) in 1922 by Ifan ap Owen Edwards? Its present membership of 50,000 in 1,500 branches, and its annual eisteddfod where 40,000 members compete has become a linchpin of a flourishing Welsh culture among young people. Was it though the formation of Plaid Genedlaethol Cymru (the National Party of Wales) in 1925? How significant was the event and its symbolic value when on 8 September 1936 (the 400th anniversary of the Act of Union with England), three eminent Welshmen, Saunders Lewis, D.J. Williams and Lewis Valentine set fire to workmen's huts at the Penyberth Bombing School on Llŷn? Their handing themselves in to the authorities, their acquittal in Caernarfon, subsequent re-trial at the Old Bailey and imprisonment in Wormwood Scrubs had powerful resonances.

What were the consequences of the drowning of the Tryweryn Valley? Liverpool, without consulting any authorities in Wales, brought forward a parliamentary bill which received royal assent on 1 August 1957. No Welsh MP voted in favour of the bill. Because it was clear that the people of Wales had no democratic voice, two young Welshmen, Emyr Llewelyn and John Albert Jones committed acts of sabotage to draw attention to the outrage. The betrayal of a Welsh-speaking rural community by an indifferent government convinced many who valued the Welsh-speaking way of life that the chains tying Wales to the centralized British state needed to be snapped. Tryweryn served as a kairos moment for all who treasured a Welsh rural identity shaped over many centuries. A similar kairos moment was to be experienced by industrialized south Wales in 1985. Just as the proud but abortive demonstration of the people of Tryweryn through the streets of Liverpool on 21 November 1956 had convinced Welsh-speaking Wales, the equally proud but abortive march of miners and their families to the pithead of Maerdy on 5 March 1985 was a sign to the people of the south Wales valleys that their future must lie in their own hands. The combination of these two peoples was ultimately to prove irresistible.

How important was Saunders Lewis' radio lecture 'Tynged yr Iaith' (the Fate of the Language) on 13 February 1962? It triggered the formation of Cymdeithas yr Iaith Gymraeg (the Welsh Language Society) later that year. How memorable was 14 July 1966 when Gwynfor Evans secured the first parliamentary victory for Plaid Cymru in the Carmarthen by-election? What have been the consequences of education through the medium of the Welsh language? The first private Welsh-language primary school was established in Aberystwyth in 1939, and in 1947 Carmarthenshire County Council opened a publicly maintained school in Llanelli. The first bilingual secondary school was at Ysgol Glan Clwyd in Flintshire in 1956. During the last decade, the number of children receiving Welsh-language education has increased in primary education from 18.81 per cent to 23.82 per cent, and in secondary education from 18.06 per cent to 20.84 per cent (2011/12 figures).

A Distinctive Form of Government

Would Wales become completely subsumed politically into England by the close of the twentieth century? No-one could have predicted any major political transformation in the sphere of Welsh self-determination. Since the Acts of Union of 1536 and 1542/3, Wales had been ruled as an indistinguishable and undistinguished part of England. It took 350 years before a Parliamentary Act acknowledged the distinctiveness of Wales. In 1881 legislation curtailed the sale of alcohol on Sundays! The collapse of Cymru Fydd in 1896 marked the end of Liberal expectations of self-government. It was not until 1925 that a party (Plaid Cymru) was formed with the specific aim of self-government. However, no significant advances were made until pressure from a few Labour MPs persuaded the Conservative government to establish the Welsh Office in 1963. James Griffiths was appointed in 1964 as the first Secretary of State for Wales. In 1969 a Royal Commission looked at the question of devolution in Wales and in Scotland. Conservatives in Wales refused to give evidence to the Commission, and the Labour Party was deeply divided. The Kilbrandon Report, published in 1973, led to the Wales Act supported by the Labour government. It advocated a Welsh Assembly with a limited range of powers.

Officially all Welsh political parties, except for the Conservatives, were in favour of devolution, but a vociferous minority of Welsh Labour MPs, led by Leo Abse of Pontypool, Neil Kinnock of Bedwellty, Donald Anderson of Swansea East and George Thomas (Lord Tonypandy) – the latter two, eminent Methodists – fiercely opposed their own government's policy. The opposition raised issues of extra cost, further administration and 'our common British-ness', but the telling argument echoed the words of Robert Bird at the Newport meeting of 1896 which had scuppered the hopes of Cymru Fydd. We will not be ruled by a minority of Welsh-speaking north Walians! We are content to be a divided people within the United Kingdom. When the result of the vote was announced on 2 March 1979, 243,048 voted in favour and 956,330 voted against. Every county in Wales had a negative majority.

That seemed the end of the affair. Wales was part of Britain – indeed part of England. Although the people of Wales seemed to have permanently destroyed any hope of a devolved Welsh government, eminent contemporary Welsh historians were perplexed and disturbed. Did 1979 mark the end of Welsh identity? Some responses were despairing:

> What seems to be clear is that a majority of the inhabitants of Wales are choosing a British identity which seems to require the elimination of a Welsh one... One thing I am sure of. Some kind of human society, though God knows what kind, will no doubt go on occupying these two western peninsulas of Britain, but that people, who are my people and no mean people, who have for a millennium and a half lived in them as a Welsh people, are now nothing but a naked people under an acid rain.[2]

Others, also frankly puzzled, hoped against hope that some form of Welsh consciousness might survive and flourish.

> But there could be little doubt that Welsh nationality, like Scottish, remained a living force in the 1970s, even after the devolution referendum of 1979, a dormant giant ready perhaps to bestir itself and to crusade anew for the destiny of a nation.[3]

Devolution day was followed during the 1980s by a centralist government's onslaught which eliminated the coal industry and contributed to the near extinction of communities created and succoured by coal for a century and a half. Half of Wales was declared redundant and needed to prepare for its endgame. The economy of the south Wales valleys was dying, as was its once-vibrant culture and religion, and its only solution seemed to be outward migration. This was in contrast to the more 'desirable' parts of Wales which were experiencing an influx of immigrants, the majority of whom were escaping from city life, attracted by good scenery, low property values and an emptying landscape. John Davies, wondering whether the nation was facing extinction, cried in a combination of despair and resolution:

> Yet the Welsh survived all the crises of their history, remaking their nation time and time again. As Wales seems to experience recurrent death and rebirth, it would almost seem as if the history of the nation is an endless journey back and fore between the mortuary and the delivery room. Thus, those who proclaim its funeral are singularly unwise, for tenacity is the hallmark of this ancient nation.[4]

The year 1979 marked both the nadir of Welsh hopes and a kairos moment. Ahead lay either extinction or renewal. A catalyst for change arrived as a most unwelcome gift. A Conservative Prime Minister, Margaret Thatcher, wedded to the ideologies of monetarism, individualism and Britishness, unintentionally became the midwife of the new Wales. In 1979 British Socialists had killed off any hope of Welsh self-determination, and later that year it was anticipated that the funeral would be presided over by the new Conservative government. It did not take long for the people of Wales to realise that they had been duped. During the General Election of May 1979, all political parties had accepted the Annan Report of 1977 which proposed the establishment of a Welsh-language television channel. In September, the new Conservative government betrayed its manifesto promise. There would be no Welsh channel. This created a furious response. Transmitters were blocked and licence fees were unpaid, but the main catalyst for action was Gwynfor Evans' threat to fast to death. Gwynfor Evans (1912–2005), a committed Christian pacifist and president of Plaid Cymru, received the support of large numbers of Welsh people, including a delegation of Welsh leaders who met the Home Secretary. The fear of chronic disorder resulted in the government restoring its original manifesto promise. The lady not for turning, turned.

The lady took her revenge on not only Welsh miners, but all miners. Although the dispute between the National Coal Board and the National Union of Mineworkers appeared to be a struggle about the future of the coal industry, at its heart it was a deliberately contrived confrontation between the government and the trade union movement. Miners and communities were pawns in a game where the main players were the ideologies and personalities of Margaret Thatcher and Arthur Scargill. The year-long strike, with its untold suffering and sacrifice, ended with the total defeat of the miners and the eventual closure of every deep mine in Wales. The day the miners walked back proudly to their pits, with their communities saluting them in solidarity, was followed by the immediate dismantling of the Welsh coal industry. Two centuries of mining were brought to an end, and the coal communities were declared obsolete.

The year-long dispute revealed that if the tools of decision-making had been within Wales, the issues would have been solved. Philip Weekes, the director of the South Wales Coalfield and Emlyn Williams, the president of the South Wales NUM had negotiated pit closures and investments for many years through processes of hard debate and eventual compromise. Their style was replaced by the deliberately confrontational methods of the British government and hardline members of the NUM. Reconciliation and compromise were dirty words. The ordinary miner, his family and community, made the sacrifices and paid the ultimate price.

Many in Wales, including the churches which played a prominent role in seeking a just settlement, recognised that neither unbridled monetarism nor hardline Marxism could provide the answer. They felt from their experience that there was another way. Most people of the coalfield were the children or grandchildren of miners. Was there 'a Welsh way of working things out', based on a combination of long-term relationships, a sense of community values and common belonging? By the 1990s, many in Wales perceived that the Westminster government had no understanding of a distinctive and distinguished Welsh language and culture, or an awareness that the Welsh experience of community and relationships provided alternate ways of negotiating. There need not be victories only for the most powerful and ruthless.

There was a renewed call for devolved government. An all-party Campaign for a Welsh Assembly was formed and although that campaign witnessed again the wearisome arguments of Robert Bird, a national referendum was held by the New Labour government on 18 September 1997. The 'Yes' vote was spearheaded by Ron Davies, the Secretary of State for Wales, and a joint campaign with the Liberal Democrats and Plaid Cymru led to a positive vote. Those in favour were 559,419 (50.3 per cent) and those against were 552,698 (49.7 per cent). Devolved government had arrived by the smallest of margins.

Wales reflected its divisions in the narrow general vote and in the way the different counties voted. The three-fold model continued. Y Fro Gymraeg and Welsh Wales voted heavily in favour. The British Wales of the south Wales coastal belt, the northern retirement areas and the old Marcher counties opposed self-determination. It was a perilous position for the people and new government of Wales. Would the new Assembly perpetuate those divisions? Would the age-old animosities re-emerge and destroy the first attempt at self-government since the Parliament of Owain Glyndŵr in Machynlleth? Would the dislike of Cardiff antagonise all those not only in the north and west, but all those further north of Nantgarw (five miles north of Cardiff)? Contrary to all expectations, a sense of growing maturity was proven twelve years later when, in 2011, Wales faced a further referendum for the extension of the Assembly's law-giving powers. This was the first national test of the popularity of the move towards self-government. In 1979, devolution had been rejected by the people of Wales by three to one, and every Welsh county had voted against the proposals. In 1997, the proposals for devolution had been passed by the narrowest of margins, with the number of counties split evenly. What would be the result in 2011? To the astonishment of most pundits, the vote in favour was 517,380 (63.49 per cent) and the vote against 297,380 (36.51 per cent). Every county, except Monmouthshire (and that failed by only one per cent) had voted a resounding 'Yes' to the Assembly. For the people of Wales, the Assembly was recognized as a process. The new government was on a journey. For the first time since the Tudors, the people of Wales were responsible for their own future. What have been the implications of these developments for the future of the Welsh people, and what has been the relationship, if any, between the changing values of the nation and the churches?

The Life of the Churches: Nonconformity

The disestablishment of the Church of England in 1920 changed the status of all Welsh churches. Nonconformity could no longer define itself as being 'not established', or 'free'. All churches were now 'free churches'. There was no established church and no official conformity. Even at the end of the Second World War, Nonconformity faced the future from a position of relative strength. As well as the four major

Nonconformist denominations, there were a plethora of smaller denominations and a large number of independent non-denominational churches. In 1946 there were 173,000 Calvinistic Methodists, 156,000 Congregationalists, 110,000 Baptists and 51,000 Wesleyans. More than half a million people were in communicant membership of the chapels. The princes of the pulpit still commanded large congregations at the 'cyrddau mawr,' the bi-annual special services. Philip Jones was described as 'the last of the princes of the Methodist pulpit in south Wales'. Elfed Lewis, the Congregationalist hymn-writer and poet, who although blind for his last 20 years, preached until his nineties. The Baptist Jubilee Young was one of four preacher brothers. Most of the 'hoelion wyth' (the select few) were 'booked to preach' many years ahead, their sermons compared and contrasted, and they were feted as eloquent religious, intellectual and communal heroes. 'But times they were a changin.'

In the 'never had it so good' society, people's expectations turned away from traditional religion. While much of England and Wales was enjoying relative materialistic prosperity, prophetic voices warned that the crises in Nonconformity and the Welsh language and culture would accentuate unless the churches radically changed. Nonconformity and the Welsh language would lurch together into oblivion. The new moralities of the affluent society would jettison the Nonconformist conscience.[5]

In many industrial valleys, the children of Welsh-speaking chapel people had not been encouraged to speak Welsh. English was the language of school, shop, workplace, political debate, cinema, dancehall and sport. Welsh survived as the preserve only of chapel worship – even Sunday schools and youth meetings were often held in English. The older generation did not share their natural tongue with their own children. The younger generation remained loyal to chapel only as long as there were strong family ties, and abandoned religion when they left their home chapels and communities. The chapels in the Valleys and the last generation of native Welsh speakers died together. In the Rhondda of 1955[6] there were 28 chapels belonging to the Undeb yr Annibynwyr (The Union of Welsh Independents). Their membership totalled 5,500, there were 2,500 in Sunday schools and there were 14 full-time ministers. In 2015 only three chapels are left with an ageing membership of less than a hundred. Similar statistics would reflect the dying of Welsh Nonconformity throughout the once-industrialized Valleys.

Nonconformity fared no better in the rural areas which witnessed a tide of inward migration from England. The wealthier and 'more successful' bought second homes with their accoutrements of English accents and culture. Others fleeing the materialistic rat race explored alternative lifestyles and spiritualities. The chapel was helpless and gave up the competition. The Welsh Sabbath did not survive. Within a generation Cei Newydd (New Quay), a home of the 1904 Revival, changed from a community where no-one walked on the beach on Sunday, to a community where you walked past the chapels to the sand and sea to partake in your own bread and wine. Language, culture and religion were disappearing rapidly. The Bible of William Morgan, the hymns of William Williams and the prayers of the heart were all being extinguished.

Since the Second World War, Welsh Nonconformity had been the home of lost causes. It fought for the Welsh Sabbath by protesting against the opening of Sunday cinemas, which arrived first at Swansea in 1950. It battled against the opening of public houses on Sundays. The Licensing Act of 1960 called for a national plebiscite and the first vote in the autumn of 1961 reflected the yawning chasm dividing Wales. Eight Welsh-speaking, rural and traditionally Nonconformist counties in the west and north voted against Sunday opening, while the more populous, industrialized, English-speaking counties of the south and east voted in favour. The battle continued every seven years until in 1996, the final area, Dwyfor, capitulated. Nonconformity was portrayed as a negative force, a killjoy preventing people having the good time which they felt they deserved. In the process, Sunday lost any distinctiveness. This once first day, red-letter day, became submerged into the weekend of shopping, sport and family gatherings. Many in today's society, with its frenetic lifestyle, secretly crave for one day of stillness, quiet leisure and opportunities for renewal! Although Nonconformists lost battles, there were no victors.

Decade by decade, Nonconformity has continued its steady decline. Sunday schools rarely exist. Children are the exception at worship. Chapels have no more adherents and their congregations are made up of the ageing faithful. Chapels close at the same pace as they opened during the first half of the nineteenth century. It seems that a chapter of Christian history will soon come to an end.

The Church in Wales

The Church in Wales entered the challenges of the post-war period with eagerness, unity and confidence. Many felt that moribund Nonconformity's state of decay was the result of its abandonment of catholic tradition and apostolic ministry. Nonconformity had been a schismatic aberration whose days were numbered. The vacuum would be replaced by Anglicanism, confident in its catholic and apostolic heritage. It had faced the ignominy of disestablishment in 1920 and was now coming into its own. Possessing Wales' ancient cathedrals and churches, the Church in Wales inherited the long tradition of Welsh Christianity. Anglicanism was in the ascendancy. The numbers of communicants increased from 155,911 at Easter 1945 to 182,864 in 1960.

This new confidence often verged on arrogance. Edwin Morris, bishop of Monmouth (later to be Archbishop of Wales, 1957–67) pronounced in his Primary Visitation Charge in 1946, that 'The Church in Wales is the Catholic Church in this land, and we cannot without denying our very nature, yield one iota of this claim.'[7] In a sermon at the consecration of Daniel

Bartlett as bishop of St Asaph in 1951, Morris antagonized Welsh Christendom:

> Both the Roman clergy and Nonconformist ministers are, strictly speaking, intruders. There may be historical reasons for their being here, but we cannot recognize their right to be here.[8]

There were, however, undercurrents of disquiet, and a crisis broke over the election of both Morris as archbishop in 1957, and John Thomas as bishop of Swansea and Brecon in 1958. Many were distressed by the fact that neither spoke Welsh, but the main concern proved to be the electoral process. Bishops Glyn Simon (recently translated from Swansea and Brecon to Llandaff) and G.O. Williams (appointed to Bangor in 1957) were disturbed by the tone of the election. Glyn Simon expressed his distress in the January edition of the Llandaff Diocesan leaflet:

> These recent elections, and utterances both before and after them, have revealed an anti-Welsh and pro-English trend and, in some cases, a bigotry as narrow and ill-informed as any to be found in the tightest and most remote of Welsh communities.[9]

This public division within the church did it no favours. Edwin Morris and Glyn Simon never reconciled their differences, and eminent lay members were deeply disturbed. Gwenallt (D. Gwenallt Jones, 1899–1968), the eminent Welsh Christian poet, left the Church in Wales and returned to his roots as a Calvinistic Methodist. 'Anglicanism is a middle way between Rome and Geneva, but it is the Englishman's middle way.'

The confidence of the Church in Wales was shaken. How could *The* Church in Wales substantiate the claim inherent in its title when it had not taken on board the aspirations of the whole nation and was neglecting its ancient roots? How could Anglicanism fulfil its vision of catholicity when it displayed a prejudice bordering on arrogance, towards both Nonconformity and Roman Catholicism? At the close of the nineteenth century Nonconformity had overreached itself by its own hubris. Anglicanism was now similarly betraying its calling by its arrogant claim to be the servant of all Christ's people in Wales. While Wales was becoming secularized, and government policy was developing depersonalized communities in the large housing estates of the 1960s, the church failed to grasp the challenge of being alongside the people in the new places of work and the new styles of community. Where was the church in industrial chaplaincies and on new council estates? In a sermon of 1961, Glyn Simon wrote:

> ... the Church is working in a world where it is not hated but regarded as irrelevant; as having nothing new to offer. It simply seems to the men and women of today either to have nothing to say to their circumstances, or to say them in a way that has no sort of meaning for them.[10]

The Roman Catholic Church

By 1945, the Edwardian triumphalism of inevitable Nonconformity had long disappeared. The vacuum was being replaced by the growing confidence of the Church in Wales and the absolute certainty of the Church of Rome that Wales was returning to its ancient catholic roots. Archbishop McGrath of Cardiff, at the consecration of John Petit as bishop of Menevia in 1947, claimed, 'Wales is not Catholic but it is fast becoming Catholicised... It is more than a dream of life that the future is with the Church of Rome in this country.'[11] New church buildings and Catholic schools were opened. The consecration of the new statue of Our Lady of Penrhys in 1953 was a sign of the church reaffirming its ancient role. The number of Catholics increased from 105,775 in 1945 to 127,000 in 1960. The consistent affirmation of catholic doctrine and social teaching gave confidence to the faithful and attracted those seeking authority. This authoritarianism affected the church's attitudes towards other Christian traditions. Catholics were not allowed to join in worship with other Christian churches. It would not be until after the reforms of Vatican II that positive steps began to be taken by the Roman Catholic Church in Wales to be engaged with other Christian bodies. At the same time, some of the Protestant denominations revealed considerable hostility towards Catholicism. There was mutual mistrust between the different Christian bodies. There could be no positive engagement amongst Christians. The Christian witness reflected a very fragmented church.[12]

An Inexorable Decline

The mainline churches declined even more steeply during the last quarter of the twentieth century. Between 1980 and 1995, the Church in Wales declined from 131,600 to 96,000, the Catholic Church from 57,000 to 47,000, Presbyterians from 91,000 to 57,100, Baptists from 51,800 to 34,200, Congregationalists/Independents from 74,600 to 53,600 and Methodists from 26,000 to 18,300. Although Pentecostal and Evangelical churches increased slightly during this period, the total number of church members fell from 455,000 to 331,300 in just 15 years.

The Gweini Report of 2007[13] estimated that 200,000 (less than seven per cent of the population) worshipped each week. The majority of worshippers were Anglican and Roman Catholic, followed by the 'big four' Nonconformist denominations, but all continued their steep decline. On the other hand 'evangelical' and Pentecostal churches (called newer denominations in the Report) were not only growing but their congregations contained a much lower average age. The over 60s constituted 35 per cent of Roman Catholic, 57 per cent of Anglicans, 60 per cent of Baptists, 62 per cent of Welsh Presbyterians, 65 per cent of Annibynwyr (Welsh Congregationalists), 67 per cent of Methodists and URC, but only 27 per cent of the newer denominations. When all denominations were looked at together, only 11 per cent were under 30, and 57 per cent over 65 years of age.

These statistics were confirmed by the 2011 census which revealed that during the decade since the previous census, the number of people describing themselves as Christian had dropped from 71.9 per cent to 57.6 per cent, and that some of the least religious parts of England and Wales were the south Wales Valleys. Although some of the denominations no longer maintained accurate statistics, in 2013 the figures for membership of the Church in Wales was 60,924, there were 25,298 Presbyterians and 9,558 Methodists. If one compares these figures with the fact that congregations are ageing, the future for Christianity in Wales seems bleak.

Many influential historians have concluded that Wales is now a post-Christian nation. They point out that Wales has reached a unique period in her long history. Wales had, from its origins as a nation, been identified with the Christian faith which remained a key element in every period of Welsh history until the close of the twentieth century. John Davies notes:

> Indeed, religious decline is one of the most striking aspects of the history of Wales in the period after the Second World War; by the last quarter of the twentieth century, with only 13 per cent of the inhabitants of Wales regularly attending a place of worship, it was difficult to claim that the Welsh were a Christian nation, an astonishing change in view of their much vaunted devotion to religious observance at the beginning of the twentieth century... By the 1970s, however, the majority of the middle class had ceased to attend a place of worship and a new phenomenon had arisen – Welsh people, wholly conscious of their Welshness, who were professed non-believers... The Welsh did not revolt against Christianity; rather did they slip from its grasp, and the empty chapels were a cause of sadness and regret even to those who had never darkened their doors.[14]

Glanmor Williams reflects that:

> For the first time since the sixth or seventh centuries AD, when the Welsh could be said to have come into existence as a separate people, being a Christian is not, for the majority of them, an essential part of being Welsh... it seems as if the end of distinctively Welsh expressions of Christianity may be in sight, as those religious values dearest to earlier generations are being more and more abandoned in a lingering but painfully inexorable

process. The fire now burns on Cambria's altars only with a smoky and fitful flame, flickering hesitantly amid fast cooling embers.[15]

D. Gareth Evans' take on it is:

On the threshold of the new millennium, it seems as if the end of the distinctively Welsh expressions of Christianity may be looming on the horizon. There is no Evan Roberts in sight to rekindle the flame of religious enthusiasm, and no charismatic or prophetic leader to inspire the land of William Morgan and William Williams, Pantycelyn, or to reawaken the Welsh from their spiritual slumbers... all the evidence suggests that Welsh society has entered a post-Christian phase.[16]

In the Preface to the second edition (2011) of *The Span of the Cross*[17] Densil Morgan writes of the continuing decline of the churches. The Roman Catholic Church, despite the healing ministry of Archbishop Smith, is 'a beleaguered communion' in which 'clergy numbers contracted, mass attendance declined and financial problems led to the closure of many churches ... Institutionalism seems to be stifling bold creativity within the Anglican Church in Wales.' Cytûn (the ecumenical body serving the mainline churches in Wales) 'is suffering from institutional fatigue and a lack of creativity. The weaknesses of each of the three mainstream traditions since 2000, Catholic, Anglican and Nonconformist, all stem from their institutionalism.'

As the diminishing Christian community staggered into the twenty-first century, mainline churches continued a decline which had begun at the beginning of the twentieth century. They seemed fixated with entrenchment – how is 'our historic tradition' to be preserved? While the churches debated details of belief, church discipline and ministry, the world journeyed rapidly towards secularism. By 2016, forecasters envisaged a Wales in which Nonconformity would disappear and Anglicanism and Catholicism retain only a minority of the faithful. Welsh people faced choices between a secular lifestyle, amorphous spiritualisms and an aggressive fundamentalist witness.

Is this analysis the only option? What has the story of Welsh Christianity to offer the twenty-first-century church and to the future of the Welsh nation? What has the Spirit been saying to the church throughout its history, and is not the same Spirit at work today?

11

THE THIRD MILLENNIUM –
WHAT KIND OF FUTURE?

OUR STORY OF Welsh Christianity has borne witness to a variety of expressions and interpretations of the Gospel. Each historic period has reflected creative tensions between 'catholic' and 'puritan' traditions. Inclusivity and separatism have been two sides of the same coin – Dyfrig and Dewi, Benedictines and Cistercians, Anglicans and Puritans, Ecumenists and Evangelicals. For some Christians the emphasis has been on a search to live in unity, tolerance, openness of mind and spirit. For others it has been the call to live in purity of belief, order and practice. Some have emphasized the common unity amongst Christians, while others have been compelled to replace the 'imperfect institutional church' with a holy, separatist community. These emphases have been expressed in almost every generation, every Welsh community, in many families and often within the same person at different moments in their spiritual pilgrimage. Twenty-first-century Wales, and many local communities in Wales today, continue to reflect both interpretations of living the faith.

An examination of these interpretations within Welsh Christianity would provide a different perspective from either traditional denominational histories or the exploration of historical periods. It would also present alternative light on what is happening today in the life of Christianity in Wales, and possibly suggest fresh ways for the church to refocus its mission. In contemporary Wales, the approaches of the 'ecumenist' and the 'evangelical' reflect deep divisions within most denominations, and particularly between 'traditional churches' and 'new expressions' of being church. There is no satisfactory terminology to describe the divisions because all churches claim to be faithful to the call of the evangel, seek to present the fundamental truth of the Gospel, are anchored in biblical authority and are eager to reflect the continuity of apostolic witness.

A perennial problem has been the way terms like 'catholic', 'apostolic', 'pentecostal', 'reformed' and 'evangelical' have been narrowed into becoming the private property either of traditional denominations or of certain contemporary movements. Is it also possible to move beyond hurtful labels like 'liberals' and 'fundamentalists'? After fruitful study of scripture, prayer and debate, the historic denominations have learned to respect each other. They rejoice that their separate histories were shaped by the Spirit of God, and that the same Spirit is now drawing them together into a deeper unity. Are there ways for all the people of God to move forward together to share the Good News with a society which has been separated from the Gospel for many generations? Faithfulness to the evangelium, the Gospel, will result in God's light and truth breaking forth from his Word.

Being Evangelical and Conservative

The 1904/5 Revival had a dramatic effect on Welsh Christian life and continues to be a source of inspiration to many contemporary Christians. Most converts entered traditional Nonconformity and re-introduced a spirit of enthusiasm with a renewed emphasis on scripture. Nantlais Williams of Ammanford helped preserve an orthodox theological tradition within Calvinistic Methodism. R.B. Jones of Porth found denominationalism too restrictive. He withdrew from his Baptist affiliation and worked through conventions, campaigns and missions. Jones and Williams jointly edited *Yr Efengylydd* (The Evangelist) and organised the annual Llandrindod

Convention. Their stance was founded on the defence of biblical inerrancy, the deity of Christ, the substitutionary nature of the atonement, personal holiness, surrender to Christ, and an emphasis on the imminent return of Christ. They were tapping into spiritual resources released during the Evan Roberts' Revival, and commanded a large following, particularly from those who felt betrayed by what they considered to be the modernism of mainline denominationalism. This vein of spirituality remained throughout the century and has been reflected in those like Nantlais Williams who remain within traditional churches and others like R.B. Jones who feel compelled to separate themselves not only from the world, but also from 'worldly churches'.

Within the Welsh student world, the growth of conservative theology emerged in the formation of the Evangelical Union in Cardiff in 1923. It was soon associated with the Inter Varsity Fellowship, whose members saw themselves as diametrically opposed to the 'liberally minded and worldly' members of the Student Christian Movement. The SCM had come into being in 1889, valuing 'openness, inclusiveness, radicalism and an open and challenging approach to the Christian faith'.[1] It had been instrumental in bringing about the Edinburgh Missionary Conference in 1910, a conference which marked the beginning of the modern ecumenical movement. The division in the 1920s between SCM and IVF reflected what proved to be a division within Welsh church life throughout the century and into the third millennium. The Evangelical Movement of Wales was formed in the 1940s to preserve as it saw it, a conservative and orthodox theology. Its articles of belief include an acceptance of

> the holy scriptures, as originally given, to be the infallible Word of God... His substitutionary, atoning death on the cross... as a result of the Fall all men are sinful by nature. Sin pollutes and controls them, infects every part of their being, renders them guilty in the sight of a holy God and subject to the penalty which, in His wrath and condemnation, He has decreed against it... That the Lord

Jesus Christ will return personally, visibly and gloriously to this earth... As the righteous Judge, He will divide all men into two, and only two categories – the saved and the lost. Those whose faith is in Christ will be saved eternally, and will enter into the joy of their Lord, sharing with Him His inheritance in heaven. The unbelieving will be condemned by Him to hell, where eternally they will be punished for their sins under the righteous judgement of God.[2]

The Evangelical Movement, as epitomised by the leadership of Dr Martyn Lloyd-Jones (1899–1981), was fiercely anti-ecumenical and determined to defend 'the purity of the Gospel' from the liberal, secular humanism dominating traditional denominations. At the National Assembly of Evangelicals at Westminster Central Hall in October 1966, Martyn Lloyd-Jones called on all evangelical believers to withdraw from their denominations and form a doctrinally pure association. Although Dr Lloyd-Jones was opposed by John Stott, a revered evangelical leader and rector of All Souls Church, Langham Place, Lloyd-Jones' call had a long-term effect on the evangelical movement in Wales. In the spring of 1967, seven candidates for the Presbyterian ministry resigned from their college at Aberystwyth. Independent evangelical churches were established, largely from members seceding from mainline congregations. The Heath Evangelical Church in Cardiff was one of the largest churches to secede. Under the leadership of its minister, Vernon Higham, it withdrew from the Presbyterian Church of Wales in 1971 and accepted the 1823 Confession of Faith of the Calvinistic Methodists as its theological standard. The Rubicon had been crossed. Elwyn Davies, the general secretary of the Evangelical Movement stated that evangelicals are

... under a solemn obligation to disassociate ourselves from all those who, though avowedly Christian, deny our Lord... Evangelical churches who [which] are associated with an ecumenical council of churches are required to terminate that association.[3]

The Welsh Revival also witnessed the creation of new denominations. The Apostolic Church, a new Pentecostal movement, originated at Penygroes in Carmarthenshire, and the Elim Four-Square Gospel Alliance was founded by George Jeffreys of Nantyfyllon, Maesteg. Both new traditions have national and worldwide influence. The last 50 years have witnessed the creation of a host of Pentecostal, evangelical and charismatic fellowships. Many of these new fellowships co-operate with 'older' evangelical churches within the Evangelical Alliance. The Alliance holds together 30 different church or denominational traditions sharing a theological position similar to that expressed by the Evangelical Movement of Wales, and including Pentecostal and charismatic fellowships. They reflect a strong commitment to service in the community. In fact, many of these new churches have changed their traditional names to become 'community churches'. There was a concern amongst evangelicals to coordinate their ministries in their community service. 'Gweini Serving the Christian Voluntary Sector' was founded in 1999. Gweini came into existence because of the initiative of Care for Wales (Christian Action, Research and Education), Cornerstone Church Swansea (a church belonging to the apostolic Pioneer network), the Evangelical Alliance for Wales and Tearfund (Relief Fund created by the Evangelical Alliance). Gweini runs under the umbrella of the Evangelical Alliance and seeks to coordinate networking, representation to government and practical activities.

In 2013 the Evangelical Alliance produced a survey of 'Twenty-First Century Evangelicals'. The survey asserts that evangelicals believe 'Jesus is the only way to God... [they] strongly agree that the Bible is the inspired word of God... their faith is the most important thing in their life... the miraculous gifts of the Spirit did not come to an end in the first century... agree that Christians should be united in truth and mission... should do some kind of voluntary work and should engage with government.'[4] The witness of evangelical churches, both those serving under the umbrella of the Evangelical Movement of Wales and those who cooperate under the aegis of the Evangelical Alliance, is highly significant in contemporary Welsh life. A key issue for the future direction of Welsh Christianity is whether those who are committed to their 'conservative evangelical' interpretation of the faith – although, in fact, they reflect a remarkable variety of theological and ecclesiological positions – will be able to recognise as fellow Christians those not sharing their theological interpretation of the Gospel. Can there be mutual recognition between them and other Christians, particularly those who might be termed 'ecumenical evangelicals'?

Being Evangelical and Ecumenical

> The ideal of a Christian community in which all Christians shall be united in the confession of a common faith, bound together by an all-embracing charity and nourished by the same Word and Sacraments, and shall bear witness to the world through a fellowship transcending every difference of race and colour and civilization, has never lost its power to attract, and endless failure to realize the ideal has not availed to dull the ardour of those who have been inspired by the vision.[5]

If this vision is lost, the history of the Christian search for unity becomes a matter of seeking compromise, preserving denominational heritage and defending hard-fought traditional positions. Although the 'modern' search for unity is often dated to the Edinburgh Missionary Conference of 1911, the more immediate search for unity emerged from the crises following the Second World War. How could the hungry be fed? How could the refugee be found a home? British and Irish Church leaders created Christian Reconstruction in Europe to alleviate suffering for ordinary people, no matter what their faith. The new movement became a department of the British Council of Churches (founded in 1942), was renamed the Department of Interchurch Aid and Refugee Service and eventually became Christian Aid. The churches worked together in unity to meet the crisis in Europe.

Parallel to the call to serve a suffering world was the belief that the disunity of the Christian community did serious disservice to the mission of the Church. Historically in Wales, denominational leaders had discounted other Christian traditions as interlopers. Church members often behaved like fanatical supporters of rival football teams, who saw other churches as opposition to be overcome. The First Assembly of the World Council of Churches met at Amsterdam in 1948 and as a consequence Welsh Christian leaders saw a new chapter opening in the Church's mission. The Council of Churches for Wales held its first meeting in Swansea in May 1956. The theological foundation of the ecumenical vision was clear:

> We confirm our belief that the Christian unity upon which we
> have set our faith and hope is rooted in the unity of God and his
> redemptive act in Jesus Christ... We are convinced that the Council
> of Churches for Wales will be an effective means of enabling the
> churches in Wales to witness together to their shared commitment
> to Jesus Christ and to co-operation in matters which call for joint
> action.[6]

The founding members of the Council were the Church in Wales, the Presbyterian Church of Wales, the Union of Welsh Independents, the Methodist Church, the Baptist Union of Wales, the Congregational Union of England and Wales, the Baptist Union of Great Britain and Ireland and the Salvation Army. The Religious Society of Friends was an observer from the beginning and the Roman Catholic Church became a consultant observer in 1968.[7] The fact that these churches, often bitter rivals in the past, had agreed to work together was a miraculous step.

The story of ecumenism in Wales since 1956 has followed two main paths: the search for organic union (leading to Enfys – The Commission of Covenanted Churches) with a common understanding of faith, sacraments and ministry; and the search for greater cooperation amongst the churches (leading to Cytûn – Churches Together). The incentive driving both approaches has been the awareness that the churches' ministry and mission are only truly effective when churches speak with one voice and act in a cooperative rather than a competitive way. In other words, when Christians reveal that they love one another.

A Uniting Church at National Level (Enfys)

The search for visible unity demanded hard thinking and hard praying. The historic principles, accidents and personalities which caused the many divisions of the church all needed to be faced, examined and reconciled. It was a slow, painful and often tortuous process, but never as painful as the inability of Christians to recognize each other as fellow members of the family of God. The 'world' has been confused and angered by the way Christians have not loved one another, and the world has walked its own way.

After a decade of debate, the Church in Wales, the Methodist Church, the Presbyterian Church, the United Reformed Church and twelve congregations of the Baptist Union of Great Britain and Ireland entered into a covenant to seek visible unity. On 18 January 1975, a service of Thanksgiving for the Covenant was held at Aberystwyth. For some observers the service was a watershed moment, but for others it marked the demise of the ecumenical vision.

> What should have been the beginning of a new and vibrant phase in the ongoing story of Welsh Christianity in fact marked its end. Despite the huge commitment of a host of able, devout and exceedingly conscientious Christian leaders, it had become embarrassingly clear that the ecumenical dream (in its church unity form) had faded almost to nothing. By the mid-1970s church union was failing lamentably to engage the imagination and the ecumenical movement generally was seen as a somewhat bourgeois preserve of middle-aged and institutionally minded males.[8]

Some have described the search for unity as synonymous with preserving and unifying dying nineteenth-century church structures. However, those seeking union have been driven by the need to recast the shape of the church to equip it for mission and service. Agreements have been reached 'in principle' on the most contentious issues dividing the churches. A common understanding has been reached on baptism, eucharist and the ministry of the people of God. If this is the case, why have the churches not put these agreements into practice? A leading ecumenist has suggested that the failure has been one of implementing decisions rather than one of general principles:

> The opportunity for experiment and advance has been provided, but it has been all too seldom seized. At the local level, the inflexibility of inherited outlooks, and at the wider levels, an indifference and unreadiness to explore actual partnership, have been seriously crippling. A Covenant that is formally accepted but not put to use soon becomes an added cause of hesitation and mistrust between the churches. [9]

The Commission of Covenanted Churches has learned from and contributed to the practice of the world church and of the successful negotiations and creation of uniting churches. There have been major advances in common discipleship and liturgical practise. However the agreed statements have failed to win the support of the churches and therefore they remain like sleeping giants. The lack of national denominational response left ecumenists within the church in a dilemma. Agreements had been reached in principle, but rejected in practice. Was there a way forward? After many years of uncertainty, the Commission called together a national gathering in Aberystwyth in 2012, where the churches reviewed their progress and disappointments, and challenged themselves to seek to create The Church Uniting in Wales:

> ... there would need to be one governing body for a Uniting Church... To move from our present differing structures of governance would take a real change in attitude; one that begins with thinking of ourselves as 'The Church Uniting in Wales', a Church that incorporates all our historic churches and denominations and preserves and celebrates all their unique traditions. One that builds on all we have done in the past and

> takes a decisive step forward... A Uniting Church of Wales that
> shares one faith, one structure, one ministry and one governance
> but that honours and celebrates the different theological emphases
> and worship traditions that constitute and enrich the greater
> whole.[10]

This vision truly incorporates the history and traditions of
Welsh Christianity, but in order for it to be implemented it will
need to be 'owned' not only by ecumenical enthusiasts, but by
the leaders and congregations of all denominational traditions.
For that to happen, it will need the impetus of the kind of
programme of Bible study, prayer and discussion which was
at the core of the 'Not Strangers but Pilgrims' movement in
1986.[11] As in the period leading to the radical move from the
Council of Churches of Wales to Cytûn, inter-congregational
groups will need to meet in all communities throughout Wales.
In the 1980s they discovered how much they already shared
in common. The churches had a long tradition of cooperating
with each other to serve the poor of the world through agencies
like Christian Aid. In more recent history, they have been
serving the less fortunate in our own communities through
soup-runs, food banks, street pastors, caring for the homeless
and in a multitude of other charitable programmes. There
is a long experience of churches receiving so much through
meaningful and enriched ecumenical worship, ministry and
mission. Theological exploration in key areas like baptism,
eucharist and ministry has been pursued vigorously and
agreements have been reached in principle. Taking all these
positive developments into consideration, is it not possible to
take a further leap of faith, and trust the Spirit to guide the
churches into more organic union? The consequence would
be a united Christian presence in every community in Wales.
There could be pastoral ministry in every community, and the
end of ever increasingly scattered pastoral ministries where
ministers of word and sacrament are unable to identify with
the communities in which they minister. The Christian voice
in society would present a more coherent and clear voice at

local, regional and national levels. A challenge facing Welsh Christianity is whether its leadership and the dwindling and ageing memberships of the mainline churches will grasp this vision and provide the determination and stamina to create a new form of united Christian community. Only then will the vision break out of its imprisonment within denominationalism and become a practical programme which could help transform the Christian presence throughout Wales.

A Uniting Church at a Local Community Level

In 1968 the British Council of Churches published a document entitled *Areas of Ecumenical Experiment*. It provided guidelines to local communities and congregations who wished to pursue a common approach to mission. There was new legal provision for buildings and resources to be shared by different denominations. Ministers were recognized by different traditions and community ministries began to come into existence. By 1989, sixty ecumenical projects existed in Wales. The BCC Agreement provided the basis for sharing ministry and mission in any community in Wales.

One of the boldest of these new ministries (several were formed in south-eastern Wales) took place in Penrhys, Rhondda, where a challenge was accepted which eventually witnessed the transformation of its congregation and its community. In 1971, an experiment had been initiated by the Free Churches and the Rural Deanery in Rhondda to provide a ministry for a new council house estate of 951 properties. Many years of thoughtful and prayerful debate at national and local level eventually resulted in agreements which enabled the Christian fellowship to be recognized as a church in 1989. The uniting church was now able to call as its minister anyone ordained by any of the eight denominations committed to the 'spirit of covenanting for unity in Wales'. The minister of Word and sacraments now served a uniting congregation, recognized by eight denominations which in previous generations had often failed to see each other as members of the same Christian body. At the same time as the denominations were struggling to create a united ministry and mission on Penrhys, in the neighbouring village of Tylorstown the same denominations were closing their chapels, all of which had been serving the community for a century since Tylorstown came into existence as a coal village.[12] The sole witness in that community is the Anglican Holy Trinity and a non-denominational fellowship. Since 1989, Llanfair Uniting Church and its ministry has been celebrated as the Christian presence for the whole community. In effect Penrhys was reverting to a pre-Reformation condition when there was one Christian presence in the community.

By 1989 the Covenant Commission had produced a sufficient measure of agreement to enable the churches in Wales to both form a Uniting Church in Wales, and to create a visible local and recognized Christian presence in each community. The challenge remains ready for implementation.

The Search for Recognition and Cooperation (Cytûn)

Alongside the search for visible union, the churches have been seeking mutual recognition and cooperation. In 1984, the British Council of Churches and the Catholic Bishops Conference of England and Wales commissioned an inter-church process called 'Not Strangers but Pilgrims'. During Lent 1986, 70,000 local groups throughout Great Britain and Ireland, prayed, studied scripture and discussed together, and the result was a groundswell of joy in recognition of a shared faith. Traditions which had been divisive now were seen as enriching a rainbow church.[13] In Wales the national gathering of Teulu Duw (God's Family) at Llanelwedd in 1986, in which 20,000 participated, was inspired by the presence of Bishop Desmond Tutu who thanked the people of Wales for their support in the struggle against apartheid in South Africa, and called on the churches and the government to press more urgently for the release of Nelson Mandela and the imposition of sanctions on the South African government. During the following year, ecumenical conferences at Bangor in March, and at Swanwick in September resulted in the replacement of national councils of churches by new instruments for cooperation. The Council of Churches for Wales was replaced by Cytûn. The creation of Cytûn was nothing short of miraculous. Bitter animosity had divided the churches even as late as the close of the Second World War. The Church of Jesus Christ had succeeded in segregating families and dividing communities. Becoming a member of Cytûn was a particularly remarkable journey for the Catholic Church. Roman Catholicism, Anglicanism and Nonconformity, the three major historic divisions within Welsh Christianity, now recognized each other and rejoiced in the gift of being parts of Christ's Body. Cytûn saw itself as an instrument by which the churches could embark on a common mission with the people of Wales to serve God's kingdom. By 1990, there existed in Wales 110 local branches of Cytûn which provided the opportunities in many communities for Christians to cooperate in programmes of nurture, service and mission.

Both Cytûn (Churches Together) and Enfys (the Covenant Commission) have grasped the hope and challenge involved in being a nation of many cultures. They are very aware of the significance of its received language, and also have grasped the fact that the many cultures within Wales need to be recognised, understood and celebrated.

> Cytûn unites in pilgrimage those churches in Wales which,
> acknowledging God's revelation in Christ, confess the Lord Jesus
> Christ as God and Saviour according to the Scriptures; and,
> in obedience to God's will and in the power of the Holy Spirit,
> commit themselves to seek a deepening of their communion with
> Christ and with one another in the Church, which is his body, and
> to fulfil their mission to proclaim the Gospel by common witness
> and service in the world, to the glory of the one God Father, Son
> and Holy Spirit.[14]

Cytûn has drawn together the widest spectrum of Christian churches and denominations. While clearly acknowledging the integrity of each denomination, Cytûn seeks to serve as the servant of those churches, so that they may work together and speak with one voice in today's society. This is of particular significance since the devolving of political power to the Cynulliad, the Welsh Assembly. Subscribing to the statement of faith are the Anglican, Baptist, Congregational, Lutheran, Methodist, Presbyterian, Roman Catholic, the Salvation Army and the United Reformed Churches. Although the Religious Society of Friends has no creedal statements in their tradition, they are committed to Cytûn.

The Social Witness of Churches Acting Together

During the past half-century the churches in Wales have debated major social, economic and political issues which have concerned the people of Wales. The Council of Churches for Wales and its successor, Cytûn, provided a forum for these debates, attempted to seek reconciliation and to speak on behalf of the churches. Its motivation was the central prayer of Jesus that 'thy kingdom come... thy will be done in earth as it is in heaven.'

When the Council debated nationalism and self-government, the Churches were often as divided as the people of Wales. There existed a fissure between Welsh-speaking and English-speaking denominations. Welsh-speaking churches, while responding to the needs of the language and culture of Y Cymry Cymraeg were not as conversant with, or sympathetic towards other cultures which are also an integral part of contemporary Wales. English-speaking churches, sometimes almost totally composed of people from outside Wales, had little understanding of, and even less sympathy towards Welshness. How could there be reconciliation between these cultural divides and animosities? The Council of Churches provided a forum for the most widely and most conscientiously held convictions. Several individual denominations, the Free Church Council for Wales and the Council of Churches for Wales have all been in the forefront of the debate and have attempted to define a Wales which would both be confident in its own distinctive heritage and contribution, and at the same time seek its rightful place within the partnership of nations. The vision of the wealth of nations is dependent on the integrity of the individual nation. The struggle for devolution and the ultimate creation of the Welsh Assembly government reflects the prophetic vision and moral debate of the churches.

From the earliest days, the Council of Churches was attuned to and expressed the needs of an industrialized society. A significant response of the Welsh churches was their initiative during the coal-mining dispute of 1984/5. Four Nonconformist ministers earned the trust of the leaders of the National Union of Mineworkers and the south Wales director of the National Coal Board, and produced a document affirming that sufficient common ground existed between unions and management in Wales for an immediate cessation of the strike. This document provided the foundation for a consensus within the Churches – through the Council of Churches and the Welsh Church leaders. During the following months, as the churches' initiative took a prominent role in the search for a solution, it became apparent to the churches, and eventually to the wider public, that there was no possibility of a 'British solution'. It was a war without compromise, and the consequence was the destruction of the coal industry, the dereliction of coal communities and the inability of the country to arrive at a long-term energy policy. This devastating experience became a factor convincing the churches and much of the Welsh population that the solution to the problems of Wales lay in a form of Welsh self-government.

The Council of Churches persevered over many years in its opposition to apartheid in South Africa. It responded to the call of the World Council of Churches to support the humanitarian programmes of groups opposing apartheid. It tried to persuade the Welsh Rugby Union not to invite so-called 'mixed' teams to play in Wales. In 1986 the Council invited Desmond Tutu to preach at the Teulu Duw Festival, and endorsed his call to support the struggle to free the people of South Africa. The churches rejoiced in the release of Nelson Mandela on

11 February 1990 and the beginning of the creation of the rainbow nation. The Council was also concerned about issues of war and peace and helped the churches to discuss issues of disarmament.

The long-term and 'permanent' gifts of the Council to Wales have included the translation and the publication of *Y Beibl Cymraeg Newydd* in 1988, the formation of Inter-Church Aid and Service to Refugees which developed into Christian Aid, and 'Christians against Torture', which for many years was a highly significant lobbying group, pioneered by Roy Jenkins, Baptist minister and broadcaster.

Conclusion

The story of Christianity in Wales reflects the story of the Welsh people. It records both a struggle of survival against the odds and an experience of renewal down through the ages. Celtic communities emerged from the ashes of the Roman Empire and created a spiritual geography which still faithfully expresses the Christian foundation of the nation. Norman Christianity added the gifts of diocesan, parish and monastic Wales. The sixteenth- and seventeenth-century renewal movements, inspired by the William Morgan Bible created Dissent, freedom of belief and worship, and the formation of the Baptist, Congregational, Quaker and Unitarian traditions. The eighteenth-century literacy programmes of Griffith Jones, coupled with the Evangelical Revival with its hymnody and seiat gave birth to Calvinistic and Wesleyan Methodism and the renewal of the churches. The nineteenth century created a Nonconformist nation. The strains and stresses of the twentieth and twenty-first centuries have witnessed the near-death experience of much of the denominational legacy but has also given birth to two fresh approaches, both rooted in Welsh history and both offering a way forward for today's expression of the Gospel. The twentieth century has seen the emergence of both the 'ecumenical evangelical' and the 'conservative evangelical' vision. Together they reflect the traditional visions of catholicity and puritanism. Is it possible that they will see each other as partners in the mission of God's people in Wales in the twenty-first century?

12

A CHALLENGE / THE END OF ALL OUR EXPLORING?

THE STORY HAS been told. The story has been visited. There has been reading, listening, looking, conversing, reflecting, participating, celebrating. What have the writer and the photographer discovered and what do they wish to share?

Sharing the Gospel

There is one Gospel. The church exists to share the Good News. In Christ, God reveals and bestows the gift of life in its fullness. The daughters and sons of God, brothers and sisters in Christ, are through the Spirit privileged to be co-workers with God, responsible for each other and the earth. The church is God's instrument. It is not a matter of saying to others 'this is how you should love one another'. It is a matter of saying, 'we love one another, and as the church of Jesus Christ, we are commissioned to live in unity to express God's purposes for humankind'.

Sharing the National Story

The past century has witnessed the erosion of Christianity in Welsh life. Although this happened more swiftly in the south-eastern industrial communities, the challenge now for the church throughout Wales is to discover fresh expressions of the message and new models of 'being church' in post-Christian societies. This is a new task in Wales' long history. From its very beginning, the people of Wales had been identified with

194

the Christian faith. When an identifiable Wales came into being during the period between the departure of the Romans and the arrival of the Normans, land, language, people, culture, law and Christianity were all interwoven into the tapestry of the emerging nation. These ingredients remained key elements in every period of Welsh history until the twentieth century which witnessed a chronicle of uninterrupted decline. The influence of Tabernacl, Treforus (Morriston), and Tabernacl, Yr Ais (Tabernacle, the Hayes, Cardiff), has been overshadowed by the Liberty Stadium and the St David's/Dewi Sant Shopping Centre with its alluring insidious invitation: 'When you can't decide what to get them – get them everything.'

This past Christian story seems a closed book. And yet, although the majority of our contemporaries are only remotely aware of the Christian faith, many remain 'religious'. They wish to celebrate births and relationships, and to respond positively to death. They seek a sense of meaning. The burning question for those who love the Gospel is how to share that Gospel within this society. We have much to receive as well as to give. During the second half of the twentieth century, the churches were gradually learning that they ought not to be competitors in a market-place, seeking 'success' in numbers, holiness, fidelity to inherited tradition or fervour in evangelism.

It is together that the churches are members of One Body, expressions of the One, Holy, Catholic and Apostolic Church. The churches belong within one family, and God is calling them to share their treasures. Gifts which often have been preserved denominationally need to be shared inter-denominationally.

Is the contemporary church capable of being reshaped? The church has remodelled itself many times during our national story and is capable of being remodelled today. The Christian community is the inheritor of different shapes of being church: the earliest centuries of the saints, medieval catholicism, the church of reformers, puritans, evangelicals, Nonconformists. The church has been through the trials and testing of the last century and is still here. Christians need to respect each other's interpretations of the story and discover together a narrative that will be appropriate for today's challenges.

On a national level, can the church urgently explore and celebrate her common story? Throughout its long history, the Welsh experience has been a chequered one, corresponding to a 'corrugated-iron sheet' theory of history. There have been ebbs and flows. Whenever it seemed the ebb was permanent, slow streams began to flow again. Whenever it seemed the flow was permanent, sand and rocks re-appeared and the waters slowly ebbed. What are the signs of God's finger today? Can historic denominations rediscover the faith of the Tradition of God's People? Can they be open to what God has been doing throughout the story of Christian Wales? It is when the churches act together that they become inheritors of the whole history of the People of God. If the churches search together into their common story and celebrate that story together, it could lead to a reinvigorated and uniting Christian life.

Sharing the Local Story

The gift of the common national story needs to be celebrated and lessons applied to contemporary ministry and mission. The same story also needs to apply locally. When the national history and the local story intertwine, new opportunities present themselves for the church to meet today's opportunities and challenges. The principles explored at national level apply locally. How are Christians to live nationally as members of One Body? How are they to live locally as members of One Body?

Nationally and locally, Christians can reflect that they are expressions of the One, Holy, Catholic and Apostolic Church. They belong within one family which God is calling to share its treasures. Gifts preserved denominationally need to be shared inter-denominationally at national and local level.

In many instances, the national denominational structures need to catch up with what is happening in many localities. People are discovering that although in the past, they worshipped and witnessed separately, fiercely maintaining denominational loyalties and preserving inherited structures, they were in fact sharing the same Gospel. It is being recognised that it is not only folly, but indeed it is a kind of blasphemy to live separately. The church is dissipating precious resources in light of the cry of the needy in our own society and throughout the world. In many communities, Christians who were separated by denominational structures (usually reinforced by a sense of family loyalties to 'our chapel') are now enjoying worshipping and serving together. Many communities are united by working together for Christian Aid and for other charities. Many share joint mission and celebration programmes in the name of Cytûn. For many women, a highlight of the year is the Women's World Day of Prayer. Many congregations are uniting regularly for worship. How good it is to be together! As churches they discover they are not betraying their past, but are sharing treasures which had been preserved separately. It is not beyond the wit of the church to loosen denominational structures and create appropriate forms of ecumenical ministerial leadership for churches already working together for the sake of the wider community. For many years this has been done in ecumenical chaplaincies in what have been depicted as areas of special challenges. Now it is clear that the whole of Wales is an area of challenge and opportunity. The breakdown of traditional patterns of ministry provides the opportunity to discover something new in God's treasure chest.

The creation and existence of Llanfair Uniting Church Penrhys is a sign that the churches can act together creatively and courageously when they place God's mission as their priority. Llanfair is an 'inter-denominational' church. In a unique act of courage and foresight, since 1971 eight of the historic denominations have cooperated together to create 'an inter-denominational church'. Llanfair is neither 'a denominational church', belonging to only one tradition, nor is it a 'non-denominational church' which has broken from the past to create 'a church of true believers'. Llanfair was created by the historic denominations in order to play a significant role in God's providential guidance within the community. What can be learned from Llanfair and can it be shared? What practical difference at ground level did it make to be a Uniting Church?

All communities can discover they share a significant, life-enhancing communal history. It was particularly important on Penrhys to discover this history because of the lack of community dignity and self-worth. It was critical to find roots that lay beyond the received history: an estate created with great optimism in 1968, in less than 20 years had become a nightmare no man's land. The exploration of local roots was no academic exercise. The consequence of discovering 'our history' changed the perception of the people of Penrhys for its residents and for outsiders. Instead of being depicted as a new-modelled, ill-fated social housing experiment of the 1960s, Penrhys began to see itself as one of the oldest communities in Rhondda, created where ancient prehistoric ridgeways crossed. This 'new view of history' was taught and celebrated, and helped physically, morally and spiritually to change Penrhys from being an estate into the Penrhys Village.

Llanfair (named to respond to Our Lady of the Magnificat) explored the roots of the story of Penrhys. It was marked by the cross of Non, the mother of Dewi. The ancient Celtic well was cleaned and restored, and when its first health centre was opened, it was called Y Ffynnon (The Well). The place of the ancient Celtic saints of Bannau Morgannwg (the Hill Country of Glamorgan) was rediscovered, and the names of Illtud, Gwynno and Tyfodwg were celebrated on a Penrhys banner and carved on the Millennium Beacon. The death of Rhys ap Tewdwr in 1097 was remembered and the new arts centre, Canolfan Rhys, dedicated in his name. The relationship between Penrhys and the Cistercians was revitalised by the links with Caldey and the annual ecumenical pilgrimage from Llantarnam to Penrhys. Along with these rediscovered-forgotten memories came a respect for Bishop Hugh Latimer,

Penrhys' connection with the Methodist Revival, the gathering of miners on Penrhys on Red Sunday, 18 September 1927, the illegal radio station of Glyn James and the struggle for the Welsh language. These all entered into the new Penrhys history and into the life of worship. Beneath Llanfair were laid eight stones from the eight denominations, from chapels and churches closed in Rhondda Fach. Llanfair was built literally on the foundation of the past.

From that foundation in the very local, residents were introduced to the story of Rhondda with its rich heritage of music, literature, art and its Nonconformist and radical politics. Rhondda applauded the courage and vision of working people who had created a new, vibrant coal community. It also realised that when the coal community died, the Valleys needed vision and courage to learn to recreate itself. It was a straightforward move from love of local community and valley to love for Wales, its land, languages, cultures and people. Llanfair showed its respect for its nation by taking adults and children on holiday to Ynys Bŷr (Caldey), Ystrad Fflur (Strata Florida), Tyddewi (St Davids), Soar y Mynydd, Tŷ'r Ysgol Rhyd Ddu (the birthplace of T.H. Parry-Williams), Manod (the home of Father Deiniol and the Orthodox Church), climbing Snowdon, being pilgrims to Aberdaron.

Alongside the love of community and nation was a love for the world. This was reflected particularly in Llanfair's relationships with the Council for World Mission, Christian Aid and Time for God. Llanfair invited four overseas volunteers to live for a year in Llanfair and work on Penrhys. Worship was enriched by the treasures of the world church, including Cistercian Caldey, Taizé, Orthodox chants, Iona and the World Council of Churches. Llanfair created and studied courses on community development, courses which inspired many in the struggle to prevent the estate from demolition and successfully transformed a housing estate into a village in which people wish to live.

A Contemporary Agenda

The unity of the church is central to an understanding of the mission of God. It is the consequence of trust in the God experienced and worshipped in Jesus Christ. In Christ, God has revealed his glorious and gracious intention for humankind, and the church has a pivotal role within this sweeping vision. Wales has been blessed in its Christian experience throughout its history. At national, regional and local levels the churches are commissioned both to pass on the heritage and remodel the life of the church for the needs of today and tomorrow. On a local level, Llanfair is a sign that mission and unity are central in the life of the church.

Christian witness in Wales has faced far more severe situations than it does today, and has, by the grace of God, always been renewed and enabled to continue its ministry and mission. The church is always capable of renewal, facing contemporary challenges and introducing the Risen Christ to the people of Wales. Revisiting the story of Llanfair can become a sign of hope to local communities. Revisiting our common Christian story can reinvigorate the Christian community in Wales.

And so we came to the end of our journey. The photographer and the writer had been commissioned to hear the message of the Lady of Penrhys and the Nameless One, the Guardian of the Valleys. Had we found anything? Was there anything at the end of the quest? Did it all end in a vanity of vanities? Did the ancient stones speak? Did the living stones speak even more eloquently?

Yes they did – both stones and living stones. Were we surprised? Overwhelmed? Grateful? Yes! This gift of God came on the final journey together. It had taken several years to get there. It had taken thousands of miles to get there. And what did God reveal at the end of the journey?

Autumn had drawn in. Most of Wales had been travelled. One last corner remained to be explored. A final chapter needed to be written and the last photographs taken. All seemed to be drawing to a close. The great door was opened and we entered the medieval wonder which is Llanfair ar y Bryn. Were we guided to the tiny narrow insignificant leper window in the chancel wall? We witnessed John Petts' gift to the church to remember the outcast, the alien, the nameless. Crimson flooded frame and floor. Who are you Lord? You do not need to ask who I am? Câr di. You are to love. Câr di. You must love. Câr di. But who am I to keep on loving?

An hour later we opened the door into Soar y Mynydd, the most remote chapel in the heart of the green desert which is the centre of Wales. We stood, and looked, and caught our breath. There was the holy answer to all our searching. Between clarity of light with hints of crimson came Duw Cariad Yw. God is Love. Here was the prayerful beseeching of Our Lady of Penrhys. Duw Cariad Yw. God is Love. Here was the Nameless One of Six Bells calling out that every name must be remembered. Duw Cariad Yw. God is Love.

Duw cariad yw. God is love. That which we learned in our first Sunday school. That which we learned from the prayers of our parents. In gratitude our response is to obey Câr Di. The Lady of Penrhys, the Nameless One of Six Bells, the window in Llanfair ar y Bryn and the writing on the wall of Soar y Mynydd all speak with one voice: Duw Cariad Yw... Câr Di.

Our journey had ended, or had it only just begun?

ENDNOTES

Preface

1   Gwilym Tew, 'Y Cymmrodor', in John Ward, *Our Lady of Penrhys*, p. 42.

2   'Six Bells' by Gillian Clarke. Interpretive panel at Guardian of the Valleys, Six Bells.

3   Thomas Rees and John Thomas, *Hanes Eglwysi Annibynnol Cymru*, Vol. 1, p. xxi. Alan Argent, 'Some Aspects of Welsh Congregationalism' lecture, St Fagans, 2012 *www.cfwales.org.uk*.

4   Gomer M. Roberts, *Y Pêr Ganiedydd: Pantycelyn*, two volumes, Aberystwyth, 1949, 1958. Meic Stephens, *The New Companion to the Literature of Wales*, article on William Williams, p. 808.

1: Origins of a People

1   Obituary in *The Times*, see *Encyclopedia of Wales*, article on E.G. Bowen (1900–83), p. 77.

2   Gwyn Alf Williams, *When was Wales?* (1985).

3   John Davies, *A History of Wales*, p. 45

4   Geraint H. Jenkins, *A Concise History of Wales*, p. 18.

2: The Shaping of a Christian People

1   Glanmor Williams, *The Welsh and their Religion*, p. 1f.

2   From the seventh-century life of Samson, see *Encyclopedia of Wales*, article on Illtud, p. 390.

3   *Hidden Histories*, Toby Driver, Discovering Early Medieval Religious Sites, p. 121.

4   T.S. Eliot, 'Four Quartets: Little Gidding'.

5   Charles-Edwards, T.M., *Wales and the Britons 350–1064*, p. 642.

6   Article by Pennar Davies, 'The Fire in the Thatch, Religion in Wales', in R. Brinley Jones (ed.), *Anatomy of Wales*, p. 107.

7   Charles-Edwards, p. 638 (quoting from Rhygyfarch's *Vita S. David* (1094)).

8   Ibid., p. 650.

9   Glanmor Williams, p. 2ff.

3: The Age of Catholicism, 1066–1509

1   R.R. Davies, *The Age of Conquest, Wales 1063–1415*, p. 172ff, cf. the monumental work of Glanmor Williams, *The Welsh Church from the Conquest to the Reformation*, Cardiff, 1962.

2   Geraint H. Jenkins, *A Concise History of Wales*, p. 64f.

3   R.R. Davies, *The Age of Conquest, Wales 1063–1415*, p. 182f.

4   See books such as T.J. Hughes, *Wales's Best One Hundred Churches*; Simon Jenkins, *Wales Churches, Houses, Castles*; Nick Mayhew Smith, *Britain's holiest places*. Note also websites: Churches' Tourism Network (*www.ctnw.co.uk*), and north Wales' holy places (*www.visitwales.com*).

5   R.R. Davies, *The Age of Conquest, Wales 1063–1415*, p. 181.

6   Ibid., p. 187.

7   Peter Lord, *The Visual Culture of Wales: Medieval Vision*, p. 62f.

8   Geraint H. Jenkins, *A Concise History of Wales*, p. 105.

9   Ibid., pp. 96–130.

10   Gwyn A. Williams, *When Was Wales?*, p. 111f.

11   *Y Mab Darogan*, a musical drama written by Derec Williams, Linda Gittins and Penri Roberts for Cwmni Theatr Ieuenctid Maldwyn to perform at the National Eisteddfod at Machynlleth in 1981. This musical reflects both on the awakening of nationhood and the folly of war. It was the first of a series of musical dramas written for Cwmni Theatr Ieuenctid Maldwyn which encourage a reappraisal and a celebration of Welsh history.

12   Peter Lord, *Medieval Vision*, p. 10f.

13   Peter Lord, *Medieval Vision*; Martin Crampin, *Stained Glass from Welsh Churches*; Martin O'Kane and John Morgan-Guy, *Biblical Art from Wales*; T.J. Hughes, *Wales's Best One Hundred Churches*.

14   Note the work of Jane Cartwright, *Feminine Sanctity and Spirituality in Medieval Wales*.

15   Christine James, 'Pen-rhys, Mecca'r Genedl' in Hywel Teifi Edwards (ed.) *Cwm Rhondda*; John Ward (ed.), *Our Lady of Penrhys*.

16   T.J. Hughes, *Wales's Best One Hundred Churches*, pp. 20, 26.

4: Reawakening and Reforming, 1509–1603

1   For a general introduction to the Reformation, see G.R. Elton (ed.), The *New Cambridge Modern History, II. The Reformation, 1520–59*, Cambridge, 1958.

2   George H. Williams, *The Radical Reformation*, London, 1962.

3   Glanmor Williams, *Renewal and Reformation Wales c.1415–1642*, p. 279.

4   A.G. Dickens, *The English Reformation*, New York, 1964.

5   Glanmor Williams, *The Welsh and their Religion*, p. 33.

6   G.A. Williamson, *Foxe's Book of Martyrs*, edited and abridged, Boston and Toronto, 1965; William Haller, *The Elect Nation, The Meaning and Relevance of Foxe's Book of Martyrs*, New York and Evanston, 1963.

7   Glanmor Williams, essay on 'Bishop William Morgan and the First Welsh Bible', in *The Welsh and their Religion*, pp. 173–229.

8   Glanmor Williams, *The Welsh and their Religion*, p. 40.

5: From Uniformity to Pluralism, 1603–1689

1   Glanmor Williams, in Williams, Jacob, Yates and Knight, *The Welsh Church from Reformation to Disestablishment 1603–1920*, Part I.

2   R. Tudur Jones, *Congregationalism in Wales*, p. 12; David Williams, *John Penry, Three Treatises Concerning Wales*, Cardiff, 1960.

3   Geraint H. Jenkins, *The Foundations of Modern Wales, 1642–1780*, p. 3.

4   John I. Morgans, *The Honest Heretique*, pp. 52–9.

5   Walter Cradock, *Glad Tydings from Heaven; to the Worst of Sinners on Earth*, p. 50

6   Geraint H. Jenkins, *The Foundations of Modern Wales*, p. 62.

7   John I. Morgans, *The Honest Heretique*, pp. 211–13.

8   William Jacob in Williams, Jacob, Yates and Knight, *The Welsh Church from Reformation to Disestablishment 1603–1920*, Part II.

9   Horton Davies, *Worship and Theology in England, Vol. II*, p. 435.

10 Ibid, p. 444.

11 Geraint H. Jenkins, *The Foundations of Modern Wales*, p. 175f.

12 John Davies, *A History of Wales*, p. 288.

13 Gwyn A. Williams, *When was Wales?* p. 137.

6: Literacy and Revival, 1689–1770

1   Nigel Yates in Williams, Jacob, Yates and Knight, *The Welsh Church from Reformation to Disestablishment 1603–1920*, p. 165.

2   Glanmor Williams, *The Welsh and their Religion*, p. 51.

3   Ibid., p. 52; Edward Samuel (1674–1748) in *Gwirionedd y Grefydd Gristnogol* (1716).

4   John Davies, *A History of Wales*, p. 307f.

5   Derec Llwyd Morgan, *The Great Awakening in Wales*, p. 10.

6   Ibid., p. 66

7   Glyn Tegai Hughes, *Williams Pantycelyn*; Sam Thomas, *William Williams Pantycelyn*.

8   Derec Llwyd Morgan, *The Great Awakening in Wales*, p. 86.

9   Gomer M. Roberts (ed.), *Hanes Methodistiaeth Galfinaidd Cymru, Cyfrol I: Y Deffroad Mawr*, p. 205f.

10   Geraint H. Jenkins, *The Foundations of Modern Wales, 1642–1780*, p. 355.

11   *Encyclopedia of Wales*, see article on Edward Williams, p. 952.

12   John Davies, *A History of Wales*, p. 337f.

7: From Dissent to Nonconformity, 1770–1851

1   John Davies, *A History of Wales*, p. 366.

2   In 1988, Cwmni Theatr Ieuenctid Maldwyn produced a musical drama, *Pum Diwrnod o Ryddid*, based on the 1839 Llanidloes Chartist Uprising.

3   *Encyclopaedia of Wales*, article on Robert Owen, p. 640; Robert Owen Museum website, *robert-owen-museum.org.uk*.

4   D. Gareth Evans, *A History of Wales 1815–1906*, pp. 80–5.

5   Nigel Yates in Williams, Jacob, Yates and Knight, *The Welsh Church from Reformation to Disestablishment 1603–1920*, p. 246f.

6   See Chapter 8 under Brad y Llyfrau Gleision for a more detailed appraisal of the Education Report.

7   Gwyn A. Williams, *When Was Wales?*, p. 158f.

8   John Davies, *A History of Wales*, p. 359.

9   A.M. Alchin, in Brendan O'Malley, *A Welsh Pilgrim's Manual*, p. 14; cf. *Praise Above All*, chapters 5 and 6; cf. Alan Luff, *Welsh Hymns and their Tunes*, pp. 117–125. See *Ann!*, a musical drama written by Derec Williams, Linda Gittins and Penri Roberts for Cwmni Theatr Ieuenctid Maldwyn.

10   John Gwynfor Jones (ed.), *The History of Welsh Calvinistic Methodism III, Growth and Consolidation*, p. 30.

11   D. Gareth Evans, *A History of Wales 1815–1906*, pp. 85–9.

12   *Encyclopaedia of Wales*, article on Temperance, p. 856.

13   D. Gareth Evans, pp. 85–94.

14   Gwyn Davies, *A Light in the Land, Christianity in Wales 200–2000*, p. 92.

8: From Nonconformity to Conformity, 1851–1903

1 Gwyn Griffiths, *Henry Richard: Apostle of Peace and Welsh Patriot*, Francis Boutle Publishers, 2012.

2 Alan Luff, *Welsh Hymns and Their Tunes*.

3 *Encyclopaedia of Wales*, article on Timothy Richard, p. 758.

4 *Cludedd Moroedd*, Ioan W. Gruffydd (ed.), particularly the article by D. Andrew Jones, pp. 55–84.

5 Frances Knight in Williams, Jacob, Yates and Knight, *The Welsh Church from Reformation to Disestablishment 1603–1920*, p. 335f.

6 Article by Owain W. Jones in David Watson (ed.), *A History of the Church in Wales*, p. 150.

7 Nigel Yates in *The Welsh Church from Reformation to Disestablishment 1603–1920*, p. 353.

8 David Egan, *People, Protest and Politics in Nineteenth Century Wales*, p. 107. Note *Er mwyn yfory*, a musical drama written by Derec Williams, Linda Gittins and Penri Roberts for Cwmni Theatr Ieuenctid Maldwyn and performed at the National Eisteddfod at Bala in 1998.

9 *Encyclopaedia of Wales*, article on The Treason of the Blue Books, p. 881.

10 Gareth Elwyn Jones and Gordon Wynne Roderick, *A History of Education in Wales*.

11 Glanmor Williams, *The Welsh and their Religion*, pp. 64–8, *passim*.

12 *Encyclopaedia of Wales*, article on Cymru Fydd, p. 186.

13 Tudur Jones, *Congregationalism in Wales*, pp. 193–5.

14 David Watson (ed.), *A History of the Church in Wales*, p. 154.

15 D. Densil Morgan, 'Theology among the Welsh Calvinistic Methodists, *c.*1811–1914', in John Gwynfor Jones (ed.), *Growth and Consolidation*, p. 77f; cf. D. Densil Morgan, *Lewis Edwards*.

16 D. Gareth Evans, *A History of Wales 1815–1906*, p. 241f.

17 D. Densil Morgan, p. 81.

18 Ibid.

9: Conformity Begins to Crumble, 1903–1945

1 M. Wynn Thomas, *In the Shadow of the Pulpit*, p. 3. Mary Davies, the grandmother of Wynn Thomas, was one of the five young women in a photograph with the evangelist.

2 For a variety of views of the 1904 Revival, see Gwyn Davies, *A Light in the Land*, p. 100f.; Frances Knight in Williams, Jacob, Yates and Knight, *The Welsh Church from Reformation to Disestablishment*

1603–1920, p. 372ff; M. Wynn Thomas, *In the Shadow of the Pulpit*.

3   D. Densil Morgan, *The Span of the Cross*, pp. 17–23.

4   John Davies, *A History of Wales*, p. 500f.

5   Robert Pope, *Building Jerusalem, Nonconformity, Labour and the Social Question inWales, 1906–1939*, p. 11.

6   Ibid., p. 53.

7   Frances Knight in *The Welsh Church from Reformation to Disestablishment 1603–1920*, pp. 316–29f.

8   Ibid., p. 319f.

9   John Davies, *A History of Wales*, p. 509.

10   D. Ben Rees (ed.), *Dilyn Ffordd Tangnefedd, Canmlwyddiant Cymdeithas y Cymod, 1914–2014*; cf. website of Cymdeithas y Cymod, The Fellowship of Reconciliation in Wales, *www. cymdeithasycymod.org.uk*.

11   Gwyn Alf Williams, *When Was Wales?*, p. 252.

12   For a perceptive description and analysis of the flight from 'chapel', see M. Wynn Thomas, *In the Shadow of the Pulpit*.

13   Robert Pope, *Building Jerusalem*, p. 176.

14   Ibid., p. 178f.

15   Harri Parri, *Tom Nefyn, Portread*.

16   D. Densil Morgan, *The Span of the Cross*, p. 154.

17   Frances Knight in *The Welsh Church from Reformation to Disestablishment 1603–1920*, p. 339f.

18   D. Densil Morgan, *The Span of the Cross*, p. 87.

19   Trystan Owain Hughes, *Winds of Change*.

10: Reaching the Millennium, 1945–2015

1   John Davies, *A History of Wales*, p. 631.

2   Gwyn Alf Williams, *When was Wales?*, pp. 303, 305.

3   Kenneth Morgan, *Rebirth of a Nation Wales 1880–1980*, p. 418.

4   John Davies, *A History of Wales*, p. 686.

5   See Ambrose Bebb, *Yr Argyfwng*, 1954 and Ivor Parry, *Ymneilltuaeth*, 1962.

6   *Congregational Year Book 1956*.

7   D. Densil Morgan, *The Span of the Cross*, p. 185.

8   Ibid., p. 186.

9   Ibid., p. 191.

10   Ibid., p. 196.

11   Ibid., p. 197.

12 The relations between Catholic and Protestant are carefully portrayed in Trystan Owain Hughes, *Winds of Change*, and the growing sense of trust is reflected in Noel Davies' *A History of Ecumenism in Wales*.

13 Evangelical Alliance website. The Welsh Evangelical Alliance through its social arm, Gweini (established in 1999), combines theological conservatism with social involvement. The Alliance initiated a nationwide report, 'Faith in Wales, Counting for Communities' (2008) which reveals the remarkable service which churches of all traditions give to the wider community. In the process, the Report provides statistics on denominations, churches and worshippers. *www.eauk.org*.

14 John Davies, *A History of Wales*, pp. 642–3.

15 Glanmor Williams, *The Welsh and their Religion*, pp. 69, 72.

16 D. Gareth Evans, *A History of Wales 1906–2000*, p. 281.

17 Densil Morgan, *The Span of the Cross*, second edition, 2011.

11: The Third Millennium – What Kind of Future?

1 Student Christian Movement website, *www.movement.org.uk*.

2 Evangelical Movement of Wales website, *www.emw.org.uk*.

3 D. Densil Morgan, *The Span of the Cross*, p. 250.

4 Evangelical Alliance website, *www.eauk.org*.

5 Stephen Neill, *A History of the Ecumenical Movement*, p. 725.

6 Noel Davies, *A History of Ecumenism in Wales*, p. 10.

7 Ibid., p. 6.

8 D. Densil Morgan, *The Span of the Cross*, p. 246.

9 Martin Conway in Noel Davies, *A History of Ecumenism in Wales*, p. 30.

10. Enfys website, *www.cytun.org.uk*. Covenanting for mission, pp. 16, 19.

11. See note 13 below, p. 121.

12 Beulah and Horeb (English- and Welsh-speaking Baptist chapels), Bethany and Ebenezer (English- and Welsh-speaking Congregationalist chapels), the Methodist Church and Moriah (English- and Welsh-speaking Methodist chapels), Seion and Libanus (Welsh Presbyterian) have all closed in recent history.

13 Colin Davey and Martin Reardon, 'Not Strangers but Pilgrims, the 1980s Inter-Church Process', Methodist Church website, *www.methodist.org.uk/downloads/ec-not-strangers-but-pilgrims.pdf*.

14 Cytûn website, *www.cytun.org.uk*.

Select Bibliography

Allchin A.M., Esther de Waal, *Threshold of Light,* London, 1986.

Allchin, A.M., *Praise Above All*, Cardiff, 1991.

Allchin, A.M., *Resurrection's Children*, Canterbury, 1998.

Amgueddfa Cymru, National Museum Wales celebrating the first 100 years, Cardiff, 2007.

Argent, Alan, 'Some Aspects of Welsh Congregationalism', 2012, *www.cfwales.org.uk*.

Ballard, Paul H. and Jones, Erastus, *The Valleys Call*, Ferndale, 1975.

Bebb, W. Ambrose, *Yr Argyfwng*, Llandybie, 1954.

Cartwright, Jane, *Feminine Sanctity and Spirituality in Medieval Wales*, Cardiff, 2008.

Charles-Edwards, T.M., *Wales and the Britons 350–1064*, Oxford, 2013.

Cole, David (ed.), *The New Wales*, Cardiff, 1990.

Congregational Year Book 1956, London, 1956.

Crampin, Martin, *Stained Glass from Welsh Churches*, Talybont, 2014.

Davies, Gwyn, *A Light in the Land, Christianity in Wales 200–2000*, Bridgend, 2002.

Davies, Janet, *A Pocket Guide to the Welsh Language*, Cardiff, 1999.

Davies, John, *A History of Wales*, Penguin Books, 1994.

Davies, John, *The Making of Wales*, Stroud, 1996.

Davies, John, and Marian Delyth, *Wales: the 100 places to see before you die*, Talybont, 2010.

Davies, John, Nigel Jenkins, Menna Baines, Peredur Lynch (eds.), *The Welsh Academy Encyclopaedia of Wales*, Cardiff, 2008.

Davies, Noel A., *A History of Ecumenism in Wales*, Cardiff, 2008.

Davies, Noel A., *Wales, Language, Nation, Faith, Witness*, Geneva, 1996.

Davies, R.R., *The Age of Conquest, Wales 1063–1415*, Oxford, 1987.

Dickens, A.G., *The English Reformation*, New York, 1964.

The Dictionary of Welsh Biography, down to 1940, London, 1959.

The Dictionary of Welsh Biography, 1941–1970, London, 2001.

Eames, Marion, *A Private Language? A Dip into Welsh Literature*, Llandysul, 1997.

Edwards, Hywel Teifi (ed.), *Cwm Rhondda*, Llandysul, 1995.

Edwards, Huw, *City Mission: The Story of London's Welsh Chapels*, Talybont, 2014.

Egan, David, *Coal Society, A History of the South Wales Mining Valleys 1840–1980*, Llandysul, 1987.

Egan, David, *People, Protest and Politics, Case Studies in the Nineteenth Century*, Llandysul, 1987.

Elton, G.R. (ed.), *The New Cambridge Modern History, The Reformation*, Cambridge, 1958.

Evans, D. Gareth, *A History of Wales 1815–1906*, Cardiff, 1989.

Evans, D. Gareth, *A History of Wales 1906–2000*, Cardiff, 2000.

Evans, Gwynfor and Delyth, Marian, *Eternal Wales*, Talybont, 2002.

Evans, E.D., *A History of Wales 1660–1815*, Cardiff, 1993.

Fishlock, Trevor, *In this place, The National Library of Wales*, Aberystwyth, 2007.

Francis, Hywel, *Miners Against Fascism. Wales and the Spanish Civil War*, London, 1984.

Francis, Hywel, *History on Our Side, Wales and the 1984–5 Miners' Strike*. Ferryside, 2009.

Francis, Hywel and Smith, David, *The Fed: A History of the South Wales Miners in the Twentieth Century*, London, 1980.

Haller, William, *The Elect Nation, the Meaning and Relevance of Foxe's Book of Martyrs*, New York and Evanston, 1963.

Harvey, John, *The Art of Piety, The Visual Culture of Welsh Nonconformity*, Cardiff, 1995.

Hilling, John B., *Cardiff and the Valleys*, London, 1973.

Hilling, John B., *The Historic Architecture of Wales*, Cardiff, 1976.

Hopkins, K.S., *Rhondda Past and Present*, Ferndale, 1975.

Hughes, Glyn Tegai, *Williams Pantycelyn*, Cardiff, 1983.

Hughes, Herbert, *An Uprooted Community: A History of Epynt*, Llandysul, 1998.

Hughes, Herbert, *Harris, Gŵr Duw a thraed o glai*, Llandysul, 2006.

Hughes, T.J., *Wales' Best One Hundred Churches*, Bridgend, 2006.

Hughes, Trystan Owain, *Winds of Change, The Roman Catholic Church and Society in Wales, 1916–1962*, Cardiff, 1999.

Jenkins, Geraint H., *A Concise History of Wales*, Cambridge, 2007.

Jenkins, Geraint H., *Protestant Dissenters in Wales, 1639–1689*, Cardiff, 1992.

Jenkins, Geraint H., *The Foundation of Modern Wales 1642–1780*, Oxford, 1993.

Jenkins, Geraint H., *The University of Wales, An Illustrated History*, Cardiff, 1993.

Jenkins, Simon, *Wales: Churches, Houses, Castles*, London, 2008.

Jones, Anthony, *Welsh Chapels*, Cardiff, 1984.

Jones, Erastus, *Croesi Ffiniau*, Abertawe, 2000.

Jones, Gareth Elwyn, *People, Protest and Politics, Case Studies in Twentieth-Century Wales*, Llandysul, 1987.

Jones, Gareth E. and Gordon, Wynne Roderick, *A History of Education in Wales*, Cardiff, 2003.

Jones Gwyn, *The Oxford Book of Welsh Verse in English*, Oxford, 1977.

Jones, John Gwynfor, *Growth and Consolidation, The History of Welsh Calvinistic Methodism, III*, Historical Society of the Presbyterian Church of Wales, 2013.

Jones, R. Brinley (ed.), *Anatomy of Wales*, Peterston-super-Ely, 1972.

Jones, R. Tudur, *Congregationalism in Wales* Robert Pope (ed.), Cardiff, 2004.

Jones, Vivian, *The Church in a Mobile Society*, Llandybie, 1969.

Lewis, E.D., *The Rhondda Valleys*, London, 1959.

Lord, Peter, *The Visual Culture of Wales, Industrial Society*, Cardiff, 1998.

Lord, Peter, *The Visual Culture of Wales, Imaging the Nation*, Cardiff, 2000.

Lord, Peter, *The Visual Culture of Wales, Medieval Vision*, Cardiff, 2003.

Luff, Alan, *Welsh Hymns and their Tunes*, London, 1990.

Morgan, Derec Llwyd, *The Great Awakening in Wales*, Dyfnallt Morgan (tr.), London, 1988.

Morgan, D. Densil, *Lewis Edwards*, Cardiff, 2009.

Morgan, D. Densil, *The Span of the Cross*, Cardiff, 1999 (second edition, 2011).

Morgan, Kenneth O., *Rebirth of a Nation, Wales 1880–1980*, Oxford, 1981.

Morgan, Kevin and Mungham, Geoff, *Redesigning Democracy, The Making of the Welsh Assembly*, Bridgend, 2000.

Morgan, Prys (ed.), *The Tempus History of Wales*, Stroud, 2001.

Morgans, John I., *The Honest Heretique*, Talybont, 2012.

Morgans, John I. and Norah, *Journey of a Lifetime*, Llanidloes, 2008.

Naylor, Barrie, *Quakers in the Rhondda, 1926–1986*, Chepstow, 1986.

Morris, Jan, *The Matter of Wales*, London, 1984.

O'Kane, Martin and Morgan-Guy, John, *Biblical Art from Wales*, Sheffield, 2010.

O'Malley, Brendan, *A Welsh Pilgrim's Manual*, Llandysul, 1989.

Osmond, John (ed.), *The National Question Again, Welsh Political Identity in the 1980s*, Llandysul, 1985.

Owen, D. Huw, *Capeli Cymru*, Talybont, 2005.

Owen, D. Huw, *The Chapels of Wales*, Bridgend, 2012.

Parri, Harri, *Tom Nefyn, Portread*, Caernarfon, 1999.

Parry, R. Ifor, *Ymneilltuaeth*, Llandysul, 1962.

Parry, Thomas (ed.), *The Oxford Book of Welsh Verse*, Oxford, 1962.

Petts, David, *The Early Medieval Church in Wales*, Stroud, 2009.

Pope, Robert, *Building Jerusalem, Nonconformity, Labour and the Social Question in Wales, 1906–1939*, Cardiff, 1998.

Redknap, Mark, *Discovered in Time*, Cardiff, 2001.

Rees, D. Ben (gol.), *Dilyn Ffordd Tagnefedd: Canmlwyddiant Cymdeithas y Cymod 1914–2014*, Lerpwl, 2015.

Rees, Ivor Thomas, *Welsh Hustings 1885–2004*, Llandybie, 2005.

Rees, Thomas and Thomas, John, *Hanes Eglwysi Annibynnol Cymru*, Cyf. 1, Liverpool, 1871.

Roberts, Alun, *Discovering Welsh Graves*, Cardiff, 2002.

Roberts, Gomer M. (ed.) *Hanes Methodistiaeth Galfinaidd Cymru, Cyfrol I: Y Deffroad Mawr*, Caernarfon, 1973.

Roderick, A.J., *Wales through the Ages, Volume II*, Llandybie, 1960.

Rouse, Ruth and Neill, Stephen Charles (eds.), *A History of the Ecumenical Movement, 1517–1948*, second edition, Philadelphia, 1967.

Sager, Peter, *Pallas Wales*, London, 1991.

Smith, Dai, *Wales! Wales?*, London, 1984.

Smith, Nick Mayhew, *Britain's holiest places*, Bristol, 2011.

Stephens, Meic (ed.), *The New Oxford Companion to the Literature of Wales*, Oxford, 1998.

Stephens, Meic, *The Literary Pilgrim in Wales*, Llanrwst, 2000.

Thomas, M. Wynn, *In the Shadow of the Pulpit, Literature and Nonconformist Wales*, Cardiff, 2010.

Thomas, Einion, *Capel Celyn, Deng Mlynedd o Chwalu: 1955–1965*, Llandybie, 2007.

Thomas, Sam, *William Williams, Pantycelyn*, Llandybie, 1991.

Vaughan-Thomas, Wynford, *Wales, A History*, London, 1985.

Wakelin, Peter, and Griffiths, Ralph A., *Hidden Histories*, Aberystwyth, 2008.

Walker, David, *A History of the Church in Wales*, Penarth, 1976.

Ward, John, *Our Lady of Penrhys*, Ystrad, 1931. (Reprinted from *Archaelogia Cambrensis*, July 1914.)

Williams, David, *John Penry, Three Treatises Concerning Wales*, Cardiff, 1960.

Williams, George H., *The Radical Reformation*, London, 1962.

Williams, Glanmor, *The Welsh Church from the Conquest to the Reformation*, Cardiff, 1962.

Williams, Glanmor, *Renewal and Reformation in Wales*, Oxford, 1993.

Williams, Glanmor, William Jacob, Nigel Yates, Frances Knight, *The Welsh Church from Reformation to Disestablishment 1603–1920*, Cardiff, 2007.

Williams, Glanmor, *The Welsh and Their Religion*, Cardiff, 1991.

Williams, Gwyn A., *When Was Wales?*, Penguin Books, 1985.

Williamson, G.A. (ed.), *Foxe's Book of Martyrs*, Boston/Toronto, 1965.

Acknowledgments

THE AUTHORS ARE grateful to the following, particularly for their help with photographs:

Mair Davies of Blaenannerch
The Dean and Chapter of St Davids Cathedral
Gerwyn Edwards (Wil Tŷ Mawr) of Tŷ Mawr Wybrnant
The Rev. Thomas Evans of Peniel, Carmarthen
D. I. Gealy of Llandovery
The Revs Llunos and Russell Gordon of Blaenannerch
Alan Griffin of Epynt
Helina Howells of Llanddowror
The Rev. Dewi Myrddin Hughes of Clydach, Swansea
Mr and Mrs Gunstone Jones of Dugoedydd
Dewi Lewis of Clydach, Swansea
Cath Morgans of Bermondsey
Jules Montgomery of the Society of Friends
Rob Moverley of Caerffili
Keith O'Brien of Trawsfynydd
Miara Rabearisoa of Penrhys
Nia Rhosier of Hen Gapel John Hughes
The Rev. Hywel Richards of Bridgend
Dewi Roberts of Pontrobert
Penri Roberts of Llanidloes
The Very Rev. John Rogers of Llandovery
Saint Michael's Centre, Llandaff
Hans Schmeinck of Yr Efail, Berriew
Sion P. Tomos of Trawsfynydd
The South Wales Miners' Library, Swansea
Angela Westacott of the Tylorstown Band
John Williams of Cefn Brith
The Williams family of Pantycelyn
Mr and Mrs Williams of Y Wernos

215

INDEX

P
Padarn 31
Pantycelyn 13, 93, 98f, 135, 175
Parry, Bishop Richard, translator
73
Patrishow, Patrisio 53
Pelagius 25f, 69
Penal Code (1401–2) 51
Penllwyn, Capel Bangor 135
Penmachno, St Tudclud 12
Penmon 25, 31, 46
Pennal (the Letter, 1406) 50f
Pennant Melangell 12, 54
Penrhys 11, 14, 32, 53f, 64, 172,
187f, 197ff
Penri, John, Puritan martyr 13,
75f, 81
Pentre Ifan 18
Penyberth 161
Penygroes, Carmarthenshire 181
Periodicals, Nonconformist 120,
141
Perrot, Thomas, Carmarthen
Academy 102
Phillips, Sir John, education
benefactor 93f
Phillips, Morgan, Douai 74
Pontrobert, Yr Hen Gapel John
Hughes 121
Poor Law Amendment Act (1834)
106
Powell, Vavasor, Puritan 84
Price, Sir John, yny lhyvyr hwn
62
Price, Richard, Llangeinor 102
Prichard, Vicar, Llandovery 73,
93
Propagation, Act for (1650) 81
Prys, Edmwnd, Salmau Cân 73
Pugh, Philip, Llwynpiod 101
Puller, F.W., Roath 124

Q
Quakers 84, 87, 111, 154, 192

R
Recusants, Catholic 68, 74, 87
Red Sunday (1935) 154, 199
Rees, Lewis, Llanbrynmair 101
Rees, Principal Thomas, Bala-
Bangor 148
Rees, Bishop Timothy 124, 155
Reform Acts (1867, 1884) 132
Revivals
Eighteenth Century, Methodist
91f, 95ff, 100f, 113, 117ff
Nineteenth Century 117ff
Twentieth Century (1904)
138ff, 144, 169, 178f, 181
Rhuddlan, Statute of (1284) 49
Rhygyfarch 28, 35f, 46
Rhys, Morgan, Cilycwm 101
Richard, Henry, Apostle of Peace
119, 147
Richard, Bishop Timothy 121
Roberts, Evan, revivalist 139,
175, 179
Roberts, John, Catholic Martyr
12, 75
Roberts, John, Ieuan Gwyllt 120
Roberts, Silyn, Tanygrisiau 142
Rowland, Daniel 79, 92, 96ff, 98,
100f
Royal Commission (1910) 109,
145

S
Salesbury, Bishop William 62,
65, 67
Samson 25, 27, 35
Samuel, Edward, Llangar 93
Seiriol 32
Seren Cymru 120
Simon, Bishop Glyn 171f
Siôn Cent 62

Also by the author:

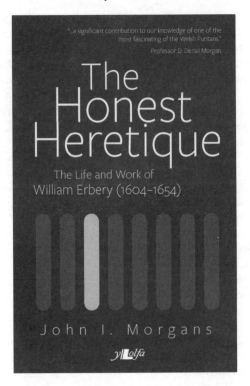

'In this splendid book John Morgans has made a significant contribution to our knowledge of the past by rehabilitating the neglected and colourful figure of William Erbery, one of the most fascinating of the Welsh puritans.'

Professor D. Densil Morgan, University of Wales Trinity St David

'William Erbery is one of Wales's hidden writers. So unorthodox and daring a theological thinker was he, and so controversial was his social outlook, that many of his own and later times dismissed him as mentally unbalanced. His rebellious originality of mind has, however, proved altogether more intriguing to recent scholarship and a full scale "rehabilitation" of him, such as that attempted in Dr Morgans' groundbreaking study, is as welcome as it is overdue.'

Professor M. Wynn Thomas, Swansea University

'This book is written to rescue a largely forgotten Welsh cleric from both obscurity and calumny. If you want a glimpse of the exhilarating chaos of mid-17th century religion, you will find it here.'

Dr Alec Ryrie, *Church Times*